AN INTRODUCTION TO CORROSION AND PROTECTION OF METALS

by
GÖSTA WRANGLÉN
Professor, Dr. Techn.
Department of Electrochemistry and Corrosion Science,
Royal Institute of Technology,
Stockholm 70, Sweden

HALSTED PRESS
A Division of JOHN WILEY & SONS, Inc.,
605 Third Avenue, New York, N.Y. 10016

To my wife Elvie

PREFACE

The brief outline of corrosion science and engineering presented here is based on an introductory course on the subject, which the author has been teaching for the past ten years to engineering students at the Royal Institute of Technology in Stockholm, Sweden.

Due to the introductory nature of this little book, I have refrained from specific references to original papers in journals. Experience seems to show that in text-books such references, which rapidly grow obsolete, are seldom used. Following some of the chapters, authoritative and modern monographs of the particular field are listed. At the end of the book there is, furthermore, a list of handbooks and journals in the corrosion field, through which the interested student may enter deeply into the subject and keep abreast of its development. All literature references pertain to publications in English.

As in my lectures, I make here diligent use of sketches, diagrams and photographs to illustrate the treatment. Photographs, above all macropictures of corrosion damage, seem particularly important in order to illustrate the subject matter to beginners without previous experience in the corrosion field. Photographic illustrations for this book were kindly supplied by the companies, organizations and individuals listed below:

AB Alfort & Cronholm: S. Berg (Fig. 05)

AB Brdr. Michaelsen: (Figs. 06, 07)

AB Elektrokoppar: A. Sandin (Fig. I2)

AGA AB: (Fig. 02)

Avesta Jernverks AB: S. Henriksson (Figs. G8, G18, H3, H4, L15)

Bartha, Stefan: (Figs. G2, G3, H10)

Gränges Essem AB: E. Mattsson (Figs. G4, G14, H2, H8, H9, H11)

KIAB Apparater AB: (Fig. 01)

Lubrizol Scandinavia AB: A. Bresle (Fig. G15)

Munters'Torkar AB. (Figs.M1, M2)

Mörrums Bruk: **P.** Isaksson (Fig. K8)

Norsk Sivilforsvar: L. Lund (Fig. M3)

Sandvik Steel Research: (Figs.G1, G10, G12)
Skarpenord A/S: F. Klingenberg (Fig. N6)
Swedish Corrosion Institute: O. Nygren (Figs. G5, L23, N7, N8, P2)
"   "   " : I. Sven-Nilsson (Fig. I1)
Swedish Institute of Steel Construction: L. Wallin (Fig. O11)
Swedish Power Administration: K.Fr. Trägårdh (Figs. L8, L11, L22)
"   "   " : Mrs. V. Victor (Figs. G7, J2)
Universal Electronics AB: (Fig. O9)

Due recognition is given in the legend of the particular photograph
These contributions are also greatfully acknowledged here. I am furthermore indebted to my secretary, Mrs. Ingrid Lilja for typing, retyping
and correcting the manuscript, to my assistants, Mr. Jaak Berendson,
Met.Eng. for careful proof-reading and Mr. Mats Linder, Met.Eng. for
preparing the index and finally to Dr. Derek Lewis for checking the
English.

Stockholm, January 1972   G. Wranglén

CONTENTS

2

NOTATION AND ABBREVIATIONS

A	ampère; area
Å	Ångström (10^{-8} cm)
a	(as a subscript) anode
b	slope of Tafel line
c	concentration; (as a subscript) cathode; centi (10^{-2})
c_o, c_e	concentration in bulk and on electrode surface, resp.
cal	calorie(4.18 Ws)
c.d.	current density (A/cm^2)
D	diffusion coefficient
d	deci (10^{-1})
E	electric potential; electromotive force (emf)
e	electrode potential; base of natural logarithms (2.718)
e_a	anode potential
e_c	cathode potential
e_h	electrode potential versus NHE
e_i	electrode potential at c.d. i
e_o	electrode potential at equilibrium (i.e. zero net current)
e^o	standard potential versus NHE
e_H, e_M, e_{O_2}, etc.	electrode potential of hydrogen, metal, oxygen etc. electrode
e_{corr}	corrosion potential
e^-	electron (charge)
equ.	equivalent (molecular weight/valency change, i.e. M/z)
F	Faraday' s constant (96500 As/equ.)
G	free energy (Gibbs')
g	gram (unit of mass); gas
I, I_a, I_c	outer (measured) net current or c.d.
I_L	limiting current density
i, i_a, i_c	real (partial) current or c.d.
i_o	exchange current or c.d.

i_{corr}	corrosion current or c.d.
K	constant
k	kilo (10^3)
l	litre ($10^{-3} m^3$); liquid
M	molecular weight; molar; metal
m	milli (10^{-3}); metre; m^2 = square metre; m^3 = cubic metre
mdd	corrosion rate, expressed in mg/dm^2, day
NACE	National Association of Corrosion Engineers (USA)
NHE	normal (or standard) hydrogen electrode
ox	oxidized state
P	pressure
p	pond (unit of weight or force, corresponding to gram)
ppm	parts per million (mg/kg, ml/m^3 etc.)
R	electric resistance; gas constant (8.3143 $Ws/^{o}C$, mole)
R_i	internal resistance in a galvanic circuit
R_e	external resistance in a galvanic circuit
red	reduced state
s	second (unit of time); solid
SCC	stress corrosion cracking
SCE	saturated calomel electrode
T	absolute temperature ($t+273$) in ^{o}K
t	time; temperature in ^{o}C
u	flow velocity
V	volume; volt
V_p	terminal voltage
W	watt
Ws	watt-second (Joule)
z	valency change in electrode process
$\alpha, \beta, \gamma, \delta$, etc.	allotropic modifications of a metal at rising temperature; phases of an alloy at rising percentage of alloying element
Δ	increase of quantity during process
δ	diffusion layer or electrode film
δ_N	Nernst diffusion layer
∂	partial differential

η	polarization (overvoltage, overpotential)
η_a, η_c	anodic and cathodic polarization resp.
η_A, η_C, η_R	activation, concentration and resistance polarization resp.
κ	conductivity (specific electric conductance)
μ	micro (10^{-6}); μm(micron) = 10^{-6}m =10^{-3} mm
μ	(also) chemical potential
$\bar{\mu}$	electrochemical potential
ν	kinematic viscosity
ρ	resistivity (in Ωcm); density (in g/cm^3)
σ	mechanical stress (in kp/mm^2)
τ	time
Ω	ohm
I,II,III,etc.	valency of atom in compound
o	(as a subscript) state of equilibrium in general
o	(as a superscript) equilibrium at standard states
[]	activity
/	contact between two phases

Certain other, less common symbols are explained in the text. For conversion factors between English and metric units, see p. 233 and 271.

INTRODUCTION

Corrosion may be defined as an unintentional attack on a material through reaction with a surrounding medium. The term can refer to a process or to the damage caused by such a process. According to this general definition, other materials than metals, such as ceramics, plastics or concrete, may also be subject to corrosion (or corrode). When no particular reference is made to the material, however, it is normally understood that a metal is being attacked. It is entirely in this limited sense that the term is used in this book.

There are good reasons for treating the corrosion of metals separately, apart from deterioration or decay of other materials. Since metals have a high electric conductivity, their corrosion is usually of an electrochemical nature. The chemical deterioration of electrically non-conducting materials, such as plastics and ceramics, is governed by other physico-chemical principles.

It is necessary to devote more attention to metallic corrosion nowadays than earlier due to

1. An increased use of metals within all fields of technology.
2. The use for special applications, e.g. within the atomic energy field, of rare and expensive metals, whose preservation requires particular precautions.
3. A more corrosive environment due to the increasing pollution of air and water.
4. The use of metallic constructions of more slender dimensions which do not tolerate corrosive attacks to the same extent as did the heavy constructions used in old days.

It is estimated that the annual costs for metallic corrosion, including measures for protection against corrosion, amount to 50-100 dollars per inhabitant in the most highly industrialized countries of the world. As direct or primary corrosion costs, we may count costs for anti-corrosive painting or other protection methods, the exchange of corroded equipment which for other reasons could have been used longer, the use of expensive metals instead of carbon steel etc. In addition, we have indirect or secondary costs, e.g. as a result of shut-downs in industries due to corroded apparatus, destruction of large constructions due to the corrosion of small details,

damage   caused by leakage of water or oil from corroded tubes and containers etc. Outside an economic evaluation we find personal injuries and health
hazards caused by corrosion. It should be noted, furthermore, that insufficient corrosion resistance of materials of construction often constitutes
an obstacle to technical development, e.g. within the atomic energy field.

From the stand-point of a nation´s economy, means allocated for research, development and education within the corrosion field are therefore
highly productive. The most rapid economic results are gained by training,
education and information since this creates the basis for a utilization of
the vast but not readily accessible knowledge of the causes of corrosion and
the means to prevent it which we already possess.

Since most corrosion processes are of an electrochemical nature, this
short review of corrosion science and engineering starts with certain electrochemical elements (Chapter A). Then follows a short chapter (B) on the structure of metals. The great importance of the environment for the corrosion process is outlined in Chapter C. In Chapter D, potential-pH diagrams as a basis
for corrosion studies are introduced. The mechanism of electrochemical corrosion in a moist environment is treated in Chapters E, F and G, whereas Chapter
H is devoted to corrosion types influenced by mechanical factors. The environmental view-point is again focussed in the three following chapters (I, J and
K), which treat corrosion in the atmosphere. in the soil and in dry gases.

Methods for corrosion prevention are then treated systematically according as the protection method involves a change of the corroding metal (Chapter
L), of the corrosive environment (Chapter M), of the electrode potential me-
tal/corrosive medium (Chapter N) or the application of a protective coating
on the metal (Chapter O). The principles of corrosion testing are outlined
in Chapter P. In Chapter Q, potential-pH diagrams for some technically important metals are presented together with a short sketch of their corrosion
properties in various environments.

The most important foundations of corrosion science are no doubt electrochemistry and physical metallurgy. With regard to corrosion prevention, knowledge of the properties of various protective coatings, organic and inorganic,
also plays an important part. The mechanical-constructional view-points of
corrosion prevention must also be considered. The outlook of the corrosion
specialist must, therefore, irrespective of his basic education, be decidedly interdisciplinary and this breadth of corrosion science makes it a particularly fascinating subject.

A. ELECTROCHEMICAL ELEMENTS

A.1 Electric conductance

A1.1 Basic concepts

Electric resistance is denoted R and is measured in ohm (Ω), resistivity or specific electric resistance, ρ, is given in ohm cm. The reciprocal of resistance is called electric conductance and its value is expressed in ohm^{-1} or mho. Conductivity or specific electric conductance,

$\kappa = \frac{1}{\rho}$, is measured in ohm^{-1} cm^{-1} or mho/cm. According to the formula

$R = \rho \frac{1}{A}$ for the resistance of an electric conductor of length 1 and area A,

the relation ohm $= [\rho] \frac{cm}{cm^2}$ is obtained between the dimensions of the quantities referred to. Hence, the dimension $[\rho]$ of ρ is Ω cm. Dimensions such as ohm/cm^3, ohm/cm etc., sometimes given for the resistivity, are incorrect.

A1.2 Different kinds of electric conductors

Electric conductors of the 1:st kind or metallic conductors have electronic conductance. Besides metals ($\kappa > 10^4$), this group comprises graphite ($\kappa = 1000$) and coke ($\kappa = 100$), carbides, nitrides etc. of transition elements and, furthermore, some common oxides and sulphides, such as PbO_2 ($\kappa = 10^4$), MnO_2 ($\kappa = 1300$), Fe_3O_4 ($\kappa = 30$), PbS ($\kappa = 335$), CuS ($\kappa = 90$) and FeS ($\kappa = 1600$). Such metallic conductors can, therefore, form the positive pole in galvanic corrosion cells with metals. Of particular importance in this respect are graphite in gray cast iron, iron carbide or cementite, Fe_3C, in carbon steel and white cast iron, sulphide inclusions in both iron and steel, and layers of magnetite, Fe_3O_4, in the form of mill-scale on steel. Silicate inclusions in steel, on the other hand, are non-conductors and do not form local cells. The conductivity of metallic conductors decreases with rising temperature and with increasing content of impurities due to impeded electron mobility.

Electric conductors of the 2:nd kind or electrolytic conductors have ionic conductance. This group comprises aqueous solutions ($\kappa < 1$) and melts

(κ<10) of dissociating (ionic) salts and acids. The conductivity rises with temperature, mainly due to a decrease of viscosity.

Electric conductors of the 3:rd kind or semi-conductors have (as a rule) both electronic and ionic conductance, the former usually prevailing. Their total conductivity is low (as a rule: 10^{-9}<κ<1) but it rises rapidly with temperature due to an increasing number of charge carriers, which may be electrons, as in so-called n-conductors, or electron holes, as in so-called p-conductors. Most metal oxides and sulphides are semiconductors due to lattice defects. In certain cases, of which examples were given above, metallic conductance dominates.

The transfer of current from an electronic conductor (electrode) to an electrolytic conductor is possible only through an electrode process, i.e. a chemical reaction, in which free electrons take part.

A.2 Electrode potentials

A2.1 Basic thermodynamic functions

Some important thermodynamic functions are

U = internal energy

S = entropy (measure of disorder)

T = absolute temperature

H = U + pV = enthalpy or heat content (p = pressure, V = volume)

G = U + pV - TS = H - TS = free energy, also called free enthalpy, Gibbs potential or thermodynamic potential

ΔG = 0 is the equilibrium condition for isothermal (T = const.) and isobaric (p = const.) equilibria

Note that $\Delta S = - \frac{\partial (\Delta G)}{\partial T}$ (p = const.)

A2.2 Chemical, electrical and electrochemical potential

The chemical potential, μ, of a substance is its free energy per mole, i.e. $\mu = \frac{\partial G}{\partial n}$. For ions, chemical and electrical potentials have to be considered separately. This is done by introducing the electrochemical potential, $\bar{\mu}$, defined according to

$$\bar{\mu} = \mu + zF \cdot E$$

with   F = Faraday's constant = 96500 As/equ.

E = electrical potential

z = change of ionic charge in an electrode process.

For the change of the electrochemical potential of an ion, taking part in an electrode process, we have

$$\Delta\bar{\mu} = \Delta\mu + zF \cdot \Delta E$$

If for example a metal is immersed in a solution containing ions of the metal a dynamic equilibrium is set up. The electrochemical potential of the ions is then equal in both phases, i.e. $\Delta\bar{\mu} = 0$ or

$$\Delta\mu + zF \cdot \Delta E = 0$$

This means that the chemical and the electrical potential differences in the phase boundary counterbalance each other so that no net transfer of ions takes place (Fig. A1). The electric potential difference ΔE can thus be expressed thermodynamically as

$$\Delta E = - \frac{\Delta\mu}{zF} \quad \text{or} \quad e = - \frac{\Delta G}{zF} .$$

ΔG is the free energy change in the electrode reaction and e is called the electrode potential. If both oxidized and reduced states of a system are present in a solution, the potential of which is measured by means of an inert electrode, such as Pt, the electrode potential is often referred to as redox potential.

For standardized conditions (pure metal, metal ion activity in solution = 1) we write

$$e^0 = - \frac{\Delta G^0}{zF} \quad \text{with } \Delta G^0 = \text{standard free energy change of the}$$
electrode process and e^0 = standard potential or normal potential.

A2.3 The physical back-ground of electrode potentials

A piece of zinc is immersed in water (Fig. A2A). Zinc is a metal with great tendency to dissolve and therefore gives off Zn^{2+}-ions, which, however, remain very close to the metal surface. Due to remaining electrons, the zinc sheet is negatively charged relative the solution. In this way, a so-called electrochemical double layer is created. This can, approximately, be considered as an electric condenser with + and - charge. The thickness of the double layer is ca 10^{-7} cm (10 Å). Since the potential difference across the double layer may amount to $\pm$ 1 V or more, its potential gradient may be as high as 10^7 V/cm.

The electrode potential of zinc, e_{Zn}, is negative and is visualized as an arrow, pointing downwards along a potential axis (Fig. A2B). In the same way, a piece of copper sheet is immersed in water (Fig. A3A). Copper

18

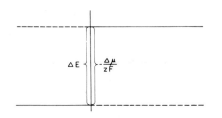

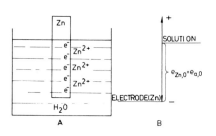

Fig. A1. The equilibrium between electric potential difference, ΔE, and chemical potential difference, Δμ, at a metal/solution interface. The electric potential difference is called electrode potential and is measured relative to an arbitrary zero point, the standard hydrogen electrode.

Fig. A2. A zinc sheet sends zinc ions into the solution (water) and therefore becomes negatively charged relative to the solution.

has a much smaller tendency to ionize. Instead, it assumes a positive potential in relation to the solution (water). Here, too, an electrochemical double layer is formed. The electrode potential of copper is positive and is shown as an arrow, pointing upwards along a potential axis (Fig. A3B).

A2.4 Electrochemical, galvanic and electrolytic cells

An electrochemical cell is a combination of the type

electronic	ionic	electronic
conductor	conductor	conductor
(metal)	(electrolyte)	(metal)

in which electrochemical processes may occur with the passage of electric current. If the electrochemical cell produces electric energy, under the consumption of chemical energy, it is said to be a galvanic cell. If, instead, the electrochemical cell consumes current from an external current source and, in effect, stores chemical energy, it is said to be an electrolytic cell.

A galvanic cell with an electrolyte bridge (a liquid junction) denoted by the symbol //, is schematically represented as shown by the example

$$Zn \ / \ Zn^{2+} \ // \ Cu^{2+} \ / \ Cu.$$

The positive pole is usually placed on the right hand side.

Some galvanic cells are given special names. Hence, a concentration cell is a galvanic cell in which the electrodes consist of the same

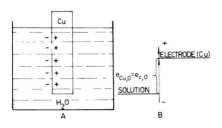

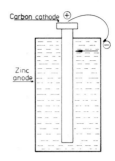

Fig. A3. A copper sheet acquires a
positive charge relative the solution
(water).

Fig. A4. Current direction in
dry cell. Note that within
the cell positive current
flows from − to +.

material (metal) but where the concentrations(activities) of the reacting
species are different at the electrodes. A corrosion cell is a galvanic
cell, the electrode reactions of which lead to corrosion. A corrosion cell
of very small dimensions (e.g. <0.1 mm) is called local cell. which may
hence be said to be a galvanic microcell. Local cells occur, for example,
on multiphase alloys or on metals with electrically conducting coatings or
inclusions of oxides, sulphides, carbon etc. The action of local cells
often leads to localized attack, such as pitting or stress corrosion cracking.

A2.5 Definition of anode and cathode

For the notation of the two electrodes in an electrochemical (galvanic
or electrolytic) cell the following general definition is valid:

The anode is that electrode through which positive current passes
into the electrolyte solution.

According to this basic definition we find, as a rule, that in an
electrolytic cell, also a storage battery under charge, the positive
electrode is the anode and the negative electrode is the cathode.

For a galvanic cell, e.g. a storage battery under discharge, on the
other hand, the negative pole is the anode and the positive pole is the
cathode.

Generally, the following rules are valid:

1) The anode reaction is an oxidation and the cathode reaction is a
reduction and

2) Anions migrate towards the anode, cations towards the cathode.

Note particularly that in a galvanic cell, e.g. a dry cell (Fig. A4), positive current flows from + to - in the outer circuit, whereas within the cell positive current, and hence a positive ion, flows from - to +.

A2.6 Standard electrode potentials

The electrode potential of a metal in a solution, e.g. water, not containing ions of the metal in appreciable concentration, is indefinite and irreversible. Such potentials are of utmost importance in the theory of corrosion, however, and will be dealt with later.

Better defined, reversible potentials are obtained if the metal is immersed in an electrolyte solution, containing its own ions. If, furthermore, the substances taking part in the electrode process are present in certain standard states (pure metals, pure gases of 1 atm. pressure, solutions of ionic activity one etc.), the potentials obtained are called standard or normal potentials. These potentials are referred to the normal or standard hydrogen electrode (NHE) as a zero point. For this electrode, the potential difference between electrode and solution is arbitrarily assumed to be zero at all temperatures (Fig. A5).

A2.7 Sign conventions for standard electrode potentials

If the standard electrode potential is conceived to be the thermodynamic quantity $\frac{\Delta G^0}{zF}$, the sign of the potential is bivariant and depends on the way of writing electrode reactions. According to a European and nowadays also international convention we write, for example

$$Zn^{2+} + 2\ e^- = Zn, \qquad e^0_{Zn} = -0.76\ V$$
$$Cu^{2+} + 2\ e^- = Cu, \qquad e^0_{Cu} = +0.34\ V$$

An older but still used American convention, on the other hand, involves the opposite order and sign according to

$$Zn = Zn^{2+} + 2\ e^-, \qquad e^0_{Zn} = +0.76\ V$$
$$Cu = Cu^{2+} + 2\ e^-, \qquad e^0_{Cu} = -0.34\ V.$$

If electrode potentials, more noble than that of the NHE are to be obtained with positive sign, the electrode reactions have to be written with the electrons on the left side. This obviously means that we put the electrode potential = the potential of the working electrode - the potential of the solution, i.e. = the potential of the working electrode - the potential of the NHE.

Fig. A5. For a normal hydrogen
electrode (NHE), consisting of a
Pt sheet, covered with Pt sponge
and immersed in a solution with
the hydrogen ion activity = 1 and
a hydrogen pressure of 1 atm.,
the potential difference is
arbitrarily taken as zero.

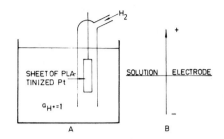

The American convention gives positive potentials to the metals which most easily form positive ions and which are therefore called electropositive. It is of greater value to the study of electrochemistry, however, that the European scale gives the correct sign of the electrodes of galvanic cells. Metals more noble than the NHE might therefore be called electrode-positive although they are usually referred to as metals with positive (or noble) electrode potential. Similarly, metals displacing hydrogen might be referred to as electrode-negative, but are usually termed metals with negative (or base) electrode potential.[x] The European convention was accepted as an international standard at a conference in Stockholm in 1953 and is therefore sometimes called the Stockholm convention for the sign of electrode potentials. With the thermodynamic concept of electrode potential, it is obviously somewhat inconsequent to write the electrons to the right and yet apply the international sign convention, as is often done. With the international sign convention, it also seems irrational to place the unnoble metals first in tables of standard potentials or to plot negative potentials upwards in potential-current diagrams.

If, on the other hand, the electrode potential is defined as the electric potential difference, e, its sign becomes invariant and the whole situation is much simplified. The direct experimental determination undoubtedly gives an electric potential difference and copper is undisputedly positive to zinc. Therefore, it seems rational to consider the

---

[x] The term electronegative, on the other hand, refers to the tendency of an element to form negative ions in chemical compounds. Electronegativity in this sense is an important concept in the theory of the chemical bond.

electrode potential as an electric quantity of invariant sign. With the electrons and the oxidized state to the _left,_ we then write $e^o = - \frac{\Delta G^o}{zF}$, with the electrons and the oxidized state to the _right_, we put $e^o = + \frac{\Delta G^o}{zF}$. With this in mind, we need no longer be so concerned about the manner of writing electrode reactions.

A2.8 _Thermodynamic_ _calculation_ _of_standard_ _potentials_

For a complete redox reaction without the appearance of free electrons, the free energy of reaction, ΔG^o, can easily be found. For an electrode process this is not a priori possible, since the ΔG^o-values of the electrons are not known. This difficulty is circumvented by _arbitrarily_ putting the free energy change $\Delta G^o = 0$ at all temperatures for the reaction

$$2 \; H^+ + 2 \; e^- = H_2.$$

According to the relation $e^o = - \frac{\Delta G^o}{zF}$, we obtain $e^o = 0$ for the NHE at all temperatures. This is the thermodynamic correspondence to the experimental zero potential reference electrode introduced in A2.6 above. Since, according to definition, $G^o = 0$ for H_2 at $25^o C$ this is true also for the sum $H^+ + e^-$.

With data from Latimer, Oxidation Potentials, we obtain, as an example, for the reaction

$$Fe + 2 \; H_2O \rightarrow Fe(OH)_2 + 2 \; H^+ + 2 \; e^-$$

ΔG^o 0   - 2·56.69   - 115.57   0

The free enthalpy change ΔG^o for the reaction is $-115.6 + 2·56.7 =$ $= -2.2$ kcal/mole $=-2200$ cal/mole. Since 1 cal $= 4.18$ Ws and in this case (with the electrons to the right) $e^o = + \frac{\Delta G^o}{zF}$, we obtain $e^o = \frac{-2200·4.18}{2·96500} =$ $= -0.05$ V at pH 0. (At pH 14 we obtain -0.88 V and at pH 7 -0.46 V according to the Nernst equation below.)

A2.9 _Nernst_equation_

Generally, an electrode reaction can be written

$$ox + z \cdot e^- = red$$

According to the thermodynamics of chemical equilibria, the free energy change in the general case (ΔG) and in the standard state (ΔG^o) are connected by the relation

$$\Delta G = \Delta G^o + RT \cdot {}^e log \; \frac{|red|}{|ox|} \; .$$

Division by $-zF$ gives for corresponding electrode potentials the equation

$$e = e^0 - \frac{RT}{zF} \; e_{log} \; \frac{[red]}{[ox]}$$

or

$$e = e^0 + \frac{RT}{zF} \; e_{log} \; \frac{[ox]}{[red]}$$

By changing from natural to decadic logarithms we obtain the so-called Nernst equation

$$e = e^0 + \frac{0.059}{z} \; log \; \frac{[ox]}{[red]}$$

since $\frac{2.303 \cdot RT}{F} = 0.059$ V at 25^0C.

The Nernst equation shows, therefore, how the electrode potential varies with the concentrations (or rather activities) of participating substances. The dependence of electrode potentials on hydrogen ion concentration or pH is of particular importance.

For the hydrogen electrode

$$2 \; H^+ + 2 \; e^- = H_2$$

the electrode potential is recalculated from pH 0 to 14 according to

$$e^0_{alkali} = e^0_{acid} + \frac{0.059}{2} \; log \; \frac{[H^+]^2}{P_{H_2}} = 0.000 - 14 \cdot 0.059 = -0.83 \; V$$

which value is, therefore, the standard electrode potential for the reaction

$$2 \; H_2O + 2 \; e^- = H_2 + 2 \; OH^-.$$

For the oxygen electrode

$$O_2 + 4 \; H^+ + 4 \; e^- = 2 \; H_2O$$

with $\quad \Delta G^0 \qquad 0 \qquad\qquad 0 \qquad\qquad -56.7$ kcal/mole

the standard electrode potential is

$$e^0 = - \frac{-2 \cdot 56700 \cdot 4.18}{4 \cdot 96500} = +1.23 \; V.$$

This value is recalculated to alkaline solution according to

$$e^0_{alkali} = e^0_{acid} + \frac{0.059}{4} \; log \; \frac{P_{O_2}[H^+]^4}{[H_2O]^2} = 1.23 - 14 \cdot 0.059 = 1.23-0.83 = 0.40V,$$

which value is, evidently, the standard electrode potential for the reaction

$$O_2 + 2 H_2O + 4 e^- = 4 OH^-.$$

Summing up the standard electrode potentials for the hydrogen and oxygen electrodes at different pH values, we obtain the following table:

	pH 0	pH 7	pH 14
$e_{H_2}^o$, V	0.00	-0.41	-0.83
$e_{O_2}^o$, V	+1.23	+0.82	+0.40

Even for other electrode reactions, in which water and hydrogen or hydroxyl ions take part, the electrode potential is displaced by 0.059 V per pH unit (if, namely, each H^+- or OH^--ion corresponds to one electron in the formula, otherwise by $(y/z) \cdot 0.059$ V, where y is the number of H^+- or OH^--ions and z the number of electrons, taking part in the reaction).

Table A1 gives standard potentials for some electrode reactions, selected with special reference to corrosion processes and usually referred to pH 7 as a standard state.

A.3 Polarization

The difference between the potentials of an electrode with and without current, or e_i-e_o (taken in this order), is called (electrochemical) polarization. Polarization is due to some kind of reaction inertia.

Electrochemical polarization is, substantially, of three different kinds:

a) Concentration polarization, η_C
b) Resistance polarization, η_R
c) Activation polarization, η_A.

Closely related to polarization is overvoltage[1], which is defined as the polarization of a definite electrode reaction, such as hydrogen evolution.

A3.1 Concentration polarization

Concentration polarization is caused by a deviation of the concentration on the electrode surface from that of the bulk solution. As an example, let us consider copper refining. Copper is deposited on the cathode resulting in a lower copper ion concentration at the cathode than in the bulk solution. At the anode, copper is dissolved, resulting in a higher concentration there than in the bulk (Fig. A6).

[1] or overpotential

TABLE A1.Standard potentials for electrode reactions.

Particular attention is paid to reactions with solid reaction products, denoted (s) in the table. pH 7, i.e. $a_{H^+} = a_{OH^-} = 10^{-7}$, is chosen as a standard state here, being of greatest relevance in corrosion reactions. For certain reactions, the electrode potentials are given also for pH 0 and pH 14. If water and its ions do not take part in a reaction, no pH value is given in the first column.

pH	Electrode reaction red = ox+z·e⁻		$e^o V$
	Ag		
–	Ag	$=Ag^+ + e^-$	+0.799
–	$Ag + Cl^-$	$=AgCl(s) + e^-$	+0.222
–	$Ag + 3CN^-$	$=\left[Ag(CN)_3\right]^{2-} + e^-$	−0.51
–	$Ag + 2NH_3(aq)$	$=\left[Ag(NH_3)_2\right]^+ + e^-$	+0.373
7	$2Ag + H_2S(g)$	$=Ag_2S(s) + 2H^+ + 2e^-$	−0.45
	Al		
–	Al	$=Al^{3+} + 3e^-$	−1.66
7	$Al + 3H_2O$	$=Al(OH)_3(s) + 3H^+ + 3e^-$	−1.96
7	$2Al + 3H_2O$	$=Al_2O_3(s) + 6H^+ + 6e^-$	−1.90
	Au		
–	Au	$=Au^+ + e^-$	+1.69
–	Au	$=Au^{3+} + 3e^-$	+1.50
–	$Au + 2Cl^-$	$=AuCl_2^- + e^-$	+1.11
–	$Au + 4Cl^-$	$=AuCl_4^- + 3e^-$	+1.00
	Bi		
7	$Bi + Cl^- + H_2O$	$=BiOCl(s) + 2H^+ + 3e^-$	−0.115
7	$Bi + 2H_2O$	$=BiOOH(s) + 3H^+ + 3e^-$	+0.07
	Cd		
–	Cd	$=Cd^{2+} + 2e^-$	−0.403
–	$Cd + 4CN^-$	$=\left[Cd(CN)_4\right]^{2-} + 2e^-$	−1.03
7	$Cd + 2H_2O$	$=Cd(OH)_2(s) + 2H^+ + 2e^-$	−0.40
	Cl		
–	$2Cl^-$	$=Cl_2(g) + 2e^-$	+1.3595

Table A1 (continued)

pH	Electrode reaction red = ox+z·e⁻		e^{o}V
	Co		
–	Co	$=Co^{2+}+2e^{-}$	-0.277
7	$Co+2H_2O$	$=Co(OH)_2(s)+2H^{+}+2e^{-}$	-0.32
	Cr		
–	Cr	$=Cr^{3+}+3e^{-}$	-0.744
7	$2Cr+3H_2O$	$=Cr_2O_3(s)+6H^{+}+6e^{-}$	-0.99
7	$Cr_2O_3(s)+5H_2O$	$=2CrO_4^{2-}+10H^{+}+6e^{-}$	+0.62
	Cu		
–	Cu	$=Cu^{2+}+2e^{-}$	+0.337
–	$Cu+Cl^{-}$	$=CuCl(s)+e^{-}$	+0.137
–	$Cu+2CN^{-}$	$=\left[Cu(CN)_2\right]^{-}+e^{-}$	-0.43
–	$Cu+4NH_3$	$=\left[Cu(NH_3)_4\right]^{2+}+2e^{-}$	-0.05
7	$Cu+H_2O$	$=CuO(s)+2H^{+}+2e^{-}$	+0.16
7	$2Cu+H_2O$	$=Cu_2O(s)+2H^{+}+2e^{-}$	+0.056
7	$Cu+H_2S(g)$	$=CuS(s)+2H^{+}+2e^{-}$	-0.62
	Fe		
–	Fe	$=Fe^{2+}+2e^{-}$	-0.440
7	$Fe+2H_2O$	$=Fe(OH)_2(s)+2H^{+}+2e^{-}$	-0.463
–	Fe^{2+}	$=Fe^{3+}+e^{-}$	+0.771
7	$Fe(OH)_2(s)+H_2O$	$=Fe(OH)_3(s)+H^{+}+e^{-}$	-0.15
7	$Fe(OH)_3(s)+H_2O$	$=FeO_4^{2-}+5H^{+}+3e^{-}$	+1.42
	H		
0	H_2+2H_2O	$=2H_3O^{+}+2e^{-}$	0.000
7	H_2+2H_2O	$=2H_3O^{+}+2e^{-}$	-0.414
14	H_2+2OH^{-}	$=2H_2O+2e^{-}$	-0.828
	Hg		
–	2Hg	$=Hg_2^{2+}+2e^{-}$	+0.792
–	$2Hg+2Cl^{-}$	$=Hg_2Cl_2(s)+2e^{-}$	+0.268
–	Hg	$=Hg^{2+}+2e^{-}$	+0.854
7	$Hg+H_2O$	$=HgO(s)+2H^{+}+2e^{-}$	+0.512
–	$Hg+S^{2-}$	$=HgS(s)+2e^{-}$	-0.69

Table A1 (continued)

pH	Electrode reaction red = ox+z·e⁻		e^oV
	Mg		
7	$Mg+2H_2O$	$=Mg(OH)_2(s)+2H^++2e^-$	-2.27
7	$Mg+H_2O$	$=MgO(s)+2H^++2e^-$	-2.13
	Mn		
7	$Mn+2H_2O$	$=Mn(OH)_2(s)+2H^++2e^-$	-1.14
	Ni		
–	Ni	$=Ni^{2+}+2e^-$	-0.25
7	$Ni+2H_2O$	$=Ni(OH)_2(s)+2H^++2e^-$	-0.30
7	$Ni(OH)_2(s)$	$=NiOOH(s)+H^++e^-$	+0.62
	O		
0	$2H_2O$	$=O_2+4H^++4e^-$	+1.229
7	$2H_2O$	$=O_2+4H^++4e^-$	+0.815
14	$4OH^-$	$=O_2+2H_2O+4e^-$	+0.401
	Pb		
–	Pb	$=Pb^{2+}+2e^-$	-0.126
7	$Pb+H_2O$	$=PbO(s)+2H^++2e^-$	-0.16
–	$Pb+2Cl^-$	$=PbCl_2(s)+2e^-$	-0.268
	Pt		
–	Pt	$=Pt^{2+}+2e^-$	+1.19
7	$Pt+2H_2O$	$=Pt(OH)_2(s)+2H^++2e^-$	+0.57
	S		
7	$HSO_3^-+H_2O$	$=SO_4^{2-}+3H^++2e^-$	-0.50
	Sb		
7	$2Sb+3H_2O$	$=Sb_2O_3(s)+6H^++6e^-$	-0.26
	Sn		
7	$Sn+2H_2O$	$=Sn(OH)_2(s)+2H^++2e^-$	-0.50
7	$Sn+2H_2O$	$=SnO_2(s)+4H^++4e^-$	-0.51

Table Al (continued)

pH	Electrode reaction red = ox+z·e⁻		e^o V
	$\underline{Ti}$		
7	$Ti+H_2O$	$=TiO(s)+2H^++2e^-$	-1.72
7	$Ti+2H_2O$	$=TiO_2(s)+4H^++4e^-$	-1.47
	$\underline{U}$		
7	$U+2H_2O$	$=UO_2(s)+4H^++4e^-$	-1.98
	$\underline{V}$		
7	$2V+2H_2O$	$=V_2O_2(s)+4H^++4e^-$	-1.23
	$\underline{W}$		
7	$W+3H_2O$	$=WO_3(s)+6H^++6e^-$	-0.32
	$\underline{Zn}$		
-	Zn	$=Zn^{2+}+2e^-$	-0.763
7	$Zn+2H_2O$	$=Zn(OH)_2(s)+2H^++2e^-$	-0.83
	$\underline{Zr}$		
7	$Zr+2H_2O$	$=ZrO_2(s)+4H^++4e^-$	-1.95

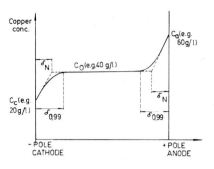

Fig. A6. Copper concentration as a function of the electrode distance in electrolytic copper refining. $\delta_{0.99}$ denotes the diffusion layer thickness reckoned out to 99 % of the concentration difference, $/c_o - c_e/$.

Without electrolysis, we have for both electrodes

$$e_o = e^o + \frac{0.059}{2} \log c_o$$

with c_o = concentration of bulk solution.

Under electrolysis, we obtain for each electrode

$$e_i = e^o + \frac{0.059}{2} \log c_e,$$

observing that $c_e < c_o$ at the cathode, $c_e > c_o$ at the anode.

Hence, the concentration polarization is

$$e_i - e_o = \frac{0.059}{2} \log \frac{c_e}{c_o},$$

which expression is < 0 for the cathode and > 0 for the anode.

The diffusion boundary layer (δ), inside which the concentration deviates from the bulk concentration, is often called electrode film. It is usually approximated with the Nernst diffusion layer δ_N, which is obtained by drawing the tangent to the concentration profile at its intersection with the electrode surface. Without agitation, the electrode film or diffusion layer has a thickness of about 0.1 mm. It must be clearly distinguished from the electrochemical double layer mentioned in A2.3 above. This has a thickness of only 10^{-6} mm.

The limiting current density, I_L, is an important quantity, connected with concentration polarization. I_L (in A/cm^2) is the highest current density (c.d.) possible for a given electrode reaction, e.g. metal deposition, due to the limitation imposed by the diffusion velocity of the reacting particle. Then another electrode process, e.g. hydrogen evolution starts. The corrosion rate in water is quite often determined by the limiting c.d. for cathodic oxygen reduction. For an anodic reaction, I_L is reached when $c_e = c_s$ = the saturation concentration of a salt, e.g. $CuSO_4$ on a copper anode. Anodic limiting c.d.:s are often an introductory step in anodic passivation. Anodic polishing is also carried out under conditions giving anodic limiting c.d. Recording of limiting c.d.:s forms the basis of polarography, which is an important method of chemical analysis.

The limiting current density is inversely proportional to the thickness of the diffusion boundary layer or

$$I_L \cdot \delta_N = const.$$

For a cathode process, the concentration polarization is given by

$$\eta_c = \frac{0.059}{z} \log \frac{c_e}{c_0} = \frac{0.059}{z} \log (1 - \frac{I}{I_L}).$$

If the limiting c.d. I_L for the cathode process is known, this equation shows how the concentration polarization varies with the applied current.

The concentration polarization decreases slowly with a rise in temperature due to an increased diffusion velocity. The concentration polarization is also reduced by stirring, since the diffusion layer δ then becomes thinner and I_L is increased. As concentration polarization is connected with diffusion it is characteristic, furthermore, that it disappears very slowly, after the lapse of several seconds, when the current is shut off.

A3.2 Resistance polarization

Resistance (or ohmic) polarization is due to an ohmic resistance in a film, e.g. an oxide film, on the electrode surface, causing an ohmic potential drop. The passivity of metal surfaces, caused by a film of an oxide (as in the case of Al, Ti, Cr, stainless steel etc.) or a salt (as on copper anodes at high c.d.), may be considered as a special case of an anodic ohmic polarization.

The ohmic polarization may be written

$$\eta_R = R \cdot I = r \cdot i$$

with   R (Ω) = film resistance for all the electrode surface

    I (amp)   = current

    r (Ωcm^2) = film resistance for the area of 1 cm^2

    i (amp/cm^2)= current density.

The ohmic polarization disappears in a few microseconds, when the current is broken.

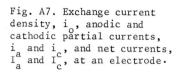 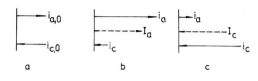

Fig. A7. Exchange current density, i_o, anodic and cathodic partial currents, i_a and i_c, and net currents, I_a and I_c, at an electrode.

Fig. A8. Polarization conditions at a non-corroding electrode.
——— = real anodic or cathodic current, i_a and i_c
------ = outer (measured) anodic or cathodic current, I_a and I_c
e_o = reversible equilibrium potential
i_o = exchange current.

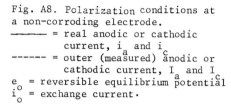 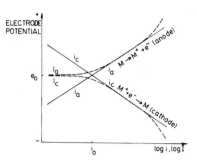

A3.3 Activation polarization

Activation polarization is caused by a certain slow step in the electrode process requiring an activation energy for overcoming the reaction hindrance. If a metal is submersed in a solution containing its own ions, a dynamic equilibrium is developed as much metal being dissolved as is redeposited in the same time (Fig. A7a). Expressed in ampères per unit area, this ion transport through the phase boundary is referred to as exchange current density and is denoted i_o.

If the electrode is made an anode in an electrolytic bath with a resulting net dissolution of metal, the cathodic partial current, i_c, is decreased while the anodic partial current, i_a, increases. The impressed net current is $I_a = i_a - i_c$ (Fig. A7b). By connecting the metal as a cathode we find, correspondingly, $I_c = i_c - i_a$ (Fig. A7c).

The equilibrium between a non-corroding metal and a solution containing its ions corresponds to the point e_o/i_o in the polarization diagram according to Fig. A8. e_o is the reversible equilibrium potential of the metal in the solution. By examining how the electrode potential of the metal deviates from the equilibrium value e_o after the application of, say, an anodic current, I_a, the following result is obtained

I. For small values of I_a (<10 i_o) and hence also of η, a linear relationship is found between η and I_a, viz.

$$\eta_A = \frac{RT}{zF} \cdot \frac{I_a}{i_o}$$

In a half-logarithmic diagram, this corresponds to a curved line, as shown by the dashed lines in Fig. A8.

II. For $I_a > 10\ i_o$, a logarithmic relationship is obtained according to the well-known Tafel's equation

$$\eta_A = b \log \frac{I_a}{i_o} = a + b \log I_a,$$

where a and b are constants, b often $2 \cdot 0.059 = 0.118$ V.
In the half-logarithmic diagram we then obtain straight lines, called Tafel lines.

III. For $I_a \gg i_o$, deviations from the Tafel lines are again obtained owing to concentration and/or resistance polarization.

The activation polarization or overpotential is strongly dependent on the composition of the solution, particularly its content of anions and inhibitors.

Anions of high total molar polarization, $P = \frac{\varepsilon - 1}{\varepsilon + 2} \cdot \frac{M}{\rho}$ (ε = dielectric constant), be it due to a permanent dipole moment or a distortion dipole moment induced by an electric field, have a strong tendency, after adsorption on metal surfaces, to promote electron exchange reactions, i.e. electrode processes, thereon. Such anions, therefore, substantially reduce both anodic and cathodic overpotential and, i.a., catalyse corrosion reactions, particularly local attacks, such as pitting and stress corrosion cracking.

Atom anions of high electron content have a high polarizability in an electric field. Relative values are obtained from electrocapillary curves, showing the surface tension of mercury as a function of electrode potential in various solutions. For some complex anions, a permanent dipole moment contributes to a high molar polarization. The total molar polarizations increase in about the following order and give the following effects:

F^-, ClO_4^-, SO_4^{2-}, CO_3^{2-}, PO_4^{3-}, CrO_4^{2-}, OH^- $\quad$ Cl^-, NO_3^-, Br^-, HS^-, I^-, SCN^-, S^{2-}

Low molar polarization	High molar polarization
Low adsorbability	High adsorbability
High overpotential	Low overpotential
Smooth, fine-grained electrodeposits	Treeing, coarse-crystalline electrodeposits
Low corrosivity	High corrosivity
Weakly peptizing	Strongly peptizing
Passivating	Activating
Weak electrocapillarity effect	Strong electrocapillarity effect
Weak hydrogen embrittlement	Strong hydrogen embrittlement

It is natural that commonly occurring anions of high molar polarization, such as chloride and sulphide ions, are particularly active in corrosion reactions. Cations mainly exert an indirect influence due to their polarizing effect on anions. It should be noted, furthermore, that the relationship between molar polarization and various effects listed above is only qualitative. It is sometimes modified and over-shadowed by other effects, such as complex formation.

The above series of molar polarization of anions is also of importance in electrodeposition of metals, since high metal overpotential gives even and fine-grained deposits of the type wanted in electroplating, whereas low overpotential in metal deposition causes coarse-crystalline, dendritic ("treeing") and rough deposits.

The polarization of anions has since long been known in colloid chemistry in the so-called Hofmeister's lyotropic series of anions, arranged after their increasing ability to adsorb on and peptize colloids. In this respect, they seem to be of importance also in corrosion reactions, namely in their varying power to penetrate and dissolve passivating oxide films.

What has been said above is valid for neutral solutions. In strongly acid solutions, the adsorption of the corresponding acids also increases from left to right, e.g. $HClO_4 < H_2SO_4 < HCl < HBr < HI$. In the corrosion of mild steel this then results in increasing polarization and inhibition as we pass from left to right. Apparently, the adsorbed anions do not facilitate electron transfer reactions if they are neutralized by hydrogen ions.

Inhibitors in general are negative catalysts. In electrochemistry, inhibitors are substances which increase overvoltage. Some anions, such as phosphate, chromate and nitrite, by forming insoluble salts or oxides with the metal exert a specific influence on anodic polarization and therefore act as powerful anodic corrosion inhibitors. Others,particularly organic substances containing sulphur and nitrogen, adsorb strongly on all the metal surface and therefore inhibit both anodic and cathodic reactions. The same types of organic substances are therefore used both as crystal growth inhibitors ("addition agents") in electroplating and as corrosion and pickling inhibitors.

The activation polarization is independent of stirring of the solution but decreases rapidly with rising temperature, since the exchange c.d., i_o, increases strongly with temperature. After current interruption, the activation polarization fades away within a few milliseconds.

A3.4 Hydrogen overvoltage

The polarization of hydrogen evolution, the so-called hydrogen overvoltage, is of particular importance since it varies between wide limits for various cathode materials. It is often the deciding factor in hydrogen evolution corrosion. Table A2 gives values of hydrogen overvoltage for a number of materials with metallic conductivity, arranged after increasing overvoltage.

The values in Table A2 explain why many metals, less noble than hydrogen, e.g. zinc, cadmium, tin and lead in pure state dissolve very slowly in acids. The dissolution rate increases very strongly, however, in the presence of small amounts of impurities of more noble metals with low hydrogen overvoltage. During dissolution in acid, these metallic impurities are redeposited on the zinc surface and will then act as efficient local cathodes for hydrogen evolution.

A more noble metal with a high hydrogen overvoltage, such as mercury, on the other hand, will not act as cathode in corrosion cells. Mercury drops on steel, for instance, do not increase its corrosion velocity in acids since the hydrogen overvoltage on Hg (about 1 V) is larger than the emf of the cell Fe-Hg (about 0.6 V). On zinc, mercury acts strongly reducing on corrosion velocity. Mercury amalgamates with zinc and also dissolves metallic impurities that would otherwise deposit and act as local cathodes.

TABLE A2. Hydrogen overvoltage in volt on various materials and at different current densities.

Material	Hydrogen overvoltage at		
	10^{-3} A/cm^2 V	10^{-2} A/cm^2 V	10^{-1} A/cm^2 V
Platinized Pt	0.015	0.030	0.04
Bright Pt	0.025	0.07	0.29
Ni_3S_2	-	0.1	0.2
NiS	0.2	0.3	0.4
Fe_3C	0.05	0.8	-
Au	0.24	0.39	0.59
Coke	0.27	0.34	0.41
Mo	0.30	0.44	0.57
Ni	0.33	0.42	0.51
Fe	0.40	0.53	0.64
Ag	0.44	0.66	0.76
Graphite	0.47	0.76	0.99
Cu	0.60	0.75	0.82
Zn	0.72	0.75	1.06
Sn	0.85	0.98	0.99
Cd	0.91	1.20	1.25
Pb	0.91	1.24	1.26
Hg	1.04	1.15	1.21

A.4 Potential-distance diagrams and potential-arrow diagrams

A4.1 For an open galvanic cell

Assume the zinc and copper sheets in section A2 above to be submersed in the same solution. An electric conductor not carrying current has a uniform and constant potential. The solution therefore has the same potential between the two electrodes. The two phase boundary potentials between the metal electrodes and the solution form an electromotive force (emf) E according to Fig. A9. This is a potential-distance diagram, obtained by placing the potential axes for the zinc and copper electrodes at a distance equal to the electrode distance. In order to find the relation

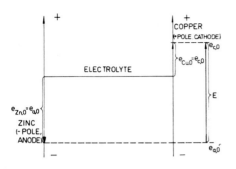

Fig. A9. Potential-distance and
potential-arrow diagram for an
open galvanic cell consisting of
a copper plate and a zinc plate
in sulphuric acid. $E = e_{c,o} - e_{a,o}$.

between various potential differences
in such a diagram, the following
procedure is used:

Go round the diagram until
the starting point is reached again. The sum of the potential differences
then passed will be zero. A potential arrow is counted positive if it is
followed in its own direction but negative if it is passed in the opposite
direction. In the present simple case we obtain:

$$E - e_{Cu} + e_{Zn} = 0 \quad \text{or}$$

$$E = e_{Cu} - e_{Zn} \quad \text{or generally } E = e_c - e_a.$$

In the further application it is also useful to put together the
emf, its components at the two electrodes and the various potential drops
referred to on one and the same potential axis. This has been done to the
right in Fig. A9. We then obtain a diagram, which is here called a potential-
arrow diagram. With the corrosion velocity or corrosion current i (strictly
speaking log i) as horizontal axis these diagrams will later be developed
to potential-current or polarization diagrams (Fig. E1, E4).

A4.2 For a resistance-circuited galvanic cell without polarization

Now connect the Zn and Cu sheets via an external resistance R_e according to Fig. A10. Assume, furthermore, that the electrolyte is a solution
of sulphuric acid and that the internal (electrolyte) resistance between
the electrodes is R_i. The tendency towards neutralization of charges causes
electrons to flow through the metal wire from Zn to Cu. This means that
positive current flows in the opposite direction. The electrons neutralize
H^+-ions on the Cu sheet with resulting hydrogen evolution. Outside the Cu-
sheet the SO_4^{2-}-ions then lose their counter-ions and migrate towards the
positive Zn^{2+}-ions outside the Zn sheet. The Zn^{2+}-ions in their turn migrate,
along with H^+-ions, towards the negative ions outside the Cu sheet. Since
positive current in the solution flows from Zn to Cu, the electric potential
must decrease in the same direction.

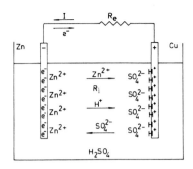

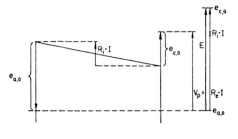

Fig. A10. Electron and ion flows
in a closed galvanic circuit.

Fig. A11. Potential-distance and
potential-arrow diagram for a
resistance-circuited, unpolarized
galvanic cell.
$E = e_{c,o} - e_{a,o} = I(R_e + R_i)$ (Ohm's law).

It should be observed that Zn^{2+}- and H^+-ions in the closed cell migrate
towards the positive Cu sheet because the solution outside this electrode
has a lower potential than the solution outside the Zn sheet. For the same
reason, the negative SO_4^{2-}-ions migrate towards the negative Zn sheet. At
the electrodes only those reactions take place which occur most easily. In
the present case this means hydrogen evolution at the cathode and zinc dissolution at the anode. It should also be observed that the definition and
rules given under section A2 above hold true: The Cu sheet is the positive
pole or + pole or cathode. The Zn sheet is the negative pole or - pole or
anode. The potential distribution in the closed cell is evident from Fig. A11.
If the terminal or cell voltage is called V_p we have

$$V_p = R_e \cdot I \quad \text{and} \quad E = I(R_e + R_i).$$

A4.3 For a resistance-circuited galvanic cell with polarization

In reality, polarization always occurs, reducing the cell voltage still
further. By polarization, the two electrode potentials are displaced towards
each other. The potential drops at the electrodes are reduced with the polarizations n_c and n_a. The correspond-
ing potential diagram is shown in
Fig. A12. The cathode polarization,
n_c, is always negative and displaces

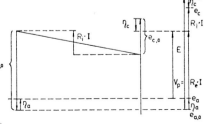

Fig. A12. Potential-distance and
potential-arrow diagram for a resistance-circuited polarized
galvanic cell.
$E = e_{c,o} - e_{a,o} = I(R_e + R_i) + n_a + /n_c/.$

the cathode potential in negative direction. In summing up the potential drops within the cell, η_c has to be taken as its absolute value $/\eta_c/$. The anode polarization, η_a, is always positive and displaces the anode potential in positive direction. With both external and internal resistance and polarization at both electrodes we thus obtain

$$E = I(R_e + R_i) + \eta_a + /\eta_c/.$$

A4.4 For a short-circuited galvanic cell (corrosion cell) with internal potential drop, corresponding to local corrosion

In a corroding metal, both resistances and corrosion currents are so small that the potential drop in the metal is negligible. This is also true if two metals are in immediate contact without separating oxide films or other high-resistive layers. For the terminal voltage we then have $V_p = R_e \cdot I = 0$. This means that a corrosion cell is short-circuited.

If anodic and cathodic surfaces appear at a significant distance from each other, corresponding to local corrosion, an internal potential drop between the electrodes is to be found in the solution (corroding medium). The corresponding potential-distance and potential-arrow diagram is shown in Fig. A13.

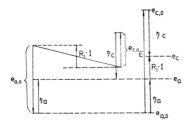

Fig. A13. Potential-distance and potential-arrow diagram for a short-circuited galvanic cell (corrosion cell) with an internal potential drop $R_i \cdot I$, corresponding to local corrosion.
$E = e_{c,o} - e_{a,o} = R_i \cdot I + \eta_a + /\eta_c/.$

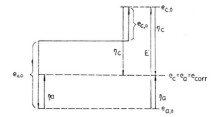

Fig. A14. Potential-distance and potential-arrow diagram for a short-circuited galvanic cell (corrosion cell) without an internal potential drop, corresponding to general corrosion. $E = \eta_a + /\eta_c'/.$ Cf. Fig. A9.

A4.5 For a short-circuited galvanic cell (corrosion cell) without internal potential drop, corresponding to general corrosion

If the corrosion attack is evenly distributed over a larger metal surface, acting at the same time as both anode and cathode, even the internal potential drop $R_i \cdot I$ in the solution is missing and all the electromotive force is nullified by polarization at the electrodes. The potential diagrams for this case are shown in Fig. A14.

A.5 Measurement of electrode potentials and polarization

In order to determine an electrode potential it is necessary to measure the emf between the test or working electrode and a reference electrode with known and constant potential. Although electrode potentials are usually referred to the NHE, this electrode is rarely used as a reference in measurements. It is more convenient to use certain other reference electrodes, some examples of which are shown in Table A3 below.

TABLE A3. Some common reference electrodes.

Designation	Composition	Electrode reaction	Potential relative to the NHE, V	Temperature coefficient, mV per ^{o}C
Saturated calomel (SCE) electrode	$Hg,Hg_2Cl_2(s)/$ $KCl(saturated)$	$Hg_2Cl_2 + 2e^- =$ $2Hg + 2Cl^-$	+0.2446	-0.76
0.1-M calomel electrode	$Hg,Hg_2Cl_2(s)/$ $KCl(0.1-M)$	$-"-$	+0.3338	-0.07
0.1-M silver chloride electrode	$Ag,AgCl(s)/$ $KCl(0.1-M)$	$AgCl + e^- =$ $Ag + Cl^-$	+0.2881	-0.65
1-M mercury sulphate electrode	$Hg,Hg_2SO_4(s)/$ $K_2SO_4(1-M)$	$Hg_2SO_4 + 2e^- =$ $2Hg + SO_4^{2-}$	+0.660	-0.80
Copper sulphate electrode, saturated	$Cu/CuSO_4(sat.soln)$	$Cu^{2+} + 2e^- = Cu$	+0.320	

In most reference electrodes, the potential is determined by the concentration of an anion (Cl^-, SO_4^{2-} etc.). The potentials of these anion electrodes can be calculated from the standard potentials of the corresponding cation electrodes (for Hg_2^{2+}/Hg + 0.792 V, for Ag^+/Ag + 0.799 V) by means of the Nernst equation and using the solubility product of the solid salt (Hg_2Cl_2, $AgCl$, Hg_2SO_4 etc.) and the concentration and activity coefficient of the conducting electrolyte of the reference electrode (KCl, K_2SO_4 etc.).

The test electrode and the reference electrode are connected to a potentiometer for measuring the potential difference between them. If a compensation circuit is used the measurement is carried out without drawing any current from the test cell and thus gives the highest accuracy. For corrosion studies, however, it is usually sufficient to use an electronic potentiometer with high input resistance, such as a pH-meter. In order to obtain a closed circuit an electrolyte bridge (a liquid junction) is required between the test electrode and the reference electrode as shown by Fig. A15.

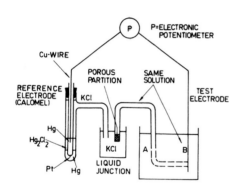

Fig. A15. Apparatus for measuring electrode potentials and polarization. A: Test electrode without outer current, as in the measurement of corrosion potentials. B: Test electrode with outer current, as in the recording of polarization curves.

In the interface between two different electrolyte solutions, a diffusion or liquid junction potential appears due to different ionic mobilities. In order to minimize the diffusion potential, KCl is usually chosen as an electrolyte in the salt bridge since the ionic mobilities of K^+ and Cl^- are about the same. Furthermore, it is suitable to place the liquid junction between the two solutions in a separate vessel. In this way, contamination of both the test solution and the reference electrode is avoided.

The measurement is somewhat different on electrodes with and without current. If the working or test electrode is currentless, as in the measurement of corrosion potentials on an evenly corroding metal surface, the electrolyte bridge may end in any place in the measurement vessel, since there is no risk of including an ohmic potential drop in this case. If, on the other hand, the measurement is carried out in a closed electrolytic or galvanic cell of macroscopic dimensions, as for instance in local corrosion, the electrolyte bridge must be drawn out to a fine capillary probe, ending as closely to the test electrode or the relevant part of it as possible. Otherwise, part of the ohmic potential drop is erroneously included. If, therefore, the capillary ends somewhere between the anode and cathode in a cell, through which current is flowing, the measured anode potential will be higher than the real one and the measured cathode potential will be lower than the real value according to Fig. A16. The ohmic potential drops, $R_a \cdot I$ and $R_c \cdot I$, included in the measurement may therefore be considered as anodic and cathodic polarizations. Fig. A16 also shows that by moving the capillary tip from anode to cathode in a local corrosion cell, the measured potential rises by the potential drop then passed, i.e. $|-R_i \cdot I|$, in accordance with Figs A11-A13.

As a matter of fact, such ohmic potential drops also are of import- ance in the determination and interpretation of potentials of evenly corrod- ing metals. On metals covered by an oxide film, the anode process takes place in the phase boundary metal/oxide whereas the measurement is carried out in the interface oxide/solution and gives a more noble value.

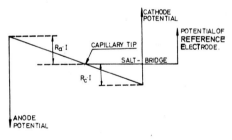

Fig. A16. If the tip of the capillary of the reference electrode is located at a cer- tain distance from the metal surface the measured potential is more noble than the real anode potential but less noble than the real cathode potential. Similarly, a metal covered with an oxide film shows a more noble potential than the oxide-free metal due to a potential drop, acting as an anodic polarization, in the oxide film or in the solu- tion in pores of the latter.

A.6 Polarization curves

Polarization curves show the relationship between electrode potential and current density and may thus also be called potential-c.d. curves. Formerly, c.d. was plotted along the vertical axis and electrode potential along the horizontal axis. The procedure followed from curves showing the current as a function of the voltage of an electrolysis cell. This method is still used in polarography. Usually, polarization curves are now plotted with electrode potential on the vertical axis and c.d. on the horizontal

axis. One example is given in Fig. E5, showing the anodic polarization
curve for iron in sulphuric acid. Considering Tafel's equation, referred
to under section A3 above, it is often suitable to plot polarization curves
in diagrams with log I on the horizontal axis.

An apparatus, allowing a regulated change of current and maintaining
it at a constant value for each point of the measurement, is called a
galvanostat. This is as a rule a simple arrangement and consists of a
large resistance in series with the electrolysis cell. In investigating
passivity phenomena it is of greater value to regulate and vary the electrode potential. This is done by means of a so-called potentiostat, which
is a considerably more complicated apparatus, as a rule electronic. If the
potential is changed continuously, the measurement is said to be potentiodynamic.

Literature

Potter, E C, Electrochemistry, Principles & Applications, Cleaver-Hume
Press Ltd, London 1961.

Kortüm, G, Treatise on Electrochemistry, Elsevier Publishing Co., Amsterdam
1965.

Hampel,CA, Encyclopedia of Electrochemistry, Reinhold, New York 1964.

Vetter, K J, Electrochemical Kinetics, Academic Press, New York 1967.

Bockris, J O'M & Reddy, A K N, Modern Electrochemistry, Plenum Press,
New York 1970.

B. METALLURGICAL ELEMENTS

B.1 Metals and alloys

The structure of metals and alloys is of deciding importance for their corrosion characteristics which cannot, therefore, be discussed without the use of metallurgical terms. In the following, some fundamental metallurgical concepts are presented. The presentation is limited to iron and steel. Special attention is devoted to stainless steels.

An alloy consists of a mixture of two or more elements of which at least one is a metal and where all occurring phases have metallic properties. Alloys may be monophasic (homogeneous) or polyphasic (heterogeneous), depending upon the mutual solubility of the metals in the solid state.

Technically manufactured metals and alloys consist of irregularly formed crystals, so-called grains. Within each grain, the orientation of the atomic lattice is constant or practically constant. The interface between two crystal grains is called grain boundary. The grain boundary is a discontinuity region in which the lattices of the two crystals are strongly disturbed (Fig. B1) and in which there are greater chances for the enrichment of impurities than in the interior of the crystal grains where the arrangement of the atoms is more regular. But even here different kinds of defects, such as dislocations and stacking faults are to be found.

In a series of atom layers which ought to be completely plane, a dislocation means a step-like defect, e.g. caused by an extra atom layer

Fig. B1. Arrangement of atoms at a grain boundary in a polycrystalline metal. ● denotes foreign (impurity) atoms.

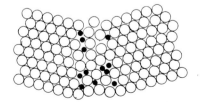

on one side of the defect (Fig. B2). If the step height, the so-called Burgers vector, is constant along all its extension, we have an edge dislocation but if it increases from the centre and outwards we have a screw dislocation. Both types play an important part in the formation and growth of crystals and also in their strength properties.

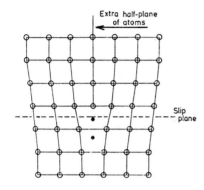

Fig. B2. Schematic illustration of an edge dislocation. ● denotes foreign (impurity) atoms, making slip more difficult.

St̲a̲c̲k̲i̲n̲g̲ f̲a̲u̲l̲t̲s̲ occur only in close-packed structures, of which the face-centered cubic one has the layer sequence ABCABC... and the hexagonal one has the sequence ABABAB... Stacking faults imply an accidental hexagonal sequence in the cubic close-packing or vice versa. Both dislocations and stacking faults play an important part in some modern theories of stress corrosion cracking.

An alloy often consists of a primary phase (as a rule a solid solution), called m̲a̲t̲r̲i̲x̲ and of dispersed particles of one or more other phases, which occur in small amounts and are called p̲r̲e̲c̲i̲p̲i̲t̲a̲t̲e̲s̲ or secondary phases. They often consist of carbides or intermetallic compounds. As well as in grain boundaries such small precipitated particles are usually found in bands, formed by so-called s̲l̲i̲p̲-p̲l̲a̲n̲e̲s̲ in the crystals. Slip-planes are atom planes in the lattice along which the metal is preferably displaced on plastic deformation. The slip-planes are always the most close-packed (most densely populated) atom planes, since these have the largest distances between them and hence the weakest cross-links.

The grain structure of a metallic material can be observed and photographed in a m̲i̲c̲r̲o̲s̲c̲o̲p̲e̲ after metallographic preparation of a specimen, comprising grinding with carbide or diamond paste, bright polishing with, for example, Al_2O_3 or MgO on a cloth disc, sometimes also electrolytic polishing, and finally etching. The e̲t̲c̲h̲i̲n̲g̲ is usually carried out by immersing the polished specimen for a short time in an acid solution, often containing hydrochloric, nitric, acetic or picric acid in alcohol but may also be done anodically. During the etching process the grain boundaries are first attacked, since these are more reactive due to lattice disturbances and enrichment of impurities. The interior of the grains is attacked differently according to their orientation and composition, resulting in a great many small reflecting surfaces. The grain boundaries therefore appear as dark lines and the etched grains as bright or dark areas on observation in reflected light through a microscope (Fig. B3). By etching it is also possible to disclose precipitates,pores, preferred orientation of crystal grains, the influence of the substrate on the structure of metallic coatings and oxide layers etc. By variation of etching agent and etching time in the investigation of one and the same specimen, one or the other effect may be emphasized. Slag inclusions are usually identified on the polished but unetched surface.

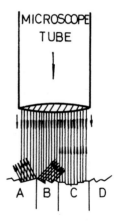

Fig. B3. Formation of light contrasts in the microscopic study of etched metal surfaces.

The etching process in itself is of great interest since it is a sort of corrosion process, occurring electrochemically and in which anode and cathode surfaces in local cells disclose the relative resistance of different phases and areas. The observation of the effect of etching is therefore of great value to the watchful student.

The etching experiment can also be carried out as a regular micro-corrosion test. A newly polished metal specimen is carefully degreased. A drop of the corroding solution, preferably containing some wetting agent, is then placed on the specimen and the resultant reaction is observed under the microscope. Hence, it is possible to show that pitting corrosion is initiated close to or around certain structural constituents, acting as local cathodes for hydrogen evolution (also in neutral media), e.g. in magnesium or aluminium alloys certain intermetallic compounds or in steel certain electrochemically active sulphide inclusions (Cf. Fig. B8 below). If the corroding solution contains some copper sulphate, metallic copper can be seen to deposit on cathodic spots.

B.2 Unalloyed steels

B2.1 Allotropic modifications of iron

In the solid state, iron occurs in three allotropic modifications, usually denoted α, γ and δ or ferrite, austenite and δ-ferrite. Each modification exists only within a certain temperature range. With iron in the molten state as a fourth modification the following ranges can be given for the existence of the various modifications.

α-iron or ferrite	- 911°C
γ-iron or austenite	911-1392°C
δ-iron or δ-ferrite	1392-1536°C
melt	1536°C-

Iron is ferromagnetic at room temperature, but with rising temperature the ferromagnetism diminishes and disappears completely at 769°C (the Curie point). The non-magnetic ferrite in the temperature range 769-911°C was earlier called β-iron but according to what we know today it does not constitute a special modification of iron.

α-iron has a cubic space-centered atom lattice (atoms in the corners and in the centre of the unit cube). δ-iron has the same atomic arrangement as α-iron and may therefore be considered as the same modification as the latter, although it has larger atom distances due to the higher temperature. γ-iron is cubically face-centered (atoms in the corners and in the centres of the faces of the unit cube). This implies a denser packing of atoms (so-called cubic close-packing) than in α-iron and therefore also a higher density. A transformation of one modification to another therefore means a change in volume which may result in internal stresses in the new modification.

B2.2 The phase diagram iron-carbon

Steels constitute alloys between on the one hand iron (more than 50 %) and on the other hand one or more alloying elements. The most important of these elements is carbon which to a larger or smaller extent is found in all kinds of steel. That part of the phase diagram iron-carbon which is of interest for steels is shown in figure B4.

The eutectoid point S at 0.80 % C and 723°C is of particular importance. The eutectoid, which is called pearlite, consists of ferrite and cementite. The latter is iron carbide of the composition Fe_3C (6.7 % C).

Fig. B4. Phase diagram for carbon steel. The eutectoid mixture of ferrite and cementite (Fe$_3$C), formed in the normal decomposition of austenite, is called pearlite.

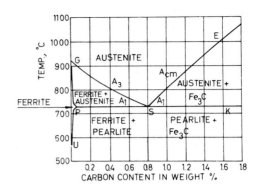

The solubility of carbon is substantially different in the different modifications of iron. The great difference in size of the iron and carbon atoms results in the formation of a so-called addition_solution, i.e. the carbon atoms are located in the empty places between the iron atoms in the lattice. The cubically face-centered lattice of austenite can provide space for considerably more carbon than the space-centered lattice of ferrite. By alloying with carbon the range of existence for ferrite is reduced while the range for austenite is widened. Carbon is therefore said to be an austenite-forming alloying element.

For the most important phase boundaries in the diagram the following notation is often used: PSK=A$_1$, GS=A$_3$, SE=A$_{cm}$.

B2.3 Definition_of_steel

Alloys of iron and carbon are usually divided into two groups, viz. steel and cast_iron. The limit between these two groups is usually given as the maximum solubility of carbon in austenite which is close to 2.0 % C. The steels, which thus contain less than 2.0 % C, can in their turn be divided into unalloyed and alloyed steels. With an unalloyed steel, or as it is often called carbon_steel, we mean a steel which besides carbon and iron contains only minor amounts of a series of elements whose presence is accidental and is dependent upon the composition of the raw materials and upon the manufacturing process. Alloyed steels contain, beside carbon, a higher content of one or more specially added alloying elements, such as Si, Mn, Cu, V, Mo, W and, particularly in the stainless and acid-proof steels, Cr and Ni. The atoms of the alloying metals are substituted for Fe atoms in the lattice and are therefore said to be in substitution_solution.

B2.4 Killed_and_unkilled_steel

Steel is produced from pig iron by refining, involving an oxidation of carbon and some other elements. In this process, a certain excess of oxygen in the iron melt is obtained in the form of dissolved FeO. The main part of this oxygen is removed by desoxidation with manganese (as ferro-manganese), silicon (as ferro-silicon) or aluminium. The remaining oxygen is given off during the casting of the steel in the solidification close to the wall of the chill and is then combined with dissolved carbon to form carbon monoxide. One then obtains so-called unkilled steel, which is characterized by a skin of a very pure ferrite low in carbon and a rim of carbon monoxide blisters inside the ferrite skin. If, on the other hand, even the last residues of dissolved oxygen are removed by a strong des-oxidizing agent, silicon or aluminium, the steel solidifies homogeneously and without the rimming zone, forming so-called killed steel.

Carbon steel with a C content higher than 0.40 % and alloyed steels are always killed, whereas carbon steel with a lower carbon content can be obtained in both conditions. Unkilled carbon steels have low silicon and aluminium contents, about 0.01 %, while killed steel contains about 0.25 % silicon or aluminium, which are partly present as finely divided oxides (SiO_2 and Al_2O_3, respectively) in the steel.

Because the unkilled steel has a skin of very pure ferrite, almost free from both cementite and slag particles, it is, as a rule, more favour-able from the corrosion point of view, since particles of cementite and some sulphides are effective local cathodes, while all slag particles jeopardize the formation of passivating oxide films and the adhesion of protective coatings. This is particularly noticeable in the application of vitreous enamels. Unkilled steels are also superior as substrates for electroplated coatings, at least for thin coatings, thanks to the soft ferrite skin. Furthermore, unkilled steels may be easily polished and may therefore pre-ferably be directly nickel-plated without a preceding copper plating. The nickel layer may then easily be obtained in a dense condition which is harder with killed steel with its non-conducting oxide inclusions in the surface, at least if the diameter of the oxide particles is larger than the thickness of the nickel layer. Even in hot galvanizing unkilled and killed steels behave in a substantially different manner, the former giving thin layers of almost pure Zn, the latter thick layers of Fe-Zn alloys.

B2.5 Austenite formation in carbon steels

A number of heat treatment operations occurring in practice involve the transformation of steel to an austenite structure, possibly containing free cementite, and a subsequent transformation of austenite on cooling or quenching (i.e. very rapid cooling).

For the austenitization of carbon steels in practice they are heated to and kept at temperatures immediately above A_3 or between A_1 and A_{cm}. Under this heat treatment the size of the austenite grains increases. This grain growth occurs more rapidly at higher temperatures. The purpose of the austenitization is to obtain a sufficiently high carbon content of the austenite (by dissolution of the cementite) without obtaining at the same time too coarse grains.

B2.6 The transformation of austenite on cooling

The rate at which the cooling of austenite occurs influences the temperature at which the transformation of the austenite ends and also the nature of the transformation products. The reason is that the decomposition of austenite varies in its nature with the temperature at which the reaction takes place, and that a more rapid cooling means that a greater part of the decomposition will occur at a lower temperature than if the cooling rate is slow. On cooling from the austenite range, ferrite is formed first at lower carbon contents and cementite at higher carbon contents. Later, a eutectoid mixture of ferrite and cementite is obtained, which at higher temperatures takes the form of pearlite and consists of alternately spaced small discs of the two phases, resulting in a pearl-like appearance of a polished and etched cross-section. Very fine pearlite is called sorbite; at lower temperatures the eutectoid takes the form of bainite, which has a needle-like structure.

In practice, the cooling rate is varied by the use of different cooling media. The slowest cooling is obtained in a furnace and may be temperature regulated. Cooling in air occurs more rapidly. For very fast cooling or quenching, the steel is immersed in oil or in water.

B2.7 Martensite formation

If austenite is cooled so rapidly that no transformation within the pearlite or bainite range can take place, the austenite undergoes a transformation of a different kind at lower temperatures. This leads to a new product called martensite, which except at low carbon contents is hard and brittle. A heat treatment comprising austenitization and quenching with the purpose of obtaining a martensitic structure is called hardening.

In its essential part, the martensite formation is not time dependent but the amount of martensite formed at a given composition of the austenite is instead dependent upon the temperature at which the quenching has taken place. Martensite constitutes a metastable, forced solution of carbon in ferrite, which thereby obtains a space-centered, tetragonal structure. On heating, it decomposes into normal ferrite and carbide. On heating or tempering the martensite at a low temperature, 200-400°C, a special, finely dispersed carbide, called ε-carbide and of the composition $Fe_{2.4}C$, is formed. Above 400°C normal cementite, Fe_3C, is formed. Like ferrite, pearlite and bainite, martensite is formed from austenite by a volume increase, which results in so-called hardening stresses.

Most stainless steels cannot be hardened. This may be due either to the fact that the structure is an austenite which is so stable that it is not transformed to martensite even at low temperatures or a ferrite which at high temperatures is not transformed to austenite.

B.3 Alloyed steels

B3.1 Influence of alloying elements on the phase diagram

In alloyed steels we find mainly the same phases as in carbon steel, viz. ferrite, austenite, martensite and carbide. The principle difference is that in alloyed steels other carbides than cementite may occur. The ranges of stability of the various phases in steel are highly dependent upon the alloying elements. An alloying element which dissolves in a certain phase in preference to another phase will stabilize the former, that is favour its formation. The alloying elements in steel are therefore divided into austenite stabilizers and ferrite stabilizers.

The principle austenite stabilizers are:

C, N, Ni, Mn

and the principle ferrite stabilizers are:

Cr, Si, Mo, Nb, Ti.

In the ferritic stainless steels, e.g. with 13 % Cr and a low carbon content, the chromium content acts so stabilizing on ferrite, that austenite cannot be formed. The austenitic stainless steels are obtained by the addition of a considerable amount of nickel. One example is the wellknown 18/8 steel. In spite of the high chromium content (18 %), the nickel content in this steel acts so stabilizing on the austenite that ferrite cannot be formed at all. It should be noticed that chromium has a space-centered cubic lattice like ferrite, whereas nickel is face-centered cubic like austenite.

Many alloying elements form carbides with carbon. The tendency to form carbides differs. For some of the most important components in stainless steels we have the following series for increasing affinity to carbon: Ni, Fe, Cr, Mo, Ti, Nb, Ta. The alloying elements may form so-called special carbides which do not contain iron, or double carbides, which contain iron as well.

B3.2 Subdivision of stainless and acid-proof steels

Depending upon the composition and heat treatment of stainless steels they can be divided into the following main groups, named after the phases that occur:

Ferritic
Martensitic
Austenitic
Ferritic-austenitic
Precipitation hardened

The three last mentioned types are often, due to higher content of alloying elements, superior to the first two types as far as resistance towards chemical attack is concerned but even the more resistant stainless steels can be attacked under certain conditions.

Table B1 lists some important stainless steels, standardized in U.S.A. and Great Britain.

B3.3 Ferritic steels

Chromium steels (13-30 % Cr) with a low carbon content are ferritic. An addition of chromium to iron suppresses the austenite phase, and an iron-chromium alloy, which contains more than about 13 % chromium, is completely ferritic, as is shown in figure B5.

Fig. B5. Phase diagram iron-chromium.
L = melt, A = austenite, F = ferrite, S = sigma phase (FeCr).

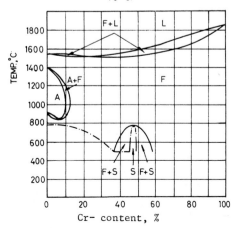

Fe -Cr

Cr- content, %

TABLE B1.Review of some standardized stainless and acid-proof steels.

American standard AISI	British standard B.S.	% Cr	% Ni	% C	% Si max.	% Mn max.	Others, %
Martensitic: body-centered tetr., magnetic, heat treatable							
403	En 56B	11.5-13		<0.15	0.5	1.0	
410	En 56A	11.5-13.5		<0.15	1.0	1.0	
414	En 57	11.5-13.5	1.25-2.5	<0.15	1.0	1.0	
420	En 56D	12-14		0.3-0.4	1.0	1.0	
431	En 57	15-17	1.25-2.5	<0.20	1.0	1.0	
Ferritic: body-centered cubic, magnetic, heat treatable							
405	713	11.5-14.5		<0.08	1.0	1.0	Al 0.1-0.3
430	En 60	14.0-18.0		<0.12	1.0	1.0	
446	En 61	23-27		<0.2	1.0	1.5	N < 0.25
Austenitic: face-centered cubic, non-magnetic, not heat treatable							
301	801A	16-18	6-8	<0.15	1.0	2.0	
302	En 58A	17-19	8-10	<0.15	1.0	2.0	
304	En 58E	18-20	8-12	<0.08	1.0	2.0	
304L	801C	18-20	8-12	<0.03	1.0	2.0	
309	En 55	22-24	12-15	<0.20	1.0	2.0	
310S	A 11	24-26	19-22	<0.08	1.5	2.0	
316	En 58 H	16-18	10-14	<0.08	1.0	2.0	Mo 2.0-3.0
316Cb	A 12 Nb	16-18	10-14	<0.08	1.0	2.0	Mo 2-3, Nb >10xC
316Ti	845 Ti	16-18	10-14	<0.08	1.0	2.0	Mo 2-3, Ti >5xC
317	En 58J	18-20	11-15	<0.08	1.0	2.0	Mo 3-4
318	845	17-19	13-15	<0.08	1.0	2.0	Mo 1.75-2.75, Nb+Ta>10xC
321	En 58B	17-19	9-12	<0.08	1.0	2.0	Ti >5xC
347	En 58F	17-19	9-13	<0.08	1.0	2.0	Nb+Ta > 10xC

In general, S < 0.03 %, P < 0.045 %. So-called easy machining, non-seizing grades have high contents of S (or Se) and P, which reduce their corrosion resistance considerably.

For a given structure the carbon content bears a relation to the
chromium content, so that for instance a steel with 13 % chromium is ferritic,
if the carbon content is lower than 0,08 %, while at higher chromium contents the carbon content may be allowed to rise as high as 0.25 % with
maintenance of the ferritic structure. The ferritic steels resemble soft
unalloyed carbon steel in their mechanical properties, although the alloyed
ferrite is harder and more brittle. The ferritic stainless steels are
magnetic.

The carbon present combines with a considerable amount of chromium to
form carbide, reducing the corrosion resistance of the matrix. The ferritic
steels should therefore be heat-treated in such a manner that the amount of
carbides is as small as possible. The ferritic chromium steels, furthermore,
have a certain tendency towards grain growth at high temperatures.

The presence of chromium implies, that the alloy assumes a more noble
potential and resists attack by the atmosphere and also of many chemicals
(Fig. B6). It is characteristic of stainless steels that they require the
presence of oxygen or other oxidizing substances to remain in the passive
state (Fig. B7).

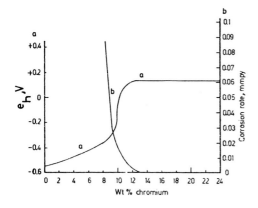

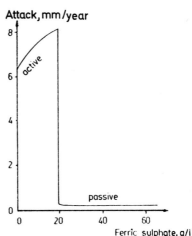

Fig. B6. a) Corrosion potentials of
Fe-Cr alloys in 4 % NaCl, room temperature.
    b) Corrosion rates of Fe-Cr
alloys in intermittent water spray,
room temperature.

Fig. B7. Corrosion of 12.5 % Cr
steel in 10 % H_2SO_4 with additions
of ferric sulphate.

B3.4 Martensitic steels

So-called martensitic steels contain chromium in the range 13-17 % as principal alloying element but they have in addition such a high carbon content that they can be given a martensitic structure by hardening, the hardness being determined by the carbon content. Due to the high carbon content of the martensitic steels, they have a great tendency towards the formation of chromium carbide. In order to be resistant towards corrosion, these steels must therefore be heat-treated at such a high temperature before hardening that all carbide is dissolved in the austenitic phase. Just like the ferritic steels, the martensitic steels are magnetic.

B3.5 Austenitic steels

These steels contain as principal alloying elements chromium (12-25 %) and nickel (8-25 %). The high nickel content in combination with a heat treatment suitable for the purpose give to these steels an austenitic structure. Accordingly, they are non-magnetic.

The high contents of chromium and nickel, furthermore, reduce the rate of the allotropic transformations so that these become very slow in the commonly used steels. According to the ternary phase diagram Fe-Cr-Ni, 18/8-steel for instance should be ferritic at room temperature but it remains in a metastable austenitic state if it is cooled rapidly from the austenite range. Its stability varies with the nickel content. If the latter is lower than 7 %,the austenite is rapidly transformed to ferrite on cold-working the steel but above 14 % nickel the austenite may be considered stable for all practical purposes. Besides its influence on the structure, nickel also gives a considerable increase of corrosion resistance if its percentage is higher than 8 %. Although the addition of nickel does not result in a higher corrosion resistance in strongly oxidizing media, such as nitric acid, it improves considerably the resistance towards non-oxidizing substances such as sulphuric acid and many organic acids.

The precipitation of chromium carbide on heating is particularly dangerous in austenitic steels, since it usually occurs along the grain boundaries of the austenite. The effective chromium content in a narrow zone along the grain boundaries may then be too low for passivation, and the steel is then sensitized towards so-called intercrystalline corrosion. In the martensitic and ferritic steels, on the other hand, the carbide precipitate is more evenly distributed which means that the resistance towards general attack is reduced.

In order to reduce the risk for intercrystalline corrosion after, for instance, welding, the austenitic steels are often alloyed with titanium, niobium or tantalum, which instead of chromium combine with carbon to form carbides and therefore counteract a local chromium depletion. Such steels are said to be stabilized. But even stabilized steels may show so-called knife-edge attacks after welding at a high temperature and exposure to certain corrosive media. A safer means to avoid intercrystalline corrosion and increase weldability is therefore to use steel with a very low carbon content, less than 0.03 % - 0.05 % C, depending upon the sensitizing conditions.

By the addition of varying amounts of molybdenum to chromium-nickel steels, a group of steels with increased resistance towards corrosion is obtained, which are particularly useful in certain organic acids and in dilute solutions of sulphuric acid, and which also have a good resistance towards pitting in chloride solutions. In order to maintain the austenitic structure, despite the addition of the ferrite stabilizer molybdenum, the nickel content of the steel must be increased at the same time. Austenitic stainless steels containing molybdenum are usually referred to as acid-proof. The effect of molybdenum is further increased by alloying with silicon and with copper. For very corrosive conditions, nickel-based alloys, containing chromium and molybdenum (e.g. Hastelloy, Chlorimet) are used.

B3.6 Ferritic-austenitic steels

These steels have a high chromium content, usually about 26 %, and a lower nickel content than the austenitic steels, usually 4-6 %, and they will therefore besides austenite also contain ferrite. The percentage of ferrite may be determined in a so-called magnetic balance. The good properties of both the ferritic and austenitic steels are in many respects combined in these steels. Grain growth at high temperatures does not occur in these steels to the same extent as in ferritic steels, and they therefore give considerably tougher welds. Furthermore, welded constructions of these steels are usually insensitive towards intercrystalline corrosion. By a further addition of molybdenum, the corrosion resistance of these steels can be improved still more and may be comparable to (or in certain cases superior to) the austenitic steels containing molybdenum.

B3.7 Precipitation hardened steels

These stainless steels can be given a very high strength by heat treatment (tempering after annealing). They contain carefully regulated amounts

of chromium and nickel but also other alloying additions such as aluminium,
copper, molybdenum and titanium.

The high strength of these steels depends upon secondary precipitates,
for instance an aluminium-nickel phase (in 17/7 PH) or a copper-rich phase
(in 17/4 PH). As usual, the figures denote the chromium and nickel contents
while PH for precipitation hardening denotes the structural characteristic
of the steel. In corrosion resistance these steels range somewhere between
the martensitic chromium steels and the austenitic steels.

B.4 Heat treatment of steels

By heat treatment in a wider sense we mean every procedure by which,
by heating and subsequent cooling,a change of the properties of the material
is brought about. For steels the principal heat treatment procedures are:
normalizing, hardening, tempering and annealing.

The normalizing of a carbon steel involves austenitization plus slow
cooling in air and leads to "normal" grain growth and "normal", lamellar
pearlite.

Hardening of carbon steels or martensitic stainless steels with high
carbon content involves austenitization plus such rapid cooling through A_1
(Fig. B4) that the pearlite formation is suppressed and martensite is
formed instead. For carbon steels, quenching in water is required for
hardening, for low alloyed steels quenching in oil is used but for martensitic stainless steels cooling in air is usually sufficient.

Tempering involves a moderate heating to a temperature below 700°C.
For hardened martensitic steels tempering has the purpose of reducing the
stresses after hardening and transforming the hardened steel to a tougher
and softer state, called tempered martensite. For precipitation hardened
steels, on the other hand, tempering produces the precipitates giving
the hardness.

For carbon steels and for ferritic and martensitic stainless steels,
a type of annealing called soft annealing is used. This treatment is
carried out at temperatures around the line A_1 (see Fig. B4), at which
the cementite lamellae are spheroidized and a structure of spheroidized
pearlite is obtained.

In order to give the stainless austenitic and ferritic-austenitic
steels their best corrosion properties they are heat treated according
to a procedure called quench annealing. The steel is then heated to a high

temperature, 1050 - 1150°C for austenitic and 950 - 1000°C for ferritic-austenitic steels. All carbides are then dissolved and a homogeneous austenitic structure is obtained after quenching.

B.5 Slag inclusions in steel

In steels considerable amounts of non-metallic inclusions, so-called slag inclusions occur. The content of slag inclusions is usually around 0.1 % but may be as high as 1 weight %. The slag inclusions usually consist of oxides, silicates and sulphides. In unkilled steels, the oxide inclusions consist of FeO, in killed steels of oxides of the killing agents, thus in general SiO_2, Al_2O_3 and MnO. MnO and SiO_2 together form manganese silicate.

The oxides and silicates mentioned are not metallic conductors and cannot therefore act as local cathodes in corrosion cells. They affect the corrosion properties of the steel in other ways, however. They may thus cause pores in electro-plated metal coatings and reduce the adhesion of various protective coatings, such as vitreous enamels. The high content of slag inclusions also reduces the possibility to attain fine and bright-polished surfaces, which is particularly important for the passivity of stainless steel. Slag inclusions may also act as stress-raisers in various types of corrosion cracking.

Regarding the sulphide inclusions they usually consist of MnS. The Mn content of various steels is usually kept high enough (0.5-2 %) to combine with the S present (often 0.03-0.05 %) to form MnS. The S content of the matrix is usually negligible. Pure MnS has a high melting point, around 1600°C. In the solidification of steel, liquid drops of FeS are first separated. In the subsequent slow cooling and soaking of large ingots FeS is gradually transformed to almost pure MnS. If the Mn content of the steel is too low, S is mainly or partly combined with Fe to form FeS, which has low melting point, around 1200°C and therefore solidifies at a rather late stage as thin films in the grain boundaries. On heating to a high temperature these sulphide layers are melted and cause cracking along the austenite grain boundaries, so-called red-shortness. In the presence of FeS, the S content of the metallic matrix is considerable, amounting to 0.01 %.

In contrast to silicate slags and most oxide inclusions, sulphide inclusions in steel are electric conductors. FeS (κ =1600 $\Omega^{-1}cm^{-1}$) is a far

58

better conductor than MnS (κ =0.1 $\Omega^{-1}cm^{-1}$). According to section A3.3 above, sulphide ions stimulate electrode processes. For example, conducting metal sulphides have low hydrogen overvoltage, see Table A2. Accordingly, sulphide inclusions act as local cathodes and initiate corrosion attack , particularly pitting. The corrosion pattern of carbon steel in water may be found to correspond closely to a so-called sulphur print. This is obtained by pressing a photographic paper, soaked in dilute H_2SO_4, against the polished steel surface and then rinsing and fixing.

By the so-called micro-corrosion test, described in p. 45 above, it may be shown that certain sulphide inclusions are considerably more effective than others in initiating corrosion attacks. As a matter of fact, active and inactive sulphide inclusions may be distinguished by this test, see Fig. B8. They usually do not differ in their own composition whereas their immediate surroundings seem to do so, active sulphides being surrounded by a fine sulphide dispersion, which stimulates anodic dissolution of the metallic matrix. Active sulphides are sometimes found in rapidly cooled steels, e.g. continuously cast steels that have not been sufficiently heat-treated before rolling. A high frequency of active sulphides corresponds to a high pitting susceptibility. With an adequate heat treatment, continuously cast steels do not show a higher content of active sulphides or a higher corrosion susceptibility than conventional, ingot-cast steels.

Fig. B8. Micro-corrosion test (30 s in 3 % NaCl-solution) on a continuously cast steel containing active sulphide inclusions, causing anodic attack in their immediate surroundings. 600X.

B.6 Some important copper and nickel alloys

It seems appropriate, finally, to list in the following two tables the designations and compositions of some copper and nickel alloys, which have been given special names.

TABLE B2. Some important copper alloys.

| Designation | Composition, % | | | | |
	Cu	Zn	Sn	Ni	Others
Red brass	85	15	–	–	–
Low brass	80	20	–	–	–
Cartridge brass	70	30	–	–	–
Muntz metal	60	40	–	–	–
Naval brass	60	39	0.75	–	–
Admiralty brass	71	28	1.00	–	0.04 As
Aluminium brass	77	21	–	–	2 Al 0.04 As
Nickel brass	65	25	–	10	–
Zinc bronze	90	10	–	–	–
Tin bronze	90	–	10	–	0.25 P
Nickel bronze	90	–	–	10	–
Aluminium bronze	92	–	–	–	8 Al
Cupro-nickel 30	70	–	–	30	–

TABLE B3. Some important nickel alloys.

| Designation | Composition, % | | | | | |
	Ni	Cr	Mo	Fe	Cu	Others
Monel 400	66	–	–	1	32	1
Inconel 600	76	16	–	7	–	1
Hastelloy B[1]	65	–	28	6	–	Si 1
" C[1]	59	16	16	5	–	W 4
" D	88	–	–	–	3	Si 9
" F	50	22	7	17	–	Co3, W 1
Illium G	56	23	6	7	6	2
Ni-o-nel 825	42	22	3	30	2	Ti 1

[1] Chlorimet 2 and 3 are similar to Hastelloy B and C respectively.

Literature

Hume-Rothery, W & Raynor, G V, The Structure of Metals and Alloys, Institute of Metals, London 1962.

Metals Handbook, American Society for Metals, 8th Ed., Vol. 1, Metals Park, Ohio, 1966.

C. METALLIC CORROSION IN VARIOUS ENVIRONMENTS

C.1 Various ways of systematization of the corrosion field

Every field of science needs systematization. Since the corrosion field is very large and varying, many different ways of division are possible, the most common being after:

1. Corrosion environments
2. Corrosion mechanisms
3. Corrosion types
4. Metals
5. Field of application or industrial branch
6. Methods of protection.

For a systematic review of the corrosion field it is most suitable to start from the corrosion environment: moist environment, dry gases, fused salts etc. This means, at the same time, a division according to mechanism: e.g. electrochemical mechanism in moist environment, chemical in dry gases. Even methods of testing and research are mainly determined by the corrosive environment. Different types of corrosion, such as pitting and stress corrosion cracking are natural subdivisions. Division after various metals is common and practical in handbooks but not very effective from a systematic point of view. Field of application or industrial branch is a special application of the environment principle. The corrosion protection methods, finally, may, according to the localization and nature of the changes made for the purpose, be divided in the following way:

1. Change of the metal itself
2. Change of the corrosive medium
3. Change of the electrode potential metal/corrosive medium
4. Separation of the metal and the corrosive medium by means of surface coatings.

C.2 Systematization of corrosion phenomena after environment

Corrosion phenomena can be divided in the following way into main groups after environment and consequently also after basic reaction mechanism in the corrosion process:

I. Corrosion in moist environments. Electrochemical mechanism.
1. Corrosion in water and aqueous solutions
2. Atmospheric corrosion
3. Soil corrosion

II. Corrosion in fused salts and slags. Electrochemical mechanism.

III. Corrosion (oxidation) in dry gases. Chemical mechanism.
1. At ordinary temperature:
a) Tarnishing and discolouration
b) Fretting corrosion
2. At high temperature:
Scaling

IV. Corrosion in water-free organic liquids and gases. Chemical mechanism.
1. In chlorinated hydrocarbons
2. In alcohols

V. Corrosion in molten metals. Physical mechanism.

C.3 Corrosion in moist environments. Electrochemical mechanism.

The environment is of very great influence on the rate of corrosion. Table Cl shows the approximate corrosion rate in μm (1 micrometer$=10^{-6}m=10^{-3}$ mm) in 10 years for some metals in various moist environments.

In moist environments, corrosion proceeds by electrode processes, as is to be expected, since the corroding medium is an electrolyte solution. The dissolution of the metal is an anode process. At the same time there must take place a cathode process, by which the corrosive agent, usually dissolved atmospheric oxygen but sometimes hydrogen ions, is consumed. Corrosion protection procedures aim at preventing one or both of these processes.

C3.1 Water and aqueous solutions

A "hard" tap water, i.e. a water of relatively high content of calcium bicarbonate causes less corrosion than a soft water, such as river water, since the deposits of calcium carbonate formed from hard water give a certain protection against corrosion.

Hot water is generally more corrosive than cold water. For steel in water the corrosion increases with temperature, due to higher diffusion rate of oxygen, to a maximum at about 80°C. At a further increase in temperature the corrosion rate decreases again due to diminishing oxygen solubility in the water.

TABLE C1. Rates of corrosion in various moist environments.

	Corrosion in μm in 10 years								
	Air			Water			Soil		
	Indust-rial	Urban	Rural	River water	Sea water	Hard tap water	Highly corro-sive	Corro-sive	Slight-ly cor-rosive
Unpro-tected steel[1]	1000	500	100	500	1000	100	1000	300	50
Zinc-coated steel	100	50	20	300	200	150	150	100	30
Aluminium alloys		10[2]	0.5[3]				350	35	5
Copper		10	5				30	15	5

[1] Pits may be 5 times as deep as the average thickness reduction
[2] " " " 10 " " " " " " " "
[3] " " " 100 " " " " " " " "

C3.2 The atmosphere

Atmospheric corrosion in general is the result of the conjoint action of two factors: oxygen and moisture (water in liquid form). If one of these factors is missing, corrosion does not occur. In dry air, as under the freezing point or at a relative humidity less than about 60 %, steel does not rust. Corrosion is therefore negligible in polar regions and in hot deserts. Indoors in heated, i.e. dry localities, steel does not rust either. In unheated premises, however, the humidity may be so high that rusting can occur.

The atmospheric corrosion increases strongly if the air is polluted

by smoke gases, particularly sulphur dioxide from fossil fuels, or aggressive salts, as in the vicinity of chimneys and in marine environments. The
atmospheric corrosion is therefore particularly strong in industrial and
coastal areas. The corrosion is, furthermore, much higher if the metal surface is covered by solid particles, such as dust, dirt and soot, because
moisture and salts are then retained for longer time.

C3.3 The soil

Table C1 shows that corrosion rates in soil may be higher than in the
atmosphere and sometimes as high as in sea water. The corrosivity of soils
is mainly determined by their electric resistivity. Low soil resistivity
usually means high corrosivity and vice versa. Low resistivity reflects the
presence of moisture and soluble salts, two factors promoting corrosion
reactions, and also means that corrosion currents flow more easily. At great
depth, however, corrosion is limited by low oxygen replenishment. Sometimes,
however, so-called sulphate-reducing bacteria may cause high corrosion rates
if oxygen is missing.

C.4 Corrosion in fused salts and slags. Electrochemical mechanism.

Relatively little is known of the attack on metals in these media.
Since the corrosion medium is an electrolyte, the mechanism is probably
electrochemical. A liquid layer of salts or slags in the presence of
oxygen and Mo- or V-compounds as oxygen carriers is particularly aggressive
and causes so-called catastrophic oxidation.

C.5 Corrosion (oxidation) in dry gases (air, smoke gases, steam at high temperature). Chemical mechanism.

From a purely formal point of view, even this "dry" corrosion can be
regarded electrochemically as a result of electrode processes in a galvanic
cell. In this the metal/oxide interface acts as anode (reaction: $Me \rightarrow Me^{2+}+2e^-$)
and the outer surface of the oxide layer as cathode (reaction: $\frac{1}{2} O_2 + 2e^- \rightarrow O^{2-}$)
while the oxide film itself, being a semiconductor, acts as both external
circuit and electrolyte solution in the galvanic cell. The oxidation rate
is usually determined by mass transfer through the oxide film: metal ions
outwards, oxygen ions (O^{2-}) inwards. Certain features of solid state physics,
viz. the theory of lattice defects and semi-conductors, are of great importance for the understanding of this type of corrosion.

Dry oxidation at a low temperature is often referred to as tarnishing, while high temperature oxidation, leading to thick, spalling oxide-layers, is often called scaling. Fretting corrosion may also be considered as a case of dry oxidation.

C.6 Corrosion in water-free organic liquids and gases. Chemical mechanism.

Such cases of corrosion are relatively unusual. Examples are to be found in the corrosion of Al in chlorinated hydrocarbons, such as CCl_4, and $CHCl_3$, and in alcohols, as ethanol, propanol and butanol, and, furthermore, of Mg and Ti in methanol. These reactions occur in the same way whether the corroding medium is in liquid or gaseous form and are obviously non-electrochemical, in accordance with the fact that the corrosion media are non-electrolytes. In fact, water acts as an inhibitor of these reactions.

It should be observed,on the other hand, that most cases of corrosion in organic liquids, such as oils, are due to the presence of small amounts of water, often containing salts or acids,and are of normal electrochemical nature.

C.7 Corrosion in molten metals. Physical mechanism.

Corrosion in molten metals involves the dissolution or cracking of solid metals in contact with liquid metals, such as lead, sodium and mercury. The attack is not caused by chemical reactions but physical dissolution with alloy formation, sometimes penetration of liquid metal into grain boundaries. In this category we find the attack of mercury on brass, leading to cracking in the presence of mechanical stress, and on aluminium, which after amalgamation is rapidly oxidized, since a protecting oxide film can no longer form.

D. POTENTIAL-pH DIAGRAMS

Most metals have a tendency to corrode due to reaction with surrounding media, such as water and air. Together with the surrounding media, such metals form a thermodynamically instable system, which has a tendency to give off energy with the transformation to a chemical compound of the metal, often an oxide or a hydrated oxide. The metal itself has been won from some of its naturally occurring compounds, an ore, usually by the supply of energy. The corrosion process thus means that the metal strives to return to the oxidized natural state. An important way of considering corrosion processes is, therefore, the thermodynamic one, which shows under which circumstances a metal can and cannot corrode.

As far as electrochemical corrosion in moist environments is concerned, potential-pH diagrams, also called Pourbaix diagrams after their originator, are of good help. Such a diagram has the redox potential of the corroding system as a vertical axis and the pH scale as a horizontal axis. Using thermodynamic data and the Nernst equation for electrode potentials it is possible to derive the boundaries of regions, within which the metal itself or some of its compounds are stable. Fig. D1 and D2 show such diagrams in simplified form for copper and iron.

For iron, as in many other cases, thermodynamic data are too incomplete and uncertain to allow a derivation of the boundaries of all stability regions. The diagrams are usually constructed for a temperature of $25^{o}C$ and a metal ion concentration of 10^{-6} moles of dissolved metal per litre of solution. If the metal ion concentration in the solution is smaller, corrosion is considered not to have occurred.

The sloping, dashed straight lines in the diagrams give the redox potentials of solutions in equilibrium with hydrogen and oxygen, respectively. They show that the redox potential of the solution in equilibrium with oxygen is 1.23 V more noble than in the presence of hydrogen. Furthermore, they take account of the fact that the redox potential of both the oxygen and the hydrogen electrode decreases with 0.059 V for a rise in pH of one unit. Generally speaking, all sloping lines in the diagram correspond to pH-dependent redox equilibria. Horizontal straight lines, on the other hand,

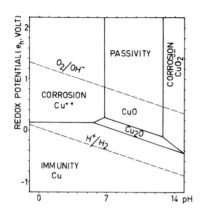

Fig. D1. Potential-pH diagram for copper in an aqueous solution containing 10^{-6} gram-atoms Cu per litre. Temperature 25°C.

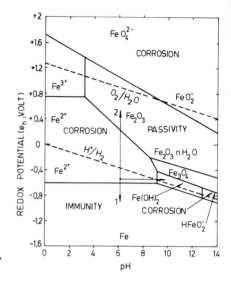

Fig. D2. Potential-pH diagram for iron. Iron concentration = 10^{-6} gram-atoms per litre. 25°C.

reflect redox equilibria, which are not pH-dependent (e.g. Cu^{2+}/Cu and Fe^{3+}/Fe^{2+}). Vertical lines, finally, correspond to equilibria, not involving valency change and hence independent of potential (for example the solubility equilibria between the amphoteric compound $Cu(OH)_2$ and acid or alkali).

If conditions are such that the metal is the stable phase, the state of immunity exists. Then corrosion cannot occur. In all cases, when a compound of the metal is the thermodynamically stable state, corrosion can take place. Under certain conditions, however, a sparingly soluble compound of the metal may form a protective film on its surface, rendering the corrosion rate negligibly small. The metal is then said to be in a state of passivity. Passivation requires that the sparingly soluble compound, often an oxide, forms an adhering and dense film on the metal. Whether a coating of a corrosion product has passivating properties cannot be derived by means of thermodynamics. It is an empirical result, more connected with reaction kinetics. Potential-pH diagrams get much more valuable, however, if experiences regarding passivity are included.

It follows from Fig. D1 that for copper the potential of the hydrogen electrode falls within the region of immunity for all pH values. This means that deaerated solutions of non-oxidizing and not complex-forming acids, salts or alkalis do not attack metallic copper. In aerated solutions, on the other hand, copper is attacked. In acid solution Cu^{2+}-ions are formed, in strongly alkaline solution CuO_2^{-2}-ions, corresponding to the amphoteric character of copper (II) hydroxide. In the pH interval 6.7-12.7, on the other hand, the copper surface becomes covered with insoluble CuO. If this oxide forms a dense and coherent film, the attack ceases rapidly. At pH values close to the borderlines between the areas of corrosion and passivity, incomplete coverage and local attacks are likely to occur. The diagram in Fig. D1 is not valid in the presence of complexing agents, such as ammonia and cyanides, in which completely different electrode reactions and potentials are established. Since the immunity region is smaller and, furthermore, copper oxides are dissolved in NH_3 and CN^-, the corrosion risks are much higher in these media.

In the case of iron, the redox potential of the hydrogen electrode lies above the immunity region along all the pH scale. This means that iron may dissolve with evolution of hydrogen in aqueous solutions of all pH values. In the pH interval 9.4-12.5, however, a passivating layer of $Fe(OH)_2$ is formed. At lower pH values, iron is corroded with the formation of Fe^{2+}-ions, at higher pH values, the ferrous hydroxide dissolves giving $HFeO_2^-$-ions. Within the latter corrosion region falls the so-called caustic cracking of steel, which is an example of stress corrosion cracking. At higher redox potentials in the corroding medium, the passivating layer consists of Fe_3O_4 or Fe_2O_3, nH_2O. In a very strongly oxidizing, alkaline medium corrosion may occur with the formation of ferrate ions, FeO_4^{2-}. Complex forming ions change the appearance of the diagram and increase the risks for corrosion also in the case of iron.

Consider now an iron specimen immersed in an oxygen-free solution with pH 6. If the electrode potential of the specimen were determined by the equilibrium between the metal and its ions in the solution, the potential would fall on the horizontal boundary line between the regions of immunity and corrosion, corresponding to said equilibrium. If, on the other hand, the iron specimen behaved as an inert metal and acted as a hydrogen electrode, its potential would fall on the dashed, sloping straight line corresponding to this electrode. In reality, the potential will fall somewhere between these equilibrium potentials. The corrosion potential established is an example of a so-called mixed potential, determined by two simultaneous and electrically coupled electrode reactions.

According to diagram D2, there are three different ways of removing the iron specimen from the corrosive region:

1. By lowering the electrode potential down into the region of immunity. This can be done by making the specimen a cathode in a galvanic or electrolytic cell. This is called cathodic protection. A lowering of the potential from the FeO_4^{2-}-region down into the passivity region is also an example of (incomplete) cathodic protection.

2. By raising the electrode potential up into the region of passivity. In some cases this can be accomplished by making the metal an anode in a galvanic or electrolytic cell. This is called anodic protection. A more common way of creating the potential increase according to this alternative is the addition of an anodic inhibitor, often an oxidizing agent, forming a passivating film on the metal surface.

3. By raising the pH or alkalinity of the solution, also forming a passivating film.

The theoretical potential-pH diagrams according to Pourbaix are an efficient means to collect and represent thermodynamic data for corroding systems. They are therefore a natural starting-point for theoretical considerations of corrosion processes. They have certain inherent limitations, however, which should always be born in mind. These include the following:

1. The Pourbaix diagram presupposes equilibria between the metal and its ions and between the ions in the solution and corrosion products containing these ions. In practical corrosion cases, conditions may be far from equilibrium, however.

2. The term passivity in the Pourbaix diagram is applied to the field of existence for oxides, hydroxides or other sparingly soluble substances, irrespective of their protective properties.

3. The pH value, referred to in the diagram is the one prevailing at the surface of the metal considered. This often varies from point to point and is usually lower at anode surfaces and higher at cathode surfaces than the (measured) value in the bulk of the corrosive solution.

4. The Pourbaix diagram gives no information on the corrosion rate, since the diagram is based on thermodynamic and not on kinetic data.

If, however, the theoretical potential-pH diagram is supplemented by experimental and experience data on passivity, we obtain empirical potential-pH diagrams, which are of greater practical importance in corrosion control (see chapter Q).

Literature

Pourbaix, M, Atlas of Electrochemical Equilibria in Aqueous Solutions, Pergamon Press, Oxford 1966.

E. THE KINETICS OF ELECTROCHEMICAL CORROSION. PASSIVITY

E.1 Electrode potentials of corroding systems. The galvanic series.

It is of fundamental importance to investigate the electrode potential, developing on a metal surface in a corrosive liquid. As a rule, this liquid does not contain any ions of the metal to begin with. The irreversible electrode potentials developing in such a case, therefore deviate considerably from the reversible equilibrium potentials of metal electrodes in solutions of their own ions.

By attack of the corroding medium on the metal, a small metal ion concentration is gradually obtained close to the metal surface, however. If a sparingly soluble compound is formed, the metal ion concentration will be determined by the solubility product of this compound. It turns out, therefore, that the electrode potentials of corroding metals can often be regarded as approximately reversible potentials and can therefore be calculated or at least estimated from the standard potentials of the corresponding cation- or anion-electrodes by means of the Nernst equation.

In solutions forming complex ions with the corroding metal, conditions corresponding to a very low metal ion concentration are obtained and, according to Nernst´s law, the electrode potential is strongly displaced in negative direction. Sometimes, the corrosion potential is mainly determined by a redox system, not comprising the metal, such as the hydrogen or oxygen electrode.

The formation of passivating oxide films usually displaces the corrosion potential strongly in positive direction. In the same way as in Fig. A16 this displacement can be regarded as an anodic, ohmic polarization caused by the ionic resistance of the oxide film (or alternatively in pores filled with electrolyte solution), whereas the cathodic polarization due to the electron resistance of the oxide layer is smaller, as a rule.

These various effects explain why the electrode potentials of corroding metals usually deviate more or less from the reversible standard po-

tentials, observed under equilibrium conditions in solutions, in which ions
of the respective metals have unit activity. The corrosion potentials of
metals and alloys in a certain specified solution, e.g. a 3 % NaCl solution,
roughly corresponding to sea water, are often put together in a so-called
galvanic series. In such a potential series, the metals appear in quite a
different order than in the so-called electromotive series, based on the
standard electrode potentials of metals (cf. Table A1). Table E1 below
shows a comparison for some common metals of a galvanic series (in 3 % NaCl)
and two electromotive series, viz. partly the usual one with potentials
Me/Me^{n+} in solutions with unit activity of the relevant metal ion, and
partly an anion electrode, Me/Me_xZ_y.

TABLE E1. Comparison of standard electrode potentials and corrosion potentials (in 3 % NaCl solution) for some common metals.

Standard electrode potential series relative to the NHE		Galvanic potential series (in 3 % NaCl solution) relative to the NHE	
	Me/Me^{n+}	Me/Me_xZ_y, pH 7	
Pt/Pt^{2+}	+1.20 V	+0.57 (Pt/PtO)	Pt +0.47 V
Ag/Ag^{+}	+0.80 V	+0.22 (Ag/AgCl)	Ti +0.37 V
Cu/Cu^{2+}	+0.34 V	+0.05 (Cu/Cu$_2$O)	Ag +0.30 V
H_2/H^{+}	±0.00 V	-0.414 (H$_2$/H$_2$O)	Cu +0.04 V
Pb/Pb^{2+}	-0.13 V	-0.27 (Pb/PbCl$_2$)	Ni -0.03 V
Ni/Ni^{2+}	-0.25 V	-0.30 (Ni/NiO)	Pb -0.27 V
Fe/Fe^{2+}	-0.44 V	-0.46 (Fe/FeO)	Fe -0.40 V
Zn/Zn^{2+}	-0.76 V	-0.83 (Zn/ZnO)	Al -0.53 V
Ti/Ti^{2+}	-1.63 V	-0.50 (Ti$_2$O$_3$/TiO$_2$)	Zn -0.76 V
Al/Al^{3+}	-1.67 V	-1.90 (Al/Al$_2$O$_3$)	

It is particularly conspicuous from a comparison of the three series
that the formation of a passivating oxide film has ennobled the potential
of Ti by more than 2 V and that of Al by more than 1 V. In the case of Pt,
Ag, Cu, Pb, Fe and Zn, oxide or chloride electrodes are developed, whose
observed electrode potentials are in good agreement with those calculated
for pH 7 or $[Cl^-] = 1$. The practically unchanged values for Fe and Zn in

the three sets of values is fortuitous.

The practical, galvanic series of electrode potentials is the relevant one as soon as corrosion is involved. Thus it turns out, for example, that in the galvanic cell Zn-Al, zinc becomes the negative pole and is dissolved or corroded. In sea water or a marine atmosphere zinc coating is therefore a cathodically protective covering on aluminium as it is on steel.

A deeper insight into the fundamental concept of corrosion potential is provided by the theory of mixed potentials. This theory takes account of the fact that the electrode potential of a corroding metal must be determined by two electrode processes occurring simultaneously, viz. oxidation of the metal and reduction of the corroding agent.

E.2 Mixed potentials. Potential-current diagrams.

The concept of mixed potential was introduced already in connection with the thermodynamic potential-pH diagrams. As indicated by the notation, such an irreversible, non-equilibrium potential is assumed to be formed by a "mixing" of the potentials of two electrode reactions, coupled by a common current. If these electrode reactions constitute a corrosion process, the mixed potential is usually called corrosion potential. How such a corrosion or mixed potential is thought to be established is shown clearly by potential-current or polarization diagrams, which therefore form the basis of electrochemical corrosion theory.

Fig. E1 shows the polarization diagram for a corroding metal, M, the cathode process being hydrogen evolution. If the attack is of a general, uniform nature, the whole surface may be considered as anode for the metal oxidation reaction and as cathode for the reaction involving a reduction of

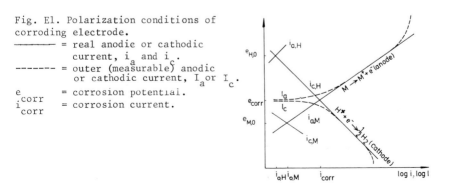

Fig. E1. Polarization conditions of corroding electrode.
———— = real anodic or cathodic current, i_a and i_c.
------ = outer (measurable) anodic or cathodic current, I_a or I_c.
e_{corr} = corrosion potential.
i_{corr} = corrosion current.

the corrosive agent. If the metal were not corroding but in a reversible ion exchange, $i_{o,M}$, with the solution it would assume the equilibrium potential, $e_{M,o}$. If, on the other hand, the non-corroding electrode were saturated with hydrogen gas in a reversible ion exchange, $i_{o,H}$, with the hydrogen ions of the solution, it would assume the corresponding equilibrium potential, $e_{H,o}$. During corrosion, these individual electrode potentials are displaced towards each other. The anode potential is displaced in a positive direction by the anodic polarization, n_a, and the cathode potential in a negative direction by the cathodic polarization, n_c. The measurable electrode potential is a common, intermediate mixed potential, the corrosion potential, e_{corr} in Fig. E1. The corrosion process is then going on with a current, i_{corr}, which, in the absence of an outer current, must be of equal size for the anodic and the cathodic reaction. The corrosion potential and the corrosion current therefore appear as the point of intersection between two rectilinear polarization curves in the half-logarithmic polarization diagram according to Fig. E1. To make this type of diagram applicable even for local attack, in which case the anode and cathode surfaces are of different size, it is necessary to plot the logarithm of the current strength on the abscissa rather than the logarithm of the current density, as is customary for individual polarization curves.

In the following, many examples will show how potential-current diagrams can be used to represent and clarify different corrosion processes. We then make use of the parts of the polarization curves lying between the exchange current and corrosion current and usually obtained by extrapolation of Tafel lines. Polarization diagrams of this type were first used by the British scientist U.R. Evans and his school and are therefore often called Evans diagrams. They constitute the most important theoretical tool of corrosion science.

The theory of mixed potentials may be said to supplement and partly substitute the old corrosion theory, entirely based on local cells, which in the case of general corrosion are assumed to be of submicroscopic dimensions. This development of electrochemical corrosion theory means that fundamental corrosion research is more and more concerned with the kinetics of electrode reactions, attempts being made to draw conclusions regarding the mechanism and velocity of corrosion processes from polarization measurements.

E.3 Experimental demonstration of the electrochemical nature of metallic corrosion

The electrochemical interpretation of corrosion processes is not only a theory which better than others explains observed phenomena. By measurements of electrode potentials and corrosion currents and by observation of anodic and cathodic corrosion products, convincing proofs of the electrochemical mechanism of metallic corrosion have been obtained. In particular, such studies were devoted to corrosion caused by oxygen concentration cells as a consequence of non-uniform supply of air and hence also referred to as differential aeration cells.

A typical example of such local electrochemical corrosion is the so-called drop corrosion, which occurs when, for instance, a drop of sodium chloride solution is placed on an iron plate (Fig. E2). Corrosion then takes place in the centre of the interface between the drop and the plate. This is interpreted as a result of a concentration cell due to non-uniform supply of air. Under the peripheral parts of the drop, the excess of oxygen is abundant and cathodic reduction of dissolved oxygen to OH^--ions therefore takes place. The excess of oxygen and the raise in pH act passivating on the cathodic parts of the steel. Centrally under the drop, the diffusion path of oxygen is longer and hence its concentration lower and a negative or anodic region develops with resultant iron dissolution. The corrosion product, primarily iron(II)hydroxide, is formed as a ring in an

Fig. E2. Drop corrosion as a result of a differential aeration cell in a drop of sodium chloride solution on a steel surface. Anodic and cathodic regions are made visible with ferroxyl indicator ($K_3Fe(CN)_6$ + phenolphtalein). Radially flowing corrosion currents are revealed by a vertical magnetic field which makes the drop rotate (Blaha´s experiment).

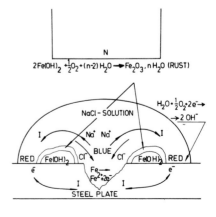

intermediate zone where iron-II-ions from the anode in the centre and hydroxyl ions from the cathode around the periphery meet as a consequence of both diffusion and ionic migration. Secondarily, the ferrous hydroxide is oxidized by atmospheric O_2 to a hydrate of tervalent iron, i.e. rust. The separate appearance of anodic and cathodic surfaces can be directly demonstrated if the sodium chloride solution contains the so-called ferroxyl indicator. This is a mixture of potassium cyanoferrate (III), giving a blue precipitate with ions of divalent iron or ferrous ions and the acid-base indicator phenolphtalein, which is coloured red by hydroxyl ions. It is then found that the solution in the corrosion pit is coloured blue, which proves the presence of divalent iron, whereas the periphery of the drop is coloured red, obviously due to alkali formed by the reduction of atmospheric oxygen. The current in the corrosion cell is transported mainly by sodium and chloride ions. Iron(II)chloride is therefore enriched in the pit, which may eventually lead to the precipitation of solid salt. Such an enrichment of a salt of the metal on small anode surfaces is an important principle, examples of which are also found in pitting corrosion of metals totally immersed in water or soil and also in local atmospheric corrosion attacks. Likewise, chloride enrichment is found in corrosion pits in boiler tubes. If the above interpretation of drop corrosion is correct, electric currents must flow radially in the drop from the centre and towards the periphery and then back to the centre via the iron plate. In fact, such radial corrosion currents are demonstrated if the experiment is carried out in a vertical magnetic field, as was first described by Blaha in 1930. It turns out that the drop rotates like a rotor in an electric motor and in a direction predicted by the orientation of the magnetic field. The concordance of all observed phenomena constitutes the proof of the electrochemical theory of corrosion in this particular case.

In the differential aeration cells referred to above, corrosion is initiated by external, geometrical factors, causing non-uniform supply of the corrosive agent. There are, however, many important cases of local corrosion attack, initiated by inhomogeneities in the metal itself, e.g. welds. With the ferroxyl indicator it can be established whether a weld is anodic or, as it should be, cathodic towards the surrounding metal.

E.4 Local and general electrochemical corrosion

From the point of view of reaction kinetics, the corrosion of metals in moist environments is evidently an electrochemical phenomenon, the corrosion process occurring as electrode reactions. If the attack is localized, anodic and cathodic surfaces of actual corrosion cells can be distinguished, sometimes to the naked eye (macro-cells) or at least under the microscope (micro-cells). Such corrosion cells may be of a chemical nature, caused by varying composition of the metal (galvanic cells) or the corroding solution (concentration cells) or of the metal surface (e.g. active-passive cells). Corrosion cells may also be of a physical nature, depending, for instance, on differences in lattice strain due to cold-working of the metal.

Quite often, however, the individual electrode surfaces have such small extension that they cannot be distinguished even under a microscope (sub-micro-cells) or they fluctuate over the metal surface in a statistical, disordered way. If this is the case it is appropriate to regard the corroding metal as one single electrode on which anodic and cathodic reactions occur simultaneously.

When separate corrosion cells can be distinguished by variations of the electrode potential over the metal surface, by the appearance of corrosion currents or of separate anodic and cathodic corrosion products, local electrochemical corrosion is said to exist. In the opposite case, general electrochemical corrosion is said to occur.

The differentiation between local and general electrochemical corrosion is mainly based on practical view-points. If corrosion takes place locally in distinct corrosion cells, metal dissolution may occur in one place and the reduction of the corrosive agent (e.g. $O_2 \rightarrow OH^-$) in a second one, whereas the corrosion product, such as rust, is formed in a third site. In such a case, it is not probable that the corrosion product will form a protection against continued attack. If, furthermore, the anode surface is small in comparison to the cathode surface, as when corrosion occurs in a pore or a crack in an otherwise protective film, the localized attack may be very strong, even if the total metal loss is small. If, on the other hand, separate anodic and cathodic surfaces do not appear or are of very small dimensions (submicro-cells) or fluctuate over the surface, the attack will be more uniform. Furthermore, there are then possibilities for the corrosion product to form a continuous film and retard continued attack. It may therefore be stated, that general electrochemical corrosion leads to uniform attack, whereas local electrochemical corrosion results in localized attack, such as pitting or cracking.

Characteristic features of general and local corrosion as well as some examples of localized attacks are listed in the following scheme:

General electrochemical corrosion

Anodes and cathodes not separated

Anode = cathode = electrode

Anode potential = cathode potential =
= corrosion potential (mixed potential)

Corrosion products may be protective

Results in uniform attack

Local electrochemical corrosion

Anodes and cathodes separated

Anode << cathode

Anode potential < cathode potential

Corrosion products not protective

Results in localized attacks

a) Initiated in the metal

Pitting
Intercrystalline corrosion
Layer corrosion
Selective corrosion
Graphitic corrosion
Stress corrosion cracking (SCC)
Corrosion fatigue

b) Initiated in the environment

Crevice corrosion (in water)
Deposit corrosion (in water)
Water-line attack
Filiform corrosion
Erosion corrosion
Cavitation corrosion

Some of the corrosion types mentioned here are schematically illustrated in Fig. E3.

As a first example of the use of Evans' polarization diagrams, general and local corrosion are illustrated in Fig. E4 by means of such diagrams. $e_{a,o}$ is the equilibrium potential that the metal would assume if it did not corrode but were in equilibrium with its own ions in the solution. $e_{c,o}$ is the equilibrium potential the metal would assume if it were inert, its potential being exclusively determined by the cathode reaction, such as hydrogen evolution, under equilibrium conditions. When the metal corrodes, polarizations occur, involving a displacement of the individual electrode potentials from their equilibrium values. The anode potential is displaced in a positive, the cathode potential in a negative direction. If only activation polarization appears, the potential changes are linear functions of the

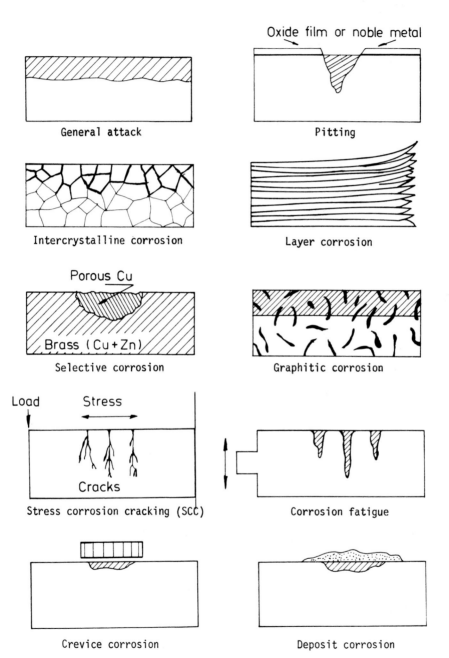

Fig. E3. Schematic illustrations of different types of corrosion.

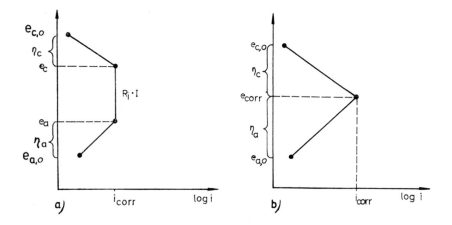

Fig. E4. a) Polarization diagram for local electrochemical corrosion, resulting in localized attack.

$$E = e_{c,o} - e_{a,o}, \quad \eta_c = e_c - e_{c,o}, \quad \eta_a = e_a - e_{a,o}$$
$$E = R_i \cdot I + \eta_a + \lceil \eta_c \rceil . \text{Cf Fig. A13.}$$

b) Polarization diagram for general electrochemical corrosion, resulting in uniform attack.

$$E = e_{c,o} - e_{a,o}, \quad e_{corr} = e_c = e_a, \quad \eta_c = e_{corr} - e_{c,o}$$
$$\eta_a = e_{corr} - e_{a,o}, \quad E = \eta_a + \lceil \eta_c \rceil . \text{ Cf Fig. A14.}$$

logarithm of current. In a semi-logarithmic diagram we therefore obtain
two straight Tafel lines.

The left hand part of Fig. E4 corresponds to local electrochemical
corrosion, resulting in localized attack, such as galvanic corrosion,
pitting, stress corrosion cracking etc. In such cases, anode and cathode
surfaces are clearly separated and have separate electrode potentials, the
difference of which constitutes an internal potential drop in the solution
of the particular corrosion cell. It is then not possible to define a common corrosion potential for all the metal surface. If we measure the potential of an oxide-covered metal with pits, we usually obtain a value e_c
corresponding to the cathode reaction occurring on the intact part of the
oxide film. The anode potential e_a at the bottom of a pit may be half a
volt lower.

The state of a generally corroding metal, on the other hand, is characterized by the point of intersection between the two Tafel lines. This
point has the abscissa log i_{corr}, i_{corr} meaning the corrosion current, and

the ordinate e_{corr}, the corrosion potential. The corrosion current must obviously be the same whether the anode or the cathode process is considered. In general electrochemical corrosion, furthermore, the corrosion cells are of submicroscopic dimensions, which means that potential drops in the solution, caused by corrosion currents, may be disregarded. This is the reason why all the corroding metal assumes a uniform mixed potential, the corrosion potential, e_{corr}.

E.5 Passivity

E5.1 Definition and subdivision

Passivity involves a strongly reduced corrosion tendency of metals due to a protecting layer of corrosion products. Passivity is of two kinds, chemical and mechanical passivity.

1. Chemical passivity appears on certain so-called passivating metals, many of which are so-called transition metals, characterized by an unfilled d-group of electrons in an inner electron shell. Passivating transition metals are, for example, the iron and platinum groups of metals, chromium, molybdenum and tungsten, titanium and zirconium. Even some non-transition metals, such as aluminium, show chemical passivity. This type of passivity is ascribed to an invisible thin but dense and semiconducting oxide film on the metal surface, displacing the electrode potential of the metal strongly (0.5-2 V) in the positive direction.

2. Mechanical passivity may occur on practically all metals in environments, where conditions are favourable to the precipitation of solid salts on the metal surface. The cause of the strongly reduced corrosion rate in this case is a thick but more or less porous salt layer, usually non-conducting in itself. The electrode potential need not be displaced in positive direction and may even, if the solubility product of the salt is low, be displaced in negative direction from the standard potential. Examples of this type of passivity are furnished by lead in sulphuric acid, magnesium in water or fluoride solutions, silver in chloride solutions etc. Phosphatizing layers on metals and calcium carbonate scale on steel in water may be considered as examples of mechanical passivity.

The chemical passivity is a general phenomenon, appearing in a great many environments for the metals concerned. The following treatment is limited to this type of passivity. The distinction between the two types is not sharp, however. Hence, the natural, invisibly thin oxide films on certain metals, such as aluminium, magnesium and tungsten, can be extended by anodic treatment (anodization) to form thick, still better protective oxide films. Chromatizing films on zinc and light metals also constitute a border-line case.

E5.2 Passivity of iron

Fig. E5 shows the anodic polarization curve of iron in 1-M sulphuric acid. Without outer current, a steady state corrosion potential develops. If the potential of the specimen is raised, an anodic net current flows from the electrode into the solution and the corrosion velocity of the specimen is increased correspondingly. At potentials around +250 mV, an anodic limiting c.d. of about 20 A/dm^2 is reached. This c.d., which is maintained up to a potential of ca +600 mV, corresponds to a steady state removal of the corrosion product, $FeSO_4$, by convective diffusion. The diffusion boundary layer (anode film) in contact with the electrode consists of a saturated solution of $FeSO_4$, from which a solid, in itself non-conducting but porous layer of $FeSO_4$ is precipitated.

On a further potential increase a higher oxide of iron is formed as a thin, non-porous, passivating oxide film. This is accompanied by a sudden and very conspicuous decrease of the corrosion current by about 6 powers of ten. The solid layer of $FeSO_4$ is dissolved in the solution and soon disappears. In the passive state the corrosion current is limited by the transport of metal ions through the oxide film. It remains at a constant value on further rise of the anode potential until the potential for evolution of oxygen is reached. The current then rises rapidly in the so-called

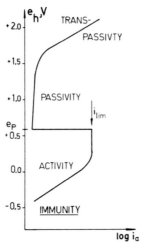

Fig. E5. Schematic anodic polarization curve for iron in sulphuric acid.

transpassive_region. The current is now mainly consumed for the evolution
of oxygen from water.

In order to change the metal from an active to a passive state, the
electrode potential has to be raised above the so-called passivation potential, i.e. that potential at which the sudden decrease of corrosion current
occurs. In principle, this can be done in two different ways, either electrically by an external current of sufficient strength or chemically by means
of oxidation agents of sufficient oxidizing power to give a mixed potential
above the passivation potential of the metal. For such an oxidizing agent,
two conditions have to be fulfilled: one thermodynamic, namely that its
redox potential is above the passivation potential, and one kinetic, namely
that its cathodic reduction occurs so easily that it creates a cathodic
limiting current stronger than the passivating current below the passivation
potential.

Passivity is therefore favoured by conditions increasing the rate of
the cathode process or decreasing the rate of the anodic metal dissolution
process below the passivation potential. Non-oxidizing anodic inhibitors,
such as orthophosphates, favour passivity by reducing the rate of the anode
process. Oxidizing anodic inhibitors or passivators, such as chromic acid
and nitric acid, act in both the ways referred to above, i.e. both by stimulation of the cathode process and by retardation of the anode process.

Once passivity has occurred, a very small passivity current is required to maintain the passive state. This is the corrosion current in the
passive region which is, in most cases, less than 1 mA/dm^2. This is very
small compared to the passivating current needed to cause passivity, amounting to ca 20 A/dm^2, reckoned on all the anode surface.

The passivation potential is pH-dependent. For pure iron at room temperature it obeys Nernst's law according to
$$e_p = 0.58 - 0.059 \cdot pH \quad V \text{ (relative to NHE)}$$
If the potential of the working electrode is lowered, the transition
from the passive to the active state takes place at a somewhat lower potential than the passivation potential. This activation potential is sometimes referred to as the Flade potential.

E5.3 Passivity of chromium

Chromium behaves electrochemically similarly to iron but certain
important differences exist. The passivation potential of chromium is substantially lower than that of iron. The passivating current of chromium is,

furthermore, a matter of a few milliamps per dm^2 whereas iron needs about 15-20 A/dm^2. Chromium is therefore passivated much more easily than iron. The fact that the passivation potential of chromium is less noble than even the equilibrium potential of hydrogen means that hydrogen ions can act as a passivator in this case.

The corrosion rate of chromium in the passive state is, furthermore, several magnitudes lower than that of iron, in spite of the fact that the passivating oxide film is probably even thinner than on iron. At a potential of about +1.25 V (NHE) the tervalent chromium in the passive film is oxidized to the hexavalent state, i.e. chromate, which is soluble in water. In this potential range, the passive film is therefore dissolved completely and the resulting so-called transpassive corrosion of the underlying metal is so rapid that, as a rule, no oxygen evolution occurs.

E5.4 Passivity of stainless steels

The fact that chromium and also nickel are readily passivated accounts for the use of these metals as alloying constituents in stainless steels. At a chromium content of only 12 to 18 % the passivity properties of chromium are approached. The value of the passivation potential has almost shifted from that of iron to that of chromium. In the passive state, the corrosion current is about two powers of ten lower than for pure iron. The result is a decided improvement of passivity and corrosion resistance.

An addition of nickel and also of molybdenum, silicon and copper reduces the passivating current and the activity range still further. This means that stainless steels containing even these alloying elements have substantially better corrosion resistance in non-oxidizing media and are also more easily transferred to the passive state.

E5.5 Properties of passive films

The passivating oxide films, e.g. on stainless steels and aluminium, are extremely thin, usually in the range 10-100 Å. This is far below the limit of optical visibility. The first step in the passivation process is probably the formation of a film of chemisorbed oxygen on the metal surface.

For iron-chromium alloys, it has been shown that chromium is enriched in the passive film although iron oxides generally predominate. For austenitic 18-8 steel, the highest corrosion resistance is obtained at a film thickness of 30-50 Å. The oxide film is then of an amorphous nature. Thicker films are more crystalline, have a higher ionic conductivity and are, re-markably enough, less protective. These thick films may be considered as hydrated oxides, as they contain up to 30 % water along with the oxides of iron, chromium, nickel and silicon.

F. HYDROGEN EVOLUTION AND OXYGEN REDUCTION CORROSION

F.1 Different cathode processes in electrochemical corrosion

For corrosion to occur it is necessary to have not only a metal which can go into solution in an anode process, but also a corrosive agent which can be reduced and thus maintain the cathode process. As a rule, this cathode process consists of hydrogen evolution or oxygen reduction, but other cathode processes may occur, as shown in the following scheme:

1. Hydrogen evolution
2. Oxygen reduction
3. Reduction of oxidizing metal ions, e.g. ferric ions in previously formed rust, acting as oxygen carriers.
4. Deposition (cementation) of more noble metals from their ions, e.g. Cu from Cu^{2+} on Fe or Al.
5. Reduction of oxidizing acids and anions (HNO_3, NO_3^- etc.).

F.2 Hydrogen evolution corrosion

Hydrogen evolution corrosion occurs mainly in acid, sometimes also in strongly alkaline solutions. Hydrogen evolution also occurs in neutral solutions on sulphide inclusions in steel, leading to localized attack (pitting). The rate of hydrogen evolution corrosion is often determined by either of the two electrode processes. If the corrosion rate is mainly determined by the cathode process, cathodic control is said to prevail. If the anode process is of greater importance for the corrosion velocity, anodic control is said to exist.

F2.1 Cathodic control

Fig. F1 corresponds to dissolution of zinc with hydrogen evolution. The zinc dissolution reaction has a low activation polarization while, on the other hand, hydrogen overvoltage on zinc is very high. On impure zinc, containing metals with lower hydrogen overvoltage, e.g. Cu or Fe, the cathodic polarization is lower and the corrosion rate higher.

If, on the other hand, zinc is amalgamated, its corrosion velocity will be reduced due to sluggish hydrogen evolution. It should be noticed, furthermore, that not only polarization but also exchange current density is changed. A high exchange current density corresponds to a small activation polarization and vice versa.

A relatively small horizontal displacement of the polarization curves in the diagrams means a large change of i_{corr}, since the scale is logarithmic. As a matter of fact, the dissolution rate of zinc in acids varies between 1 and 1.000, depending upon the nature and amount of impurities in the metal. If we measure the corrosion potential, we find, in accordance with Fig. F1, that a decrease in corrosion rate is connected with a more negative corrosion potential. If amalgamation were to interfere with zinc dissolution and not with hydrogen evolution, the corrosion potential would be displaced in a positive direction with a fall in corrosion rate. This shows that the corrosion velocity is determined by the cathode process.

F2.2 Anodic control

An anodic control of the corrosion process seems to prevail in the dissolution of a passivated metal such as aluminium or stainless steel in dilute acids. In these cases, metal ions have to penetrate an oxide film, corresponding to a high anodic polarization. The polarization diagram is shown in Fig. F2.

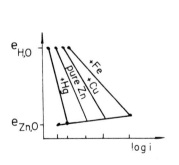

Fig. F1. Dissolution of pure and contaminated zinc in acid. Cathodic control.

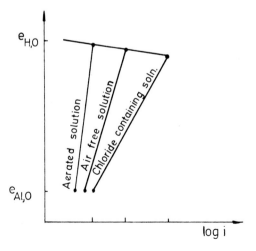

Fig. F2. Corrosion of aluminium in weak acids. Anodic control.

For metals with a passivating oxide film, the corrosion rate is usually increased greatly in the presence of chloride ions. This is probably due to the pronounced dipole character (large electric polarizability) of the chloride ion which results in its specific adsorption on the surface of the oxide film. Surface compounds, containing chloride ions (oxide-chlorides instead of pure oxides) are probably formed, which due to lattice defects and a higher solubility lead to a local break-down of the oxide film. The chloride ions will then also promote the ionization of the metal by repelling electrons (Cf. A3.3).

As a rule, the presence of oxygen in a solution reduces the corrosion velocity of metals with a passivating oxide film (aluminium, stainless steel, titanium), since defects in the oxide film will then be more easily repaired.

F2.3 Mixed control

A mixed cathodic and anodic control exists in the hydrogen evolution corrosion of iron and steel, since anodic and cathodic polarization are then of about the same magnitude. Fig. F3 shows polarization curves for pure iron and for carbon steel of various compositions.Both anodic and cathodic polarization,at a given c.d., are lower on carbon steel than on pure iron, which means that the corrosion rate of carbon steel is higher for two reasons. This is a local cell effect which is increased by cold-working and it is higher in tempered steel (with many small carbide particles) than in hardened, untempered steel (with carbon in solid solution in martensite) or in soft-annealed steel (with large and few carbide particles), see Fig. F4.

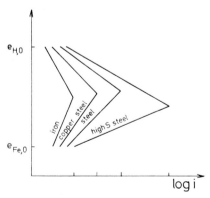

Fig. F3. Hydrogen evolution corrosion of iron and carbon steels. Mixed control.

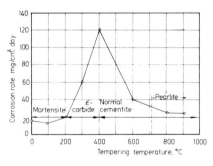

Fig. F4. Effect of heat treatment on corrosion of a 0.95 % C steel in 1 % H_2SO_4. Specimen area 18.5 cm^2. Specimen weight 29 g. Tempering time 2 hrs.

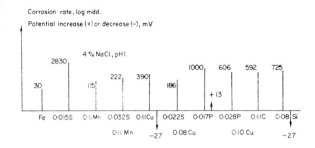

Fig. F5. Corrosion rate (mdd) for Fe, pure and alloyed with stated percentages of S, Mn, Cu. P, C and Si in acid NaCl solution. In three cases, the change in corrosion potential is also shown. Data according to Stern.

Sulphur always exerts a more or less detrimental influence on the corrosion of steel, particularly in acid solutions, as do sulphides derived from the environment. Contrary to what might be expected a small content of copper in the steel exerts a beneficial influence under the same conditions.

Figure F5 shows some data derived from Stern. The addition of 0.015 % S to pure Fe increases its dissolution rate in acids very strongly, about 100 times. Two effects may be assumed to be active:

(A) Action of microgalvanic cells (local cells) Fe(of high S content)-FeS, which is shown by the fact that this alloy corrodes with pitting.

(B) Dissolution in the acid of FeS, particularly that in solid solution in the iron, with the release of sulphide ions, which due to their high molar polarization (or pronounced dipole character) are adsorbed on metal surfaces and strongly catalyze electrochemical processes and hence corrosion reactions. The addition of small amounts (a few ppm) of sulphide to acid has a similar, stimulating effect on the dissolution of iron. Cf. p. 33.

According to Fig. F5, addition of Mn or Cu to pure Fe (1) per se accelerates the dissolution rate but (2) counteracts the detrimental effect of S. Mn addition may be assumed to counteract the detrimental effects of S (1) by forming low-conducting MnS and (2) by reducing the S content of the ferrite. On the other hand, MnS is more soluble in acids than FeS.

Addition of Cu eliminates the effect (B) above. Dissolved Cu is redeposited on to the iron surface where it reacts with sulphide ions to form Cu_2S, insoluble in acids (solubility product = 10^{-48}). The catalyzing influence of adsorbed sulphide ions is thus eliminated.

A small addition of P, which will occur in solid solution in the iron (solubility in ferrite about 1 %), exerts a stimulating effect, comparable to that of S, on the dissolution in acids, apparently due to the formation and adsorption of hydrogen phosphide or phosphide ions, catalyzing electrode processes just like sulphide ions do. The detrimental effect of P cannot be mitigated by Mn and Cu since these metals do not form definite phosphides under these conditions.

In Fig. F5 changes in corrosion potential brought about by some alloying additions are also shown. These data serve to illustrate the fact that there is no relation between corrosion potential and corrosion rate and that measurements of corrosion potential cannot, generally, be used to judge the relative corrodibility of different steels, as is sometimes done in practice.

Polarization studies show that both P and S reduce the cathodic polarization much more than the anodic polarization. A shift of the corrosion potential in positive direction would therefore be expected. This holds true only for P, however, which is present in solid solution in the iron and leads to general corrosion. With S, present as sulphides and leading to localized attack, shifts in the negative direction are found. This is undoubtedly due to the pitting character of the corrosion in this case.

Sulphide inclusions and Cu content are also of importance for the corrosion of stainless steels. Pitting and SCC of 18/8 stainless steels in chloride solutions are usually initiated at sulphide inclusions. Free-cutting Cr/Ni steels containing 0.2-0.3 % S should not be called stainless. An addition of Cu to stainless steels improves their passivity and reduces their pitting tendencies.

Regarding cathodic, anodic and mixed control we find that there is no simple correlation between corrosion velocity and corrosion potential, since at increased corrosion velocity

1. Cathodic control gives a more noble corrosion potential
2. Anodic control gives a less noble corrosion potential
3. Mixed control may give a more noble or less noble corrosion potential according to circumstances.

F.3 Oxygen reduction corrosion

F3.1 Cathodic diffusion control

The oxygen reduction corrosion in neutral aqueous solutions and in water is of greater practical importance than the hydrogen evolution corrosion in acids. Whereas in the latter case activation polarization dominates both the cathode and the anode process, a new factor occurs in the oxygen reduction type of corrosion, viz. concentration polarization. This is due to the limited solubility of oxygen in water and in aqueous solutions. Corrosion velocity in these media will therefore, as a rule, be limited by the diffusion velocity of oxygen. The corrosion rate will then coincide with the limiting c.d. for cathodic reduction of dissolved oxygen (Cf. A3.1). This is illustrated by figure F6, which shows schematically how the Tafel line, corresponding to activation polarization, merges into a vertical line, corresponding to the limiting c.d. for O_2 reduction. The diagram shows the conditions corresponding to two different oxygen concentrations and also explains why the corrosion potential is lower at lower oxygen content.

If diffusion of dissolved oxygen determines the corrosion velocity, we have a case of pronounced cathodic control, since within certain limits the corrosion current will then be independent of the slope and position of the anodic polarization curve. Figure F7 illustrates this fact for three different alloys (A, B and C). This explains why the velocity of general corrosion in water is practically the same for different types of steel, e.g. ship's plate, independent of the composition (within certain limits), cold work and heat treatment. This also means that local cells are of little importance for general corrosion of the oxygen reduction type. This

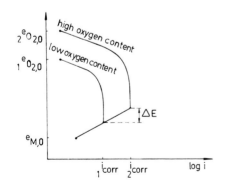

Fig. F6. Diffusion controlled, oxygen-consuming corrosion at two different oxygen contents. ΔE = decrease in corrosion potential due to lowering of oxygen concentration.

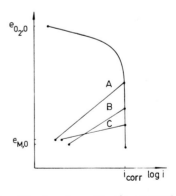

Fig. F7. Purely cathodic control in oxygen-consuming corrosion may give the same corrosion velocity for different alloys.

is what we have to expect if oxygen diffusion determines the corrosion velocity. Popularly expressed: The dissolved atmospheric oxygen, diffusing
towards the steel surface knows nothing about the composition of the steel.
Instead, other factors, determining the solubility and diffusion velocity
of oxygen,will be deciding, viz. temperature, viscosity, salt content and
flow-rate.

On the other hand, the analysis and structure of C-steels may exert
a deciding influence on local corrosion in water, such as pitting, crevice
corrosion and weld corrosion. In these cases, the cathode area and hence
the oxygen diffusion current is very large in relation to the active anode
area and the corrosion rate will therefore be influenced by the slope and
position of the anodic polarization curve and also by an IR-drop, proportional to the corrosion rate (Fig. F8). In practice, an intermediate case
is often found. Hence, weld corrosion of ship's plate is greatly influenced
by the composition of both the plate and the weld electrode but is also
raised by increasing speed, i.e. an increase of the diffusion-controlled
rate of cathodic oxygen reduction.

Whereas the corrosion velocity of carbon steel is usually determined
by the diffusion-limited current of oxygen reduction, the corrosion rate
and corrosion potential of copper is determined by the intersection of the
anodic polarization curve with the Tafel line for oxygen reduction according to Fig. F9. For very unnoble metals, on the other hand, such as Zn,
Mn or Mg, the corrosion rate and corrosion potential is determined by
both oxygen reduction and hydrogen evolution.

In atmospheric corrosion, which is of the oxygen reduction type, the
composition of steel is of great importance.

Even in this case, sulphur exerts a detrimental influence which may
be compensated by an addition of 0.1-0.2 % Cu (slow-rusting copper-steel).
The beneficial effect of Cu is particularly pronounced in industrial atmospheres, which create acid conditions and where S is also supplied by the
environment. The detrimental effect of the high S content of free-cutting
steels may also be reduced by Cu addition. Unlike S, the detrimental effect
of P on the corrosion of steel in acid solutions is not retained in corrosion under atmospheric conditions. On the contrary, P then exerts a more
or less beneficial influence, probably because P is oxidized to phosphates
that act as inhibitors. A high P content contributes to the often remarkably good corrosion resistance of old and ancient wrought iron in the atmos-

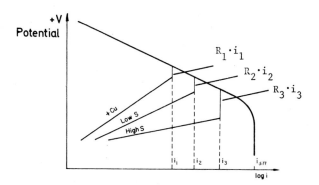

Fig. F8. Evans polarization diagram, showing schematically that the rate of local corrosion in water, such as pitting and crevice and weld corrosion, is strongly dependent on steel composition.

Fig.F9. Schematic polarization diagrams for corrosion in neutral solution with
1) oxygen reduction with activation control (Cu)
2) oxygen reduction with diffusion control (Fe)
3) oxygen reduction + hydrogen evolution (Mn).

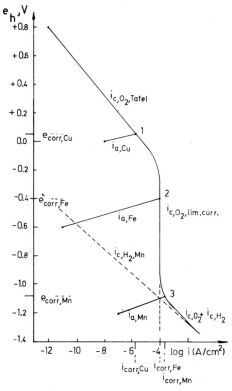

phere, e.g. the Delhi pillar. The beneficial effect of Cu and P may be further strengthened by small additions (0.1-1 %) of Cr, Si and Ni, giving so-called weathering steels, which develop dense and adhering rust films in the atmosphere. Since these low-alloyed steels show not only good corrosion resistance but also high tensile strength, they have become known under the trade-name of Cor-Ten steels. Coatings of paints and lacquers also show considerably longer life on such low-alloyed steels than on ordinary carbon steels. They may preferably be used unpainted in the atmosphere, however.

F3.2 Temperature dependence

The predominant importance of the diffusion of oxygen for corrosion in water also explains why the rate of general and pitting corrosion of iron and steel reaches a maximum at about 80^0C. Starting from room temperature, we first find an increase in corrosion rate with an increase of temperature due to diminishing viscosity ν and hence increasing diffusion coefficient D according to the relation D x ν = constant. At temperatures approaching the boiling point, the corrosion velocity diminishes again since the solubility of oxygen in water is then greatly reduced. This holds true for an open system at atmospheric pressure. In a closed system, in which the pressure increases with temperature and in which the oxygen cannot escape from the solution, we find a steadily increasing corrosion rate with increasing temperature. Cf. Fig. F10.

For zinc we find a very sharp maximum in corrosion velocity at about 60^0-70^0C, which seems to be caused mainly by a structural change in the zinc oxide film corresponding to a considerable elevation of the corrosion potential of zinc at high temperature.

F3.3 Concentration dependence

For similar reasons, sodium chloride solutions show a maximum in corrosion rate at about the composition of sea water (a good example of the law of Nature's perversity).With increasing salt concentration, corrosion will first increase due to increasing electric conductivity. At quite high salt concentrations, the corrosion rate will be reduced again as a result of a decrease of the solubility and diffusion rate of oxygen. Cf. Fig. F11.

F3.4 Corrosion in flowing media

Since diffusion and concentration polarization are strongly dependent on flow conditions, this is also the case with oxygen reduction corrosion. An increased flow velocity means that the diffusion layer, δ, at the metal surface will be thinner. Oxygen transport will then occur more easily and the limiting current density, I_L , will increase (Cf. A3.1).

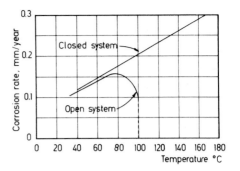

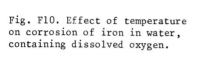

Fig. F10. Effect of temperature on corrosion of iron in water, containing dissolved oxygen.

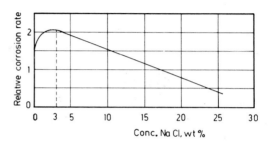

Fig. F11. Effect of NaCl concentration on corrosion of iron in aerated solutions.

The theory of convective diffusion also explains why at the transition from laminar to turbulent flow at the so-called critical Reynolds number a sudden change of corrosion velocity occurs. If this turbulence occurs locally, erosion corrosion or turbulence corrosion results. For copper and copper alloys in neutral media the corrosion velocity is not determined by the transport of oxygen to the metal surface but instead by the transport of corrosion products away from the metal surface, which in this case is the slower process. Figure F12 shows how the corrosion velocity may vary with the flow velocity of a corroding solution. The corrosion rate increases slowly within the laminar range, then faster in the turbulent range, but only up to a certain limit, at which the limiting current density for oxygen reduction is so high that the anodic polarization curve intersects with the Tafel slope, corresponding to the activation polarization of oxygen, according to figure F13. Regarding cavitation corrosion, see below, chapter H.

For passivating metals, such as stainless steels, on the other hand, a moderate increase in flow-rate often leads to a reduced corrosion rate. This is because passivity is more easily obtained with good and uniform supply of oxygen, which is favoured by stirring. Cf. Fig. F14.

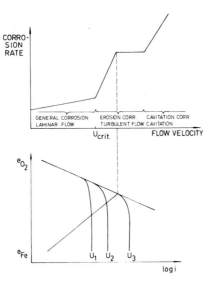

Fig. F12. Corrosion velocity and corrosion type as a function of flow velocity. U_{crit} corresponds to the critical Reynolds number.

Fig. F13. Potential-current diagram at different flow velocities, for which $u_1 < u_{crit} < u_2$.

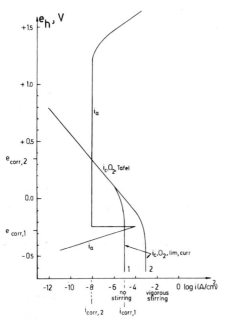

Fig. F14. Increased stirring may cause the limiting current density for oxygen diffusion to exceed the critical current density for passivation and hence change a stainless steel from the active to the passive state.

G. SOME IMPORTANT TYPES OF ELECTROCHEMICAL CORROSION

G.1 Corrosion cells, acting in electrochemical corrosion

For corrosion to occur two things are required: Firstly a potential difference between anode and cathode surfaces, secondly a substance which can maintain the cathode process. The latter was dealt with in the previous chapter. Let us now consider various types of corrosion cells. According to size, corrosion cells may be divided into

1. Macro-cells, leading to localized macro-attacks. Examples are differential aeration cells and galvanic cells between different metals.

2. Micro-cells, leading to localized attacks, examples of which are given below.

3. Submicro-cells, leading to general corrosion. An example of general corrosion is shown in Fig. G1.

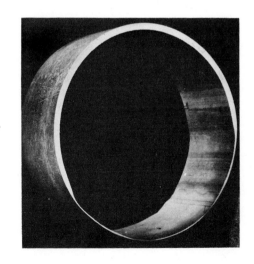

Fig. G1. General corrosion of 18-8 stainless steel tube, carrying acid water, containing 0.5 % H_2SO_4 and 0.5 % HNO_3 and at 100^oC. Tubing was horizontal and filled to about 1/3. In about 1 year, wall thickness decreased from 4.5 mm to negligible. Courtesy: Sandvik Steel Research.

Corrosion cells leading to localized attack may be classified in the following manner:

- A. Galvanic macro-cells metal-metal: Galvanic corrosion
- B. Galvanic micro-cells (local cells) within a metal: At the initiation of
   - a) intercrystalline corrosion
   - b) selective corrosion
   - c) stress corrosion cracking (SCC)
   - d) pitting
   - e) graphitic corrosion
   - f) layer corrosion
- C. Oxygen concentration cells (differential aeration cells, usually macro-cells):
   - a) waterline attack
   - b) crevice corrosion
   - c) deposit corrosion
   - d) drop corrosion
   - e) filiform corrosion
- D. Metal ion concentration cells (macro-cells): Erosion corrosion of copper and copper alloys
- E. Active-passive cells + differential aeration cells: In the propagation of
   - a) pitting of passive metals
   - b) crevice corrosion of passive metals
   - c) intercrystalline corrosion of passive metals
   - d) stress corrosion cracking of passive metals
- F. Electrolytic cells (macro-cells):
   - a) intentional: anode corrosion
   - b) non-intentional: stray-current corrosion.

G.2 Galvanic macro-cells. Galvanic corrosion.

The so-called galvanic corrosion, occuring at a contact of two different metals or alloys with different electrode potentials is probably the best known of all corrosion types. One example is provided by brass details in contact with hot water tubes of copper, in which case the brass forms the anode in the galvanic cell and is therefore de-zincified (an example of selective corrosion according to paragraph G.3 below). If a brass detail is instead connected to a galvanized steel tube, the zinc coating in the vicinity of the contact will become anodic and be dissolved away. The steel is then attacked for the same reason, whereas the brass in both combinations is under cathodic protection. Another common example is galvanic corrosion of plain carbon steel in contact with stainless steel (Cf. Fig. G2).

Fig. G2. Galvanic corrosion of a valve spindle in sea water after 10 months on board ship in the Sound. Valve spindle (1) of carbon steel, valve cone (2) of acid-proof steel (AISI 329). Courtesy: S. Bartha.

Cu may cause galvanic corrosion on a light metal even if it is not in direct contact with the latter. Cu may corrode and dissolved Cu ions may then diffuse to the light metal and deposit as metallic Cu on the latter, creating small but efficient galvanic cells and severe local attacks. This may be called indirect galvanic corrosion.

Galvanic effects can usually be neglected if the potential difference is smaller than 50 mV. The electrode potentials of relevance are not the often theoretically calculated potentials listed in the series of standard potentials, but rather the experimentally determined corrosion potentials in the actual electrolyte, eventually arranged in a so-called galvanic series, which may also comprise alloys (see table E1). This explains why Al is, as a rule, more noble than Zn and causes galvanic corrosion in contact with a Zn coating on galvanized steel, e.g. in so-called Feral cables. After the steel has been exposed it may in turn cause galvanic corrosion of the Al. Sometimes, however, corrosion potentials cannot be used to judge the relative distribution of corrosion in a galvanic couple. For example, a high carbon steel dissolves more rapidly in acids and at a more positive potential than a low carbon steel and this is still true after galvanic coupling of the two steels. In some cases, galvanic effects may be quite small in spite of large potential differences, due to an insulating oxide film on the cathodic member, e.g. titanium.

The combination small anode - large cathode, exemplified by brass
bolts in a copper plate, is particularly dangerous in connection with
galvanic corrosion. The opposite combination: large anode - small cathode
should be aimed at. Screws, bolts, nuts and welds should therefore always
be made from a more noble material, e.g. a low-alloyed chromium-nickel
steel if the basic material is plain carbon steel. The bolt, weld etc.
will then be cathodically protected.

The conductivity of the corroding solution is of great importance.
If large surfaces of the metals are in contact with an aqueous solution
of high conductivity, such as sea water, the attack on the baser metal
may spread to a long distance from the contact and hence be less severe
but in soft water and under atmospheric conditions the attack is often
localized in the vicinity of the metallic contact and is then more dangerous

In atmospheric corrosion, galvanic effects are operative mainly
under marine conditions. In a coastal climate, carbon steel causes galvanic
corrosion on aluminium, but this is not the case in an urban or mild industrial atmosphere.

In the absence of dissolved oxygen or hydrogen ions for the maintenance of the cathode process, galvanic corrosion does not occur. It is
therefore possible to combine steel and copper in closed hot water systems
(e.g. central heating systems) without very severe corrosion.

G.3 Galvanic micro-cells (local cells)

Within one and the same piece of metal or alloy, there exist, as a
rule, different regions of varying composition and hence different electrode
potential. This is true for different phases in heterogeneous alloys. Graphite in grey cast iron and cementite in white cast iron and in carbon
steel are examples of cathodic phases. If one phase is present in a small
amount, it is often referred to as precipitates or secondary phase. Such
precipitates are often carbides or intermetallic compounds, which have been
formed in the solid state during heat treatment of alloys. They tend to
collect along grain boundaries or slip bands in the metal. Even if detect-
able amounts of such precipitates do not occur, e.g. in pure metals and
homogeneous alloys, the grain boundaries still have a different composition
(e.g. larger concentration of low melting components or impurities) or at
least a higher lattice energy. That the grain boundaries are as a rule less

noble than the interior of the crystal grains is shown by the fact that they are usually attacked more strongly on etching. Local cells in grain boundaries are of deciding importance for the initiation of inter-crystalline corrosion.

A typical example of corrosion caused by micro-cells, formed by different phases in an alloy is so-called graphitic corrosion (also called graphitization or spongiose), which is a form of corrosion unique for grey cast iron. The iron is transformed to rust which together with graphite flakes forms a spongy mass, easily cut with a knife. This type of corrosion is common in grey cast iron in contact with water or soil. Fig. G3 shows a micrograph of grey cast iron with a corroded, graphitized layer in the upper part.

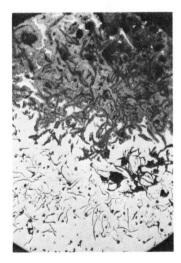

Fig. G3. Graphitic corrosion (graphitization) of grey cast iron in ship condenser after 8 months in the Baltic Sea. Lower part of micrograph (50X) shows unaffected cast iron with graphite flakes, upper part graphitized area with graphite flakes embedded in rust. Depth of graphitized layer was 8 mm. Courtesy: S. Bartha.

An example of corrosion, caused by varying composition within one and the same phase is so-called layer corrosion or exfoliation, which is an attack on rolled materials, e.g. copper-containing Al alloys, localized to certain layers, usually parallel to the surface. The attacks, which are often inter-crystalline in nature, may cause bulging and even bursting of the surface layer due to the formation of voluminous corrosion products. Cf. Fig. G4.

Also in selective corrosion (i.e. dissolution of the baser component

Fig. G4. Layer corrosion (exfoliation) of heat-affected zone along welds in Al alloy, Al Zn 5 Mg 1, aged (precipitation hardened) at ordinary temperature and exposed to sea water for 4.5 years. Cross section of blister. 50 X. Courtesy: E. Mattsson, Gränges Essem AB.

in a two-component alloy, e.g. zinc in brass) the process probably starts because of local variations in the composition. Since the more noble metal is retained or re-precipitated, the corrosion process itself generates a galvanic cell, consisting of the more noble metal as the cathode and the alloy as the anode. Selective corrosion occurs only in alloys, in which two or more metals form a solid solution. In the corrosion process only the less noble component is dissolved to a noticeable extent, while the remainder appears in metallic form even after the corrosion, although with a greatly reduced strength. The corrosion resistance of the alloys is dependent on their composition and it usually increases with increasing concentration of the more noble component of the alloy. If this concentration is higher than a certain critical value, the so-called"parting limit",the alloy has about the same resistance as its more noble component in pure form.

In dezincification of brass in aqueous solutions the zinc of the alloy passes into solution, while the copper remains as a porous metal mass with little mechanical strength (Fig. G5). The process is assumed to occur in local cells, in which zinc is dissolved at the anodes while the cathode process consists of reduction of dissolved oxygen in the solution. The copper is assumed to form mobile ad-atoms which diffuse on the metal surface and recrystallize in a structure, resembling electrodeposited copper (Fig. G6).

The remedy against de-zincification is certain alloy additions, often called inhibitors. The addition of a few hundredths of a percent arsenic, antimony or phosphorus makes α-brass practically resistant towards de-zincification.

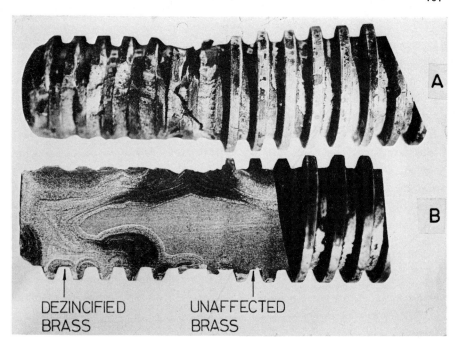

Fig. G5. Dezincification of brass. Valve spindle in domestic hot water tubing, 65-70°C, 4 years. A surface appearance, B longitudinal section. Courtesy: O. Nygren, Swedish Corrosion Institute.

Fig. G6. Schematic picture, showing the reaction process in selective corrosion (de-zincification of brass) in its initial state.

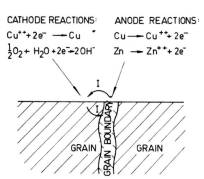

G.4 Oxygen concentration cells (differential aeration cells)

Corrosion cells need not always consist of galvanic cells, formed between different metallic phases but can also consist of concentration cells. As a rule, such corrosion cells are formed by solutions with different concentrations of dissolved oxygen. Parts of the metal surrounded by a high oxygen concentration form positive poles or cathodes, whereas parts

in contact with a solution of low oxygen concentration form negative poles
or anodes in the corrosion cells. According to what may be called the pa-
radox of corrosion science, corrosion occurs on those parts which are protected from the corroding substance, dissolved oxygen. Since the corrosion
current follows the law of least resistance, however, the attack will occur
in places close to the boundary of the oxygenated, cathodic surfaces. While
these are passivated by oxygen and by the alkali formed in the cathode reaction, the anode surfaces are activated by anions, e.g. chloride ions,
migrating with the corrosion current towards the anode,and by hydrogen ions,
formed by hydrolysis of metal ions formed in the anode process. Differential aeration cells are therefore autocatalytic (cf. the mechanism of pitting below).

Corrosion cells formed by an uneven supply of atmospheric oxygen are
very common, particularly in neutral waters and aqueous solutions. So-called
drop corrosion was treated above in paragraph E.3. Another common case is
so-called crevice corrosion (Fig. G7), i.e. attack on a metal in thin crevices between different metallic objects or between a metal and a non-metallic material. In such narrow crevices the replenishment of oxygen is
very difficult and it therefore forms an anode, while exposed surfaces of
the metal with a good supply of oxygen form cathodes. In a similar manner,
so-called deposit corrosion (Fig. G8) occurs in water and in aqueous solutions under deposits of sand, dead leaves, paper and similar things, which
make the replenishment of oxygen to the metal surface difficult. The para-
dox in these examples just referred to is that the corrosion attack occurs
just on those surfaces which are the most protected from the corrosive
agent, i.e. the aerated aqueous solution; however, this is explained by the
electrochemical mechanism.

Fig. G7. Crevice corrosion of bolt
and nut of 17 % Cr steel after 3
years in sea water. 18 Cr 12 Ni
3 Mo should be used instead. The
thread could be protected by passivating chromate putty. Courtesy:
Mrs. V. Victor, Swedish Power Administration.

Another typical case of a differential aeration cell leads to so-
called water-line attack (Fig. G9), i.e. corrosive attack just below the
liquid level on metals immersed in water, a surface tension meniscus on

Fig. G8. Deposit attack on plug
of stainless 17 Cr 2 Ni steel
under sludge in water from the
Sound. Temperature 50°C, water
velocity 2.5 m/s. A before, B
after cleaning. Courtesy:
S. Henriksson, Avesta Jernverks AB.

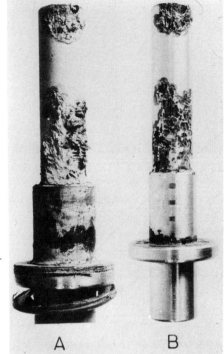

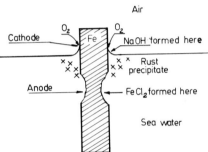

Fig. G9. Water-line attack,
caused by a differential
aeration cell.

the metal forming effective cathode surfaces with short diffusion paths for
dissolved oxygen. In a similar way, a steel pole driven into the soil is
particularly attacked just below the ground water level. A steel pole
driven into the bottom of the sea is most strongly attacked just below the
bottom level since the part of the pole in contact with the oxygenated sea
water serves as a cathode and is attacked less strongly.

Differential aeration cells also cause so-called filiform corrosion
which leads to irregularly developed hair-fine lines of corrosion products
below coatings of lacquer, paint or rubber (Fig. G10). Drops of concentrated electrolyte solution (perhaps salt crystals, which have absorbed moisture
from the atmosphere) under the film move forward by capillary forces with
corrosion under their centres and cathodic formation of alkali at the periphery, where the supply of oxygen occurs more easily. This movement forward

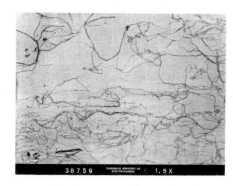

Fig. G10. Filiform corrosion below rubber coating on transport band of carbon steel, appearing after sea freight. Courtesy: Sandvik Steel Research.

is facilitated by the alkali, which lowers the surface tension and sometimes saponifies the paint film, which is then dislodged from the metallic substrate.

G.5 Metal ion concentration cells

Concentration cells may also be formed by differences in metal ion concentration. A copper rod in contact with one dilute and one concentrated copper salt solution will corrode at the part in contact with the dilute solution. Such metal ion concentration cells are, in fact, important in the corrosion of copper and its alloys in flowing media. Parts of a surface exposed to a more quickly-moving liquid will be negative and thus anodic due to a more rapid transport of copper ions away from the metal. Metal ion concentration cells therefore play an important part in the erosion corrosion of copper and its alloys, which, according to p. 93 and fi F12 above, occurs if the flow of the corroding liquid becomes turbulent on some part of the metal surface.

G.6 Active-passive cells

A common cause of local corrosion cells are defects in passivating oxide films. Such defects may be due to inhomogeneities in the composition of the metal, such as secondary phases in aluminium alloys and sulphide inclusions in steel, which determine the location of pitting corrosion, and precipitates in grain boundaries, which give rise to intercrystalline corrosion and stress corrosion cracking. As active-passive cells we may also consider corrosion cells formed between metal and mill scale, when the latter is damaged.

It should be noted that while an initiating potential difference arises in an active-passive cell this is not enough to maintain the corrosion process. It is also necessary to have a substance, as a rule dissolved oxygen, that maintains the cathode process. In this way, an active-passive cell is developed into a differential aeration cell.

G6.1 Pitting

Pitting is a localized attack, as a rule on an oxide-covered metal surface, which occurs due to a stimulation of the anode reaction by activating anions and of the cathode reaction by the presence of oxidizing agents and by effective cathode surfaces with low polarization. In order for a pitting attack to occur on a metal, a certain minimum corrosion potential, the so-called pitting or break-through potential, must be attained (Fig. G11). This potential is lower than the transpassive potential, however, and is thus situated within the passive range of the metal. A pit is initiated by the adsorption of activating anions, particularly chloride ions, on certain defect sites in the oxide film, such as slag inclusions or precipitates of secondary phases. When the pitting potential is attained, the electric field strength above the thinnest parts of the oxide film will be so high that the chloride ions can penetrate the film with the formation of oxide-chloride and a subsequent local dissolution (peptization) of the oxide film. As soon as a pit has been formed, it will continue to grow autocatalytically. In a vicious circle, the pit creates conditions

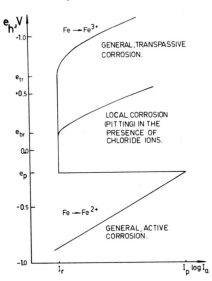

Fig. G11. Influence of pitting on anode polarization curve of passive metals.

e_p = passivation potential,

e_{br} = break-through potential,

e_{tr} = transpassive potential,

I_p = passivating current,

I_r = residual current in passive region (passivity current).

which promote its further growth. Pitting is a very common type of corrosion of stainless steels in solutions containing chlorides (Cf. Fig. G12). In commercial steels, pits are usually initiated around sulphide inclusions.

Fig. G12. Pitting corrosion inside an 18-8 stainless steel tube in a gelatin evaporator after four years of service. Pitting caused by a small amount of NaCl in the gelatin. Courtesy: Sandvik Steel Research.

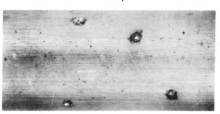

Figure G13 illustrates the mechanism of pitting attack on aluminium. In principle, it is apparently the same in the pitting of carbon steel and stainless steel. As shown in figure G13, the self-generating conditions for pitting are:

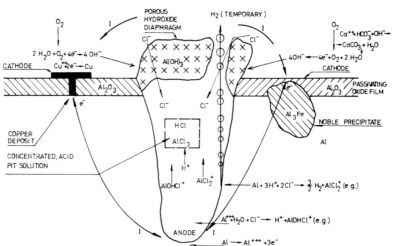

Fig. G13. Electrochemical mechanism of pit growth on aluminium, showing its autocatalytic self-stimulating nature.

1. Within the corrosion pit and preventing repassivation:
   a) enrichment of chloride ions in the pit by migration with the corrosion current, generated by the pit cell
   b) the generation of an acid solution within the pit, by the hydrolysis of metal ions, and a consequent local rise in the passivation potential
   c) high conductivity in the concentrated salt solution in the pit
   d) limited O_2 supply, partly due to low O_2 solubility in the concentrated pit electrolyte.

2. In the pit mouth:
   The formation of a crust (dome, tubercle) of hydrate, counteracting the dilution of the pit solution by diffusion and convection and hence strengthening   the factors listed above.

3. Around the pit and preventing general corrosion:
   a) cathodic protection by the corrosion current
   b) passivation by alkali formed in the cathode reaction, particularly in the presence of calcium hydrogen carbonate
   c) deposition of more noble metals, such as copper, on local cathodes, increasing their efficiency, so that the cathode potential is maintained above the pitting potential. The anode potential within the pit clearly has to be in the active region, which is facilitated by a local rise in the passivation potential within the pit (cf. 1b above).

   Remedies against pitting on aluminium are:

˙ Decreasing the contents of Si, Fe and Cu,which give noble precipitates, i.e. effective local cathodes, of Si and $FeAl_3$ and of Cu and $CuAl_2$.

2. Alloying with Mn or Mg,which will combine with Fe and Si respectively to form less noble phases.

3. Avoiding annealing temperatures around 500^oC, which gives a maximum of cathodic precipitates.

4. Plating aluminium alloys with pure aluminium, which is resistant against pitting and protects the substrate cathodically.

Pitting of aluminium in the atmosphere is usually self-healing (Fig. G14).

Fig. G14. Pitting of Al alloy, AlMg 2.5, after 10 years in an industrial atmosphere, containing copper dust. Pitting of Al in the atmosphere is usually "self-healing". 50 X. Courtesy: E. Mattsson, Gränges Essem AB.

Characteristic for pitting on carbon steel is the formation above the pits of rust warts, formed by concentric layers, and the collection of salt in the pits (Fig. G15). This salt usually consists of iron(II)chloride in marine atmospheres and of iron(II)sulphate in industrial atmospheres.

Fig. G15. Rust tubercles above pits in the bottom of a vertical cylindrical oil tank after 10 years. Courtesy: Å. Bresle, Lubrizol Scandinavia AB.

G6.2 Crevice corrosion and deposit attack

The mechanism of crevice corrosion and deposit attack is very similar to that of pitting. Consider, for example, the case of stainless chromium steel in aerated, neutral sodium chloride solution (cf. Fig. G7). Dissolved oxygen within the crevice is rapidly consumed, resulting in local break-down of the passivating oxide film. The whole of the cathode process (oxygen reduction) therefore takes place on the free surface whereas within the crevice mainly metal dissolution occurs. By hydrolysis of dissolved metal ions (Fe^{2+} and Cr^{3+}) the solution within the crevice is acidified to pH 3 - 4. The passivation potential of the steel within the crevice is raised accordingly (cf. E5.2) and the crevice is thus maintained in the active state, although the potential difference between crevice (anode) and free surface (cathode) is often quite small, only 50-100 mV (Fig. G16). Three conditions are necessary for the occurrence of crevice corrosion on stainless steels:

1. The presence of an oxidizing agent, usually oxygen, forming a concentration cell.

2. The presence of activating ions, usually chloride ions.

3. A low enough buffer capacity to allow the build-up of a considerable pH-difference between crevice and free surface.

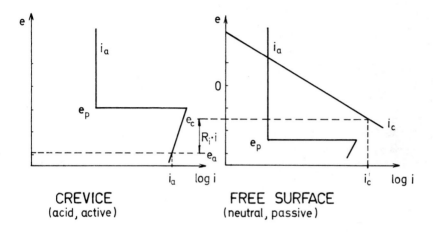

CREVICE
(acid, active)

FREE SURFACE
(neutral, passive)

Fig. G16. Polarization diagram for crevice corrosion of stainless chromium steel in aerated NaCl solution. $i_a' = i_c' = i_{corr}$. $e_c - e_a = R_i \cdot i_{corr}$. Note that the passivation potential (e_p) within the crevice is raised due to acidification.

G6.3 Intercrystalline corrosion

Intercrystalline or intergranular corrosion is of particular importance in austenitic 18/8 steel with a carbon content of, for instance, 0.08 - 0.10 %. These steels are sensitized to attack by certain corrosive media if they are heated to temperatures between 400^0 and 800^0C or if they are cooled slowly through this temperature range. This attack occurs preferentially at the grain boundaries and in extreme cases it may undermine the grains so that the metal is transformed to a powder. Media favouring this attack are, above all, acid solutions and also neutral chloride solutions, such as sea water. As a reagent for disclosing sensitization for intercrystalline corrosion a mixture is used which contains sulphuric acid, copper sulphate and copper powder (Strauss' test). More rapid results are obtained by potentiostatic etching (Fig. G17).

Fig. G17. 18-8 steel (0.033 % C), sensitized towards intercrystalline corrosion by annealling for 317 hrs at 600°C. Etched potentiostatically for 5 min. at a potential of +80 mV relative NHE, in a solution containing 5 % H_2SO_4, 0.01 % NH_4SCN (cf. P6.6 C).

Intercrystalline corrosion of austenitic steels is common near welds, around which there always exists a zone which has been kept in the dangerous temperature range for a short time. This may result in a pronounced attack in a zone on each side of the weld and at a certain distance from it (so-called weld decay). Cf. Fig. G18.

The sensitization for intercrystalline corrosion seems to be due to the formation of chromium carbide ($Cr_{23}C_6$), precipitated at the grain boundaries, which,even from the beginning,have a higher carbon content. In the vicinity of the grain boundaries the amount of Cr in solid solution in the matrix will therefore be reduced and consequently even the tendency towards passivation will be reduced (Fig. G19).

The methods of protection against intercrystalline corrosion aim at eliminating chromium carbide or preventing its formation. The methods of protection are therefore essentially the following:

1. Dissolution of chromium carbide by heat treatment above the susceptibility range and subsequent rapid cooling. For natural reasons this method is applicable to small objects only.

2. Lowering the carbon content to 0.05 % - 0.02 % according to requirements. If an 18/8 steel contains less than about 0.02 % carbon it is not sensitive to intergranular corrosion even after a long period of annealling at 700°C. Such steels are often referred to as ELC (extra low carbon) steels. Cf. Fig. G18.

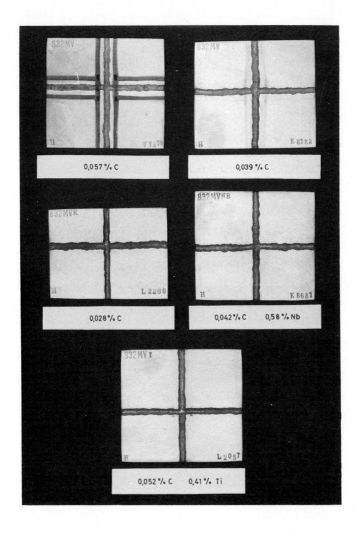

Fig. G18. Intergranular attacks (weld decay) in sensitized zones along welds in 2 mm 18-8 stainless steel. Manual welding by the tungsten-inert-gas (TIG) method. Testing for 4.5 hrs in 15 % HNO_3, 3 % HF at 80°C. The first three specimens show clearly the effect of decreasing carbon content. Note the unbroken attack along the second (vertical) weld in the first photograph. No attack occurs at the lowest carbon content (0.028 %) or in the niobium-stabilized steel, whereas the titanium-stabilized steel, at four points close to the first (horizontal) weld seam, shows knife-line attack. This is a special form of intergranular corrosion in stabilized steels occurring in a narrow region close to the weld seam, where the steel has been heated to such a high temperature that the stabilized carbide (e.g. TiC) is dissolved and is then not reprecipitated due to rapid cooling. Instead, Cr carbide forms at a somewhat lower temperature. Courtesy: S. Henriksson, Avesta Jernverks AB.

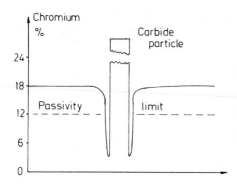

Fig. G19. Schematic representation of chromium distribution along a grain boundary in a sensitized 18-8 stainless steel. Precipitation of chromium carbides has caused a depletion of chromium around the carbide particles.

3. Addition of carbide-forming alloying elements, so-called stabilizers, the most important being titanium and niobium, which have a higher affinity for carbon than has chromium. Since the atomic weights are 48 for Ti and 93 for Nb, the contents of these alloying elements should be about five respectively ten times the carbon content of the steel. If the steel is now kept in the dangerous temperature range, carbon will form carbides with Ti and Nb, which prevents the depletion of Cr close to the grain boundaries. Cf. Fig. G18.

4. Generation of ferrite islands in the austenite. This method consists of modifying the relative contents of Cr and Ni in the steel, or generally the contents of ferrite and austenite formers respectively, so that the steel will contain a certain amount of ferrite instead of having a purely austenitic structure. In these ferritic-austenitic steels the precipitation of carbides occurs within the islands of ferrite and does not cause sensitization.

G.7 Electrolytic cells

Corrosion may also be caused by electrolytic cells, partly intentional cells, as in attack on so-called insoluble anodes for cathodic protection with impressed current or in industrial electrolysers, and partly unintentional electrolytic cells, caused by stray currents.

G7.1 Anode corrosion

Anode corrosion on permanent anodes in electrolytic cells is a particularly difficult corrosion problem caused by a combination of anodic current and, as a rule, aggressive electrolyte solutions. Very few metallic materials, which under other conditions are passivated by electron-conducting oxides, can be used. Quite often, non-metallic materials with good electronic conductivity, such as graphite and oxides, are used. The standard anode material for chloride solutions is graphite and for sulfate solutions lead.

G7.2 Stray-current corrosion

Stray-current corrosion is usually caused by direct current. Great damage may thus be caused by the direct current from welding generators used in electric welding, particularly if the circuit is closed through earth, but also by current leaking from the weld electrode via the object back to the generator (Fig. G20). Another source of stray-currents is electric trains (Fig. G21).

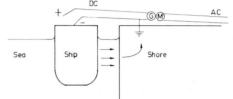

Fig. G20. Stray-current damage caused by welding generator. To reduce damage, the motor-generator should be placed on board ship.

Even alternating current may cause stray-current corrosion as a result of irreversibility, because metal which has been dissolved during one half-cycle is not redeposited during the next half-cycle. In particular, passivated metals such as platinum are sensitive to alternating current because their surface oxides are in this way reduced to spongy metal which is no longer passivated. Alternating current is particularly dangerous if it has a low frequency. as is often the case with the current used for electric trains.

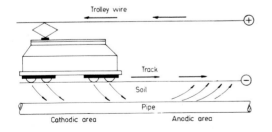

Fig. G21. Corrosion attack on buried tubing, caused by DC current from electric train. The steel tube is dissolved in the anodic area.

Literature

Staehle, R W (Editor), Localized Corrosion, Proceedings of Conference, Williamsburg, Va., 1971, Publ. by NACE 1973.

H. CORROSION TYPES, INFLUENCED BY MECHANICAL FACTORS

Corrosion types caused by a conjoint action of chemical and mechanical factors demand a chapter of their own. Depending on the nature of the mechanical forces the following cases may be distinguished:

1. Mechanical forces within the metal

    a) stress corrosion cracking (due to tensile stress)
    b) hydrogen cracking (due to tensile stress plus atomic hydrogen)
    c) corrosion fatigue (due to cyclic stress)

2. Mechanical action of a liquid on the metal

    a) erosion corrosion (due to shearing or frictional forces between a liquid and the metal)
    b) cavitation corrosion (due to the hammering action of a liquid, caused by implosion of vapour bubbles)

3. Mechanical action of a solid body on the metal

    a) fretting oxidation (due to vibrations under pressure), in contrast to the foregoing cases usually of non-electrochemical nature.

H.1 Stress corrosion cracking

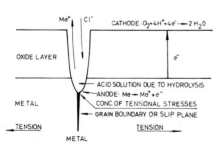

AQUEOUS SOLUTION, CONTAINING CHLORIDE IONS AND OXYGEN.

Me^+ | Cl^- CATHODE : $O_2 + 4H^+ + 4e^- \longrightarrow 2 H_2O$

OXIDE LAYER | e^-

ACID SOLUTION DUE TO HYDROLYSIS
ANODE: $Me \longrightarrow Me^+ + e^-$
METAL CONC. OF TENSIONAL STRESSES
GRAIN BOUNDARY OR SLIP PLANE
TENSION TENSION
METAL

Fig. H1. Stress corrosion cracking of oxide-covered metals (stainless steel, Al-alloys etc.).

Stress corrosion cracking (SCC) (Fig. H1) consists in a conjoint action between an internal or external static tensile stress and a local corrosion attack, resulting in cracking. Compressive stress, which can be generated by, for example, steel blasting of the metal surface, has, on the other hand, an inhibiting action.

SCC never or seldom occurs in pure metals but in many two- or multi-component systems (alloys), in which there are greater chances for local corrosion in galvanic micro-cells (local cells). SCC is sometimes connected with precipitates of intermetallic compounds in grain boundaries or slip bands. By the anodic attack there are formed narrow etch grooves with a wedge-shaped section. Due to the high stress concentration in the bottom of such etch grooves the metal will flow. New small anodic surfaces are form-ed, the formation of a passivating oxide film is prevented and the corrosion attack is intensified.

The electrochemical nature of SCC as regards both the initiation of cracks and their growth (propagation) is clearly demonstrated by cathodic polarization of the metal which prevents the occurrence of SCC and the pro-pagation of cracks already started.

Just like pitting, SCC usually occurs on alloys covered by a passivat-ing oxide film. On austenitic steels, for instance, which have been com-pletely activated, there is no tendency at all for SCC but only general corrosion. Due to the existent oxide film most local cells seem to be passivated so that the attack is concentrated to a few exposed local cells. As in the case of pitting, the first step in SCC is the action of the specific agent, often chloride ion, on the passive oxide film. Whether the attack later develops to pitting or to SCC depends on other factors, parti-cularly the level of tensile stress but also the corrosion potential. As with pitting, a certain critical potential must often be exceeded for SCC to occur.

SCC leads to brittle fracture, i.e. fracture without contraction of the fracture region. According as the cracks propagate along grain boundaries or slip planes, we distinguish intercrystalline (Fig. H2) and transcrystal-line cracking (Fig. H3). The cracks seem to propagate by a conjoint, some-times alternating, action of both electrochemical and mechanical processes. Of importance for the propagation of SCC is the generation of a concentration cell (usually an oxygen concentration cell) between the bottom of a crack (as a small anode) and the outer surface of the metal as a large cathode. The electric current, generated by this corrosion cell, transports active anions, often chloride ions, into the crack, in which there is formed a concentrated electrolyte solution, which is, furthermore, acidified by hydrolysis. This means that the process of SCC is autocatalytic like pitting and crevice corrosion.

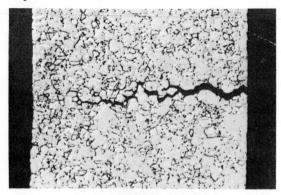

Fig. H2. Intercrystalline stress corrosion crack in deep-drawn cup of brass (Cu 37 Zn) exposed for three months to a rural atmosphere, containing traces of ammonia. 250 X. Courtesy: E. Mattsson, Gränges Essem AB.

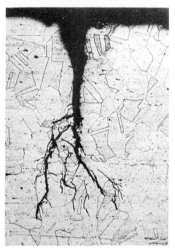

Fig. H3. Transcrystalline stress corrosion cracks in stainless 18-8 steel, developed after testing in 40 % $CaCl_2$ solution at 100°C. 300 X. Courtesy: S. Henriksson, Avesta Jernverks AB.

It is characteristic of SCC that it is connected with certain special corrosion media, which are able to cause local attacks and to dissolve corrosion products and thus prevent repassivation. Hence, SCC occurs in carbon steel in strong alkali solutions (caustic brittleness) and in nitrate solutions (nitrate brittleness), in austenitic stainless steels, as well as in aluminium and magnesium alloys in the presence of chloride ions and in brass under the influence of traces of ammonia, e.g. given off by plastics or lacquers, containing amines or amides. If SCC of brass is connected with residual internal stresses, it is sometimes termed "season cracking", since it follows the wet season and also resembles the seasonal cracking of wood.

SCC of a̲u̲s̲t̲e̲n̲i̲t̲i̲c̲ 18/8 s̲t̲e̲e̲l̲ in chloride solutions is of particular importance (Fig. H4). This system has therefore been investigated thoroughly, particularly by potentiostatic technique (Fig. H5, H6). It has been found

Fig. H4. Coffee-boiler of stainless 18-8 steel showing stress corrosion cracking. The chloride content of the water in the heating jacket was originally below 50 mg/1 but was increased considerably through evaporation. Courtesy: S. Henriksson, Avesta Jernverks AB.

σ, kp/mm^2 τ, min

10   106

20   43

25   28

Fig. H5. Increase of the number of stress corrosion cracks with increasing tensile load at constant anodic polarization (e_h = 0 mV) of test wires, ϕ 1.5 mm, of austenitic steel (18 Cr 9 Ni, annealed, $\sigma_{0.2}$ = 31 kp/mm^2, σ_B = 82 kp/mm^2). σ = applied tensile stress, τ = time to fracture. Test solution: 45 % MgCl$_2$, bp. 154°C, thermostated at 140°.

Fig. H6. Increase of the number of stress corrosion cracks with increasing anodic polarization of stressed (σ = 30.5 kp/mm^2) test wires, ϕ 1.5 mm , of austenitic steel (18 Cr 9 Ni, annealed, $\sigma_{0.2}$ = 31 kp/mm^2, σ_B = 82 kp/mm^2) e_h = test potential relative NHE. τ = time to fracture in min. Test solution 45 % MgCl$_2$, bp. 154°C, thermostated at 140°C.

that a certain time elapses before the first cracks show up. During this induction period (incubation period) a break-through of the passivating oxide film on the steel surface occurs. The reactions going on during the induction period are little influenced by the stress conditions of the metal. The end of the induction period is marked by the occurrence of the first crack. The length of the induction period decreases considerably at rising chloride concentration and at rising temperature. Below 80°C, SCC of austenitic steel does not occur at all. The induction period is considerably longer than the crack period, during which the cracks pro-pagate. The induction period is therefore the dominating time factor for an austenitic material which is subjected to SCC. A cathodic current pro-longs the induction period and a sufficient cathodic current prevents the occurrence of the crack period entirely. Contact of the stainless steel with a less noble metal, such as aluminium, zinc, carbon steel or lead has the same effect.

Besides chloride ions, oxygen or some other oxidizing agent for main-tenance of the cathode process must be present in the solution in order that SCC of stainless steel shall occur. Oxidizing inhibitors as chromate may counteract SCC by passivation, however. If the oxygen content increases,

a smaller amount of chloride is necessary to cause crack formation. Vice
versa, if the chloride concentration increases, less oxygen is necessary.
It has therefore been suggested that the product of chloride concentration   and oxygen concentration have   to   attain a certain minimum for
SCC to occur. The presence of pure hydrogen or nitrogen above the solution
eliminates SCC of austenitic steels entirely. On the other hand, the active
metal exposed within the advancing crack reacts with the acidified crack
solution and hydrogen is evolved. It therefore seems possible that embrittlement due to atomic hydrogen plays a part in the SCC of austenitic
steels.

H.2 Hydrogen_embrittlement_and_hydrogen_cracking

Hydrogen_embrittlement means embrittlement of metals caused by atomic
hydrogen, which locks dislocations and makes plastic flow more difficult.
If internal cavities exist, a catalytic process on their surfaces may lead
to the formation of molecular hydrogen, causing high pressure and blister
formation, which can sometimes be seen on stainless cutlery. If a metal
embrittled by hydrogen is subjected to tensile stresses above a certain
critical value hydrogen_cracking takes place. The critical stress is lower
the higher the hydrogen content. Sometimes the necessary tensile stress is
caused by the hydrogen itself and cracking takes place independently of an
outer load, e.g. longitudinal cracks in stressed wires, subjected to hydrogen embrittlement.

The atomic hydrogen may have been formed by corrosion of the metal
itself or by corrosion of a baser metal in direct contact with the former.
The hydrogen may also have entered the metal during some manufacturing
process, such as pickling, cathodic cleaning or electrodeposition. Hydrogen
embrittlement in steel is made worse by the presence of the following
elements in the order: Bi, Pb, S, Te, Se, As (As most dangerous), since
these inhibit the reaction $H + H = H_2$, resulting in high concentrations of
atomic hydrogen on the steel surface. Hydrogen sulphide causes many cases
of corrosion cracking in the petroleum industry. Hydrogen cracking occurs
in carbon steel, but particularly in low-alloyed, high-strength steels,
furthermore in martensitic and ferritic stainless steels and in a number
of metals forming hydrides. In high-strength, low-alloyed steels with a
martensitic structure, tempering at a somewhat higher temperature, e.g.
at $400^{\circ}C$ instead of $250^{\circ}C$, which lowers the strength but slightly, is an

effective means to eliminate susceptibility to hydrogen embrittlement. By tempering at the higher temperature, normal cementite is formed from the special tempering carbide, ε-carbide, whose composition is sometimes given as $Fe_{2.4}C$ and which seems to absorb hydrogen easily.

Hydrogen embrittlement may be distinguished experimentally from SCC by cathodic polarization, which enhances hydrogen embrittlement due to hydrogen evolution but prevents SCC.

H.3 Corrosion fatigue

Corrosion fatigue arises from the conjoint action of corrosion attack and cyclic stresses, e.g. rapidly alternating tensile and compressive stresses. In contrast to purely mechanical fatigue, which often takes place only above a certain critical value of the cyclic stress, the so-called fatigue limit, corrosion fatigue may occur also at very low stresses, as is shown in Figure H7.

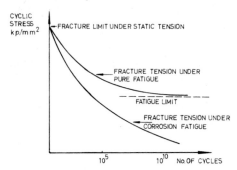

Fig. H7. Diagram, showing fracture tension as a function of the number of cycles in purely mechanical fatigue and in corrosion fatigue.

In contrast to SCC, corrosion fatigue occurs in most aqueous media and is not connected with special combinations of ion and metal. The mechanism seems to involve an exposure of oxide-free, cold worked metal by extrusion of slip bands in grains in the metal surface. These parts of the metal become anodes and result in corrosion grooves, which gradually develop to transcrystalline cracks.

Corrosion fatigue may be prevented by cathodic protection (e.g. by a zinc coating), which makes the anode surfaces immune, or by inhibitors (e.g. chromate), which passivate them. For steels, particularly titanium-alloyed steels, surface hardening by nitriding is an efficient means against corrosion fatigue.

H.4 Erosion corrosion (turbulence corrosion)

Erosion corrosion was described above as connected with turbulent flow. Another designation   is therefore turbulence corrosion. If caused by a jet of liquid, impinging upon a metal surface, it is denoted impingement attack. Turbulence increases the supply of the corrosive agent and the transport through the solution of corrosion products from the metal surface. In addition, there is a purely mechanical factor, viz. the tearing away of corrosion products from the metal surface by the shearing stress between the metal and the liquid, which is particularly high under turbulent conditions. In special cases, this mechanical moment of erosion corrosion is strengthened by air bubbles or by suspended solid particles, such as sand.

Localized attacks due to erosion corrosion usually have bright surfaces, free from corrosion products. The pits are often under-cut in the direction of the flow and their cross-sections exhibit an under-cut surface zone pointing against the flow. Sometimes these pits have a characteristic horse-shoe shape as from a horse running upstream(Figs. H8, H9).

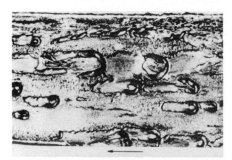

Fig. H8. Erosion corrosion of hot water copper tube. Horseshoe shaped pits. Flow direction from right to left. 2 X. Courtesy E. Mattsson, Gränges Essem AB.

Fig. H9. Erosion corrosion in wall of copper tube for domestic hot water. Flow direction from right to left. Cross-section of horseshoe pit. 50 X. Courtesy: E. Mattsson, Gränges Essem AB.

Turbulence attacks are common in water circulation systems with copper tubing and brass components. It is usually connected with irregularities (protruding parts, bends etc.), causing local turbulence (Figs.H10, H11).

Fig. H10. Erosion corrosion of valve cone of brass, subjected to flowing sea water for 15 months in cooling system on board ship. Left: Corroded cone. Right: New cone. Material: Die-cast brass, 38.5 % Zn, 2.5 % Pb, balance Cu. Courtesy: S. Bartha.

Fig. H11. Perforations, caused by erosion corrosion in creased bend of copper tubing. Courtesy: E. Mattsson, Gränges Essem AB.

H.5 Cavitation corrosion

Cavitation corrosion is also a result of the conjoint action of high liquid flow rate and corrosion. Cavitation denotes the occurrence of vapour bubbles in a liquid, when its velocity u becomes so high that its static pressure p according to Bernoulli´s law ($p + \rho u^2/2$ = const.) is lower than the vapour pressure of the liquid. If these vapour bubbles collapse (implode) on a metal surface, the result is a strong hammering action, which destroys passivating oxide films and also damages the underlying metal. The exposed, cold worked metal is corroded and the process is repeated.

Although cavitation attack sometimes, e.g. on plastics and ceramics, may be of a purely mechanical nature (cavitation erosion), it always seems to involve a corrosion moment on metals in water. This is shown by the fact that cavitation corrosion

    1. may be prevented by cathodic protection

    2. may be reduced by inhibitors

    3. is more pronounced in salt water than in soft water.

H. 6 Fretting oxidation

Fretting oxidation (or fretting corrosion) occurs at the interface between two solid bodies, one or both being metallic, that,
under considerable normal pressure and without a lubricant, make small
relative movements in relation to each other, e.g. due to vibration.
Irregularities in one of the surfaces scrape off the oxide layer on the
other and the exposed metal oxidizes, whereafter newly formed oxide is
scraped off again etc. The process requires oxygen but not moisture, which,
on the contrary, exerts a retarding effect on the attack, probably due to
a lubricating action and because oxide hydrates are less hard than oxides.
The mechanism is therefore apparently rather purely chemical than electrochemical. It is characteristic for fretting oxidation that the corrosion
product is oxide (on steel Fe_2O_3), not hydroxide.

Literature

Staehle, R W, Forty, A J & van Rooyen, D, Fundamental Aspects of Stress
Corrosion Cracking, Proceedings of Conference, The Ohio State University,
1967, Publ. by NACE 1969.

I. ATMOSPHERIC CORROSION

Atmospheric corrosion varies quite considerably within different geographical areas and with local conditions (Fig. I1). With regard to climatic conditions, the earth is divided into temperate, tropical and arctic areas. Tropical regions are in turn usually divided into dry and moist regions. With regard to local atmospheric conditions, the usual division is into marine, industrial, urban and rural climates. In an industrial area, the corrosion velocity may be more than one hundred times as high as in a desert or in an arctic region.

Fig. I1. A famous example of long preservation of a metallic object in the atmosphere is the 1600 years old "rustless" pillar of wrought iron (0.15 % C, 0.25 % P) at Delhi, India. It is covered with a magnetite film, 50-600 μm thick. Reasons for the good state of preservation of the Delhi pillar are
1. Dry and un-polluted climate.
2. Favourable composition of the iron (low in S, high in P).
3. Large mass and heat capacity of the pillar.
Courtesy: I. Sven-Nilsson, Swedish Corrosion Institute.

Within limited local areas quite different atmospheric conditions may occur, sometimes referred to with the term micro-climates. Even the geographical orientation is important. It is often observed, for instance, that the eastern and southern sides of a construction corrode less than the western and the northern ones, since those sides which are exposed to the sun dry up faster after they have been wetted by rain and dew. The opposite may be true for painted surfaces, however, to which sunshine is often more damaging than moisture.

Within coastal areas with a marine climate, common salt is a naturally occurring corrosive pollutant in the air. Corrosion decreases with increasing distance from the coastal line due to the diminishing salt content of the air. The salt content and the corrosion velocity increase, on the other hand, with height above the ground to begin with. The reason is apparently that immediately above the ground the vegetation (trees,bushes) slows down the wind and removes salt water drops (Fig. I2).

Fig. I2. Hot-galvanized steel stay ropes for wooden power pylon on the Swedish west coast, about 1 km from the sea. All of the 20 ropes were heavily rusted on their upper parts whereas the zinc layer remained on. their lower parts. Courtesy: A. Sandin, AB Elektrokoppar.

The most dangerous air pollutant from the present point of view is sulphur dioxide, which occurs in the smoke gases from combustion of coal and oil and various motor fuels. Since the fuel consumption is higher during the colder season, the SO_2-content of the air and usually the corrosion rate also is higher during the autumn and winter months. The SO_2-content varies within urban and industrial districts from 0.1 to 100 mg/m^3.

Fig. I3 shows the results of laboratory corrosion tests with polished steel plates in both pure and SO_2-containing air with increasing relative humidity. In some of the tests, some solid particles were placed on the test plates to imitate the deposit of solid pollutants from the air. The results show the following:

a) In very pure air, rusting is small and increases but slightly with increasing humidity.

b) In polluted air, rusting is also small as long as the relative humidity of the air is not higher than 70 %. In the presence of SO_2, the corrosion rate increases strongly at high relative humidities.

c) Solid particles of ammonium sulphate and soot, which constitute common air pollutants within industrial areas, accelerate attack.

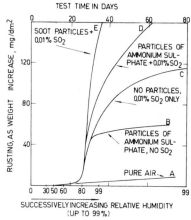

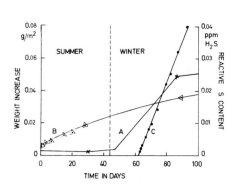

Fig. I3. Rusting of polished steel specimens with successively increasing relative humidity during the time of the test. The experiment illustrates the effect of various impurities (sulphur dioxide and particles of ammonium sulphate and soot). After Vernon.

Fig. I4. The effect of initial exposure conditions on subsequent corrosion (of copper).
A = sulphur content of air
B = specimens put out in summer
C =   "   "   "   " winter

In polluted air condensation takes place if the relative humidity exceeds about 70 %. In the thin electrolyte films then formed the electrochemical corrosion processes can occur. If the temperature is below the freezing point steel practically does not rust at all since the electrochemical processes require water in liquid form. Remains from old polar expeditions have been found to contain cameras and other instruments in very good condition after decades in arctic ice. For the same reason, a car left out in winter and covered by ice and snow rusts less than if it is placed in a badly ventilated garage.

The initial corrosion, which varies with the season, is of great, sometimes dominating influence on the continued corrosion process. The total corrosion after a given number of years is not the same for test plates put out during the winter as for test plates put out during the summer. A striking example of this is shown by investigations of the corrosion of copper out of doors in London according to figure I4. Test plates put out in the summer (curve B) show a parabolic weight increase which was not influenced by the strong increase of the sulphur content of the air due to burning fossil fuels (curve A). Test plates put out in the winter (curve C), on the other hand, show a rapid linear weight increase.

Literature

Metal Corrosion in the Atmosphere, ASTM, STP No. 435, Philadelphia, 1968.

J. CORROSION IN SOIL

The corrosivity of soil is mainly determined by its electric resistance. If the supply of air to the soil is relatively high, as in its upper layers, so that lack of oxygen does not limit the cathode process or favour the occurrence of sulphate reducing bacteria, the corrosivity of the soil is roughly inversely proportional to its electric resistivity. It is therefore possible to divide surface soils into different corrosivity groups, according to table J1.

TABLE J1. Relation between resistivity and corrosivity of surface soils (pH >6).

Soil resistivity, ρ,ohmcm (in leach water 1:1)	Salt content, mg/l (in leach water 1:1)	Corrosivity	Average corrosion rate for steel, µm per year
$<10^2$	>7500	Very high	>100
$10^2 - 10^3$	7500 – 750	High	100 – 30
$10^3 - 10^4$	750 – 75	Low	30 – 4
$>10^4$	<75	Very low	<4

The surface of a steel construction in the upper layers of the soil constitutes a great many differential aeration cells as a consequence of the changing composition and particle size of the soil from one point to another. Many cases of corrosion of steel tubes and lead cable sheathing in the soil are caused by such differential aeration cells, formed where the tubes or cables pass through soils of different water and oxygen content. Such cases of corrosion are particularly pronounced where clay is in contact with soils of larger particle size. The anode in these aeration cells is formed by tube or cable in contact with the clay, where-

as cathodic parts of the tube or cable are surrounded by sand or gravel.
Fig Jl shows a schematic diagram of such a corrosion cell.

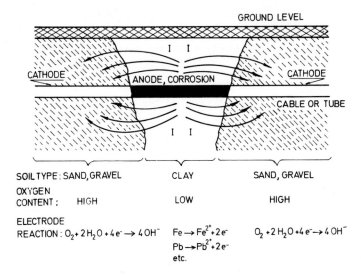

SOIL TYPE: SAND, GRAVEL CLAY SAND, GRAVEL

OXYGEN CONTENT: HIGH LOW HIGH

ELECTRODE REACTION: $O_2 + 2H_2O + 4e^- \rightarrow 4OH^-$ $Fe \rightarrow Fe^{2+} + 2e^-$ $O_2 + 2H_2O + 4e^- \rightarrow 4OH^-$
  $Pb \rightarrow Pb^{2+} + 2e^-$
  etc.

Fig. Jl. Differential aeration cell on cable or tube in soil at the passage
from an aerated to a non-aerated soil.

Above ground water level, air is transported by diffusion and convection
in the gas phase which is a comparatively rapid process. Below ground
water level oxygen can be transported only by diffusion through the water
in the soil which is slower by several powers of ten. This is also a common
cause for the formation of differential aeration cells, an example of which
is shown in Fig. J2.

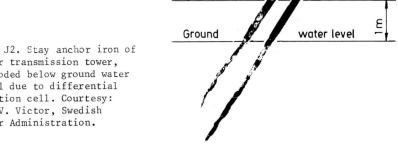

Fig. J2. Stay anchor iron of
power transmission tower,
corroded below ground water
level due to differential
aeration cell. Courtesy:
Mrs.V. Victor, Swedish
Power Administration.

The air in the soil porosity differs from the composition of atmospheric air due to biological processes in the soil. Mouldering of organic

substances as well as the breathing of plant roots consumes oxygen and generates carbon dioxide. The oxygen content therefore decreases rapidly below ground level while the carbon dioxide content instead increases, particularly if the exchange with the atmosphere is hampered. During the winter, frost and water constitute a barrier between the outer atmosphere and the air in the soil.

At greater depths (more than 10 m) corrosion rate is therefore not determined by the electric resistivity of the soil but, as a rule, by the diffusion of dissolved oxygen in soil water, and sometimes by sulphate reducing bacteria. Even in deep soils with low resistivity the corrosion rate is therefore, as a rule, low due to a low supply of oxygen. In the presence of sulphate reducing bacteria, on the other hand, the corrosivity may be quite high even in deep soils.

In summing up, it is possible to form the conception of corrosion conditions above and below ground water level that is shown in figure J3.

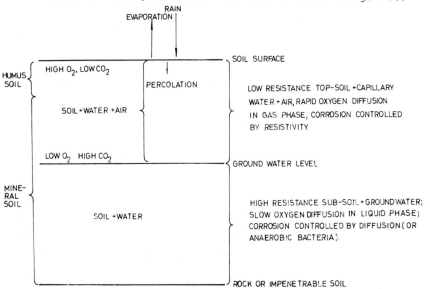

Fig. J3. Schematic view of corrosion conditions in soil above and below ground water level.

Literature

Romanoff, M, Underground Corrosion of Steel. NBS Circular 579, 1957.

K. CORROSION IN DRY GASES

The deciding question in high temperature oxidation proves to be whether the oxide layer formed constitutes a protection against continued oxidation or not. One important point of view is whether the oxide film forms cracks or remains dense. In this connection, the relative volumes of oxide and metal play an important part. If the oxide has a smaller molar volume than the metal, cracks appear in the oxide film and the oxidation continues practically unhampered. This is the case with alkali and alkaline earth metals. If, on the other hand, the oxide has a volume, which is considerably larger than that of the metal, such high compressive forces are built up in the oxide film that the latter, at a certain critical thickness, forms blisters,cracks and scales off. This is the rule for heavy metals. The most favourable conditions occur if the volume ratio between oxide and metal is just a little higher than 1. This is the case for aluminium and titanium.

Although the volume ratio oxide/metal is important, it does not give any higher degree of correlation with oxidation rate. Even dense oxide films show very different growth rates. In order to explain this it is necessary to study the transport of matter through the oxide. It should then be observed that an oxide is, as a rule, formed by an ion lattice. Through this lattice, metal ions may migrate outwards (1) or oxygen ions inwards (2). In certain cases both processes may take place simultaneously (3). Under all conditions, electrons must migrate outwards through the oxide film in order to maintain electro-neutrality (Cf. Fig. K1). The various cases referred to may be distinguished by experiments in which an inert substance (Cr_2O_3, Pt) is placed on the surface of the metal to be examined. In case 1, the inert particles are to be found between the metal and the oxide after the oxidation experiment; in case 2, on top of the oxide film and in case 3, within the oxide layer. Conditions seem to be similar in the anodic formation of oxide films.

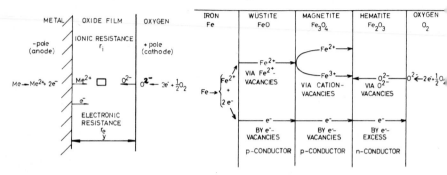

Fig. K1. An oxide film on a metal surface may be considered as a galvanic cell with

$$emf = E = - \frac{\Delta G^{O}_{MeO}}{zF}$$ and the potential gradient $= \frac{E}{y}$. The oxide film, serving as both electrolyte and external resistance of the galvanic cell, grows by ion migration via lattice defects.

Fig. K2. Schematic representation of phases and conditions of diffusion in the oxidation of iron above 570°C.

Conditions are often complicated by the occurrence of two or more oxide films on top of each other. In high temperature oxidation of iron and steel, three successive oxide films appear, viz. from within and outwards FeO, Fe_3O_4 and Fe_2O_3, as shown in figure K2.

In order for an oxide film to grow it must apparently have both ion and electron conductivity. As a matter of fact, most metal oxides are so-called semi-conductors of which this duplex conductivity is typical. This is due to a deviation from the stoichiometric composition, so that they show either excess or deficit of metal. An excess of metal ions in the lattice must be compensated by the equivalent amount of negative charge carriers or electrons and these semi-conductors are therefore called n-conductors. Among metal oxides, two types of n-conductors are known, illustrated in Figs. K3 and K4. Those semi-conductors that show a deficit of metal ions also have a deficit of electrons which corresponds to positive charge carriers. These semi-conductors are therefore called p-conductors. Only one type of p-conductors among oxides is known, illustrated by Fig. K5.

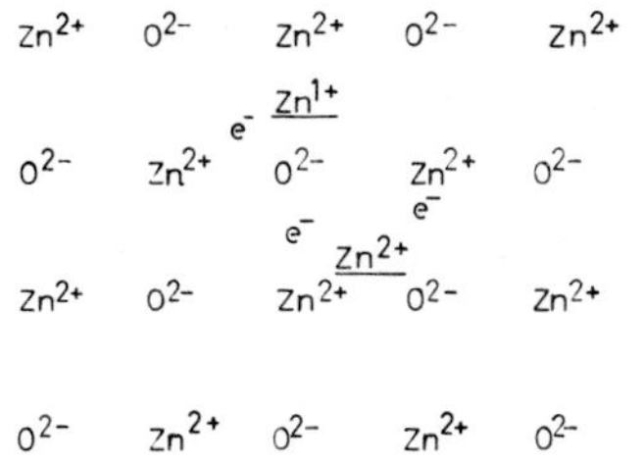

Zn²⁺ O²⁻ Zn²⁺ O²⁻ Zn²⁺

      e⁻ <u>Zn¹⁺</u>

O²⁻ Zn²⁺ O²⁻ Zn²⁺ O²⁻

      e⁻ e⁻ <u>Zn²⁺</u>

Zn²⁺ O²⁻ Zn²⁺ O²⁻ Zn²⁺

O²⁻ Zn²⁺ O²⁻ Zn²⁺ O²⁻

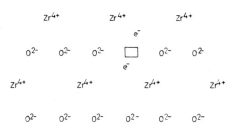

Fig. K3. Oxide semi-conductor with metal excess (n-conductor) due to <u>interstitial cations</u> (examples underlined). Metal ions migrate outwards interstitially in the lattice.

Fig. K4. Oxide semi-conductor with metal excess (n-conductor) due to <u>anion vacancies</u> (example framed) and equivalent free electrons. Oxygen anions migrate inwards via anion vacancies.

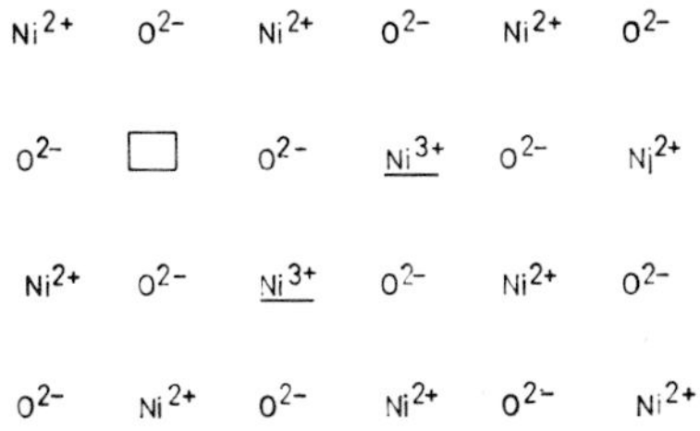

Ni²⁺ O²⁻ Ni²⁺ O²⁻ Ni²⁺ O²⁻

O²⁻ ☐ O²⁻ <u>Ni³⁺</u> O²⁻ Ni²⁺

Ni²⁺ O²⁻ <u>Ni³⁺</u> O²⁻ Ni²⁺ O²⁻

O²⁻ Ni²⁺ O²⁻ Ni²⁺ O²⁻ Ni²⁺

Ni²⁺ O²⁻ <u>Li⁺</u> O²⁻ Ni²⁺ O²⁻

O²⁻ <u>Li⁺</u> O²⁻ <u>Ni³⁺</u> O²⁻ Ni²⁺

Ni²⁺ O²⁻ <u>Ni³⁺</u> O²⁻ <u>Li⁺</u> O²⁻

O²⁻ Ni²⁺ O²⁻ <u>Ni³⁺</u> O²⁻ Ni²⁺

Fig. K5. Oxide semi-conductor with metal deficit (p-conductor) due to <u>cation vacancies</u> (example framed), compensated by cations of higher valency (underlined).

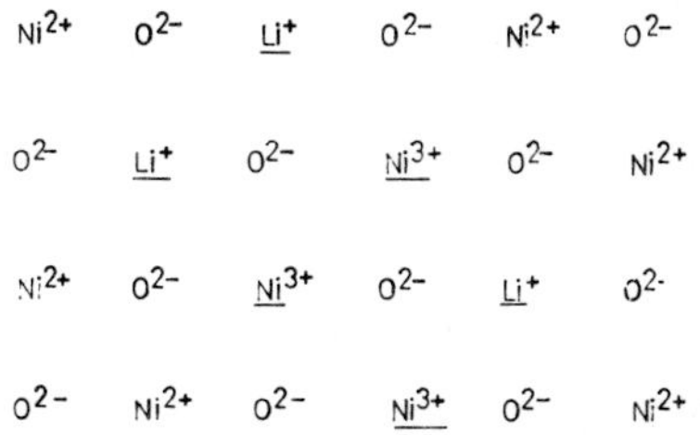

Fig. K6. Addition of Li_2O to NiO decreases the ionic conductivity (by filling cation vacancies), and increases the electronic conductivity (by forming new Ni^{3+}-ions).

While the number of lattice defects is the same for ions and for electrons, the electron conductivity is, as a rule, about a thousand times higher than the ion conductivity due to the higher mobility of the electrons. In general, therefore, ion transport is the rate determining step in oxidation.

The influence of foreign metals on lattice defects and hence on electronic and ionic conductivity and oxidation rate is of great importance. One example is given in Fig. K6. The whole situation is summarized in Table K1, which presents the so-called <u>Hauffe's valency rules</u>.

The increase of the electron conductivity of NiO by an addition of Li_2O has long been known and practically utilized in the positive electrode plate of alkaline Ni-Fe storage batteries. Experimentally, it has also been shown that the oxidation of nickel is slower in the presence of Li_2O.

TABLE K1. Influence of the valency of an alloying metal on the oxidation rate of the basic metal. Hauffe's valency rules.

Type of semi-conductor oxide	Typical oxides	The valency of the alloying metal in relation to that of the basic metal	Change of electron conductivity	Change of ionic conductivity and oxidation rate
1. <u>n</u>-conductors (metal excess)				
a) with interstitial cations	ZnO, CdO	Lower	Decreases	Increases
b) with anion vacancies	Al_2O_3, TiO_2 Fe_2O_3, ZrO_2	Higher	Increases	Decreases
2. <u>p</u>-conductors (metal deficit)				
a) with cation vacancies	NiO, FeO, Cu_2O	Lower	Increases	Decreases
	Cr_2O_3, Fe_3O_4	Higher	Decreases	Increases
b) with interstitial anions	Not known			

The rate at which the thickness (y) of an oxide film increases with time (t) is of deciding importance. A great number of <u>growth laws</u> have been formulated which show how oxide film thickness increases with time and which try to explain an abundance of experimental data. Figure K7 shows a schematic representation of various growth laws.

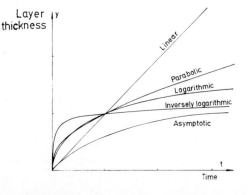

Fig. K7. Schematic representation of different growth laws.

As a rule it is not possible to derive numerical values for the constants in the growth laws by theoretical means. For the parabolic law, $y^2 = k \times t$, which is often valid at higher temperatures, such a derivation can be carried out according to the so-called Wagner electrochemical oxidation theory.

The use of unalloyed steels at higher temperatures is limited by the composition of iron oxides. Below $570^{\circ}C$, there occur in air only Fe_3O_4 and Fe_2O_3 which are relatively protective. Above $570^{\circ}C$ the oxide layer consists to the greater part of FeO with numerous lattice defects and hence a high diffusion rate of the Fe^{2+} ions. Hauffe's valency rules apparently point to one method for raising the resistance of steel against high temperature oxidation, viz. alloying. Another method consists in adding the alloying elements which have a greater tendency to oxidize than iron. The oxide of the alloying element will then form a protective layer between the steel and the iron oxide. Fireproof steels may therefore be obtained by alloying with Cr, Si, Al and also Mo. On copper, dense protective oxide films may be obtained by alloying with Al, Be and Mg.

As well as by the use of suitable alloys, protection against high temperature oxidation may be obtained by the use of surface coatings. At lower temperatures, it is possible to use certain polymer coatings, for example silicon lacquers, particularly those with aluminium pigment, and also low-melting metals, such as Pb, Zn and Al. Al, forming a protective oxide (Al_2O_3) is particularly useful for the purpose (Cf. Fig. K8).

Fig. K8. Effect of spray-coating aluminium onto heater tubes of heat-resistant Cr-Mo steel in soda furnace at a sulphate pulp mill. Steam temperature within tubes $450^{\circ}C$. Photograph shows difference between coated and un-coated part of tubes. Coating lasts about 3 years. Courtesy: P. Isaksson, Mörrums Bruk.

At higher temperatures, it is possible to use metallic, metal-ceramic or purely ceramic coatings. The latter may be refractory oxides, carbides or borides. By flame-spraying with an acetylene-oxygen flame, for example, it is possible to spray materials with melting points up to 2500°C. For still higher temperatures, plasma_spraying with a direct current arc is used. In this way, all available materials, even the most refractory ones, may be applied as coatings. Table K2 gives examples of protective coatings for steel and other metals.

TABLE K2. Protective coatings against high temperature oxidation.

Coating	Highest temperature in use
Silicon lacquer	300°C
Silicon lacquer, Al-pigmented	550°C
Lead	300°C
Al	600°C
Al-Al$_2$O$_3$, on steel	900°C
80/20 Ni-Cr alloy	1.000^{o}C
Kanthal (Fe-Cr-Al-Co alloy)	1.300^{o}C
Ni-Al$_2$O$_3$	1.800^{o}C
Ni-MgO	1.800^{o}C
SiO$_2$	1.710^{o}C
Cr$_2$O$_3$	1.900^{o}C
Al$_2$O$_3$	2.000^{o}C
TiO$_2$	2.130^{o}C
ZrO$_2$	2.700^{o}C
ThO$_2$	3.300^{o}C

Reference

Hauffe, K, Oxidation of Metals, Plenum Press, New York 1965.

Kubaschewski, O & Hopkins, B E, Oxidation of Metals and Alloys, Butterworths, London 1962.

Kofstad, P, High Temperature Oxidation of Metals, John Wiley & Sons, New York 1966.

L. CORROSION PROTECTION BY CHANGE OF METAL AND BY DESIGN

L.1 Change of composition, structure and stress condition of the metal

The corrosion resistance of a metallic material may often be considerably improved by changing its composition (by alloying additions or by refining operations), by changing its structure (by heat treatment) or by changing its stress condition (by heat treatment or cold-working).

Alloying additions for increasing corrosion resistance may be:

a) Passivating, e.g. Cr (at least 11 %),Ni and Mo in stainless and acid-resistant steels.

b) Cathodic, facilitating passivation, e.g. Cu, Ag, Pd or Pt in acid-resistant steels; Pd and Pt in titanium; Pt and Ag in zirconium; Ni in aluminium. Cf. galvanic anodic protection below.

c) Neutralizing, e.g. Ti, Nb and Ta as stabilizers (carbide formers) in austenitic stainless steels; Mn and Cu for neutralizing S in steels; Mg and Mn for neutralizing Fe and Si in aluminium.

d) Oxide-forming, e.g. Cr, Al and Si in heat-resistant steels; Al, Be and Mg in copper to improve its oxidation resistance.

e) Oxide-improving, reducing lattice defects according to Hauffe's valency rules, e.g. Li in Ni, Al in Zn.

f) Inhibiting, e.g. As or Sb in brass to prevent dezincification.

Refining operations for increasing corrosion resistance may involve, for example, lowering the content of S and P in various steels, of C in stainless steels, of Fe, Si and Cu in aluminium etc.

Heat treatment for increasing corrosion resistance by changing the structure of the alloy may consist of an annealling operation, aiming at dissolving secondary phases (intermetallic compounds or carbides), followed by rapid cooling (quenching).

Elimination of tensile stresses in order to reduce the risk for stress corrosion cracking or hydrogen cracking may be carried out by stress-relief annealling. Annealling conditions (temperature, time) should be such that a satisfactory stress-relief is obtained without substantially reducing the strength of the material.

Creation of compressive stresses in the surface layer, on the other hand, is favourable for the resistance of a material against stress corrosion and corrosion fatigue. It is possible to introduce compressive stresses or at least reduce tensile stresses by various mechanical means, such as shot peening and special rolling, so-called reeling.

L.2 Design for corrosion prevention

L2.1 Corrosion prevention starts with design

The main task of the designer or construction engineer is, of course, to give the construction a proper design with regard to function, fabrication and mechanical strength. Many constructions will be placed in locations where the environment is more or less corrosive, however, which means that protective measures have to be foreseen. Since the cost of corrosion control of a construction is strongly dependent upon its design, the designer or construction engineer should always include the aspects of corrosion prevention in his work.

The most economical construction is obviously that which during its life has drawn the lowest total costs per year. Maintenance costs, particularly costs for repainting, often constitute a very important part of the total cost. It is therefore by no means sure that the construction which is the cheapest in fabrication is also the most economical one. Quite often, it is economically more sound to choose an alternative that is more expensive in fabrication but cheaper in maintenance.

All corrosion protection work should therefore start at the design stage. It may be impossible to protect a steel construction effectively by painting or some other surface treatment if it is inadequately designed from a corrosion point of view. On the other hand, the most efficient and cheapest way to avoid corrosion is often to design the construction in a proper way, not favouring corrosion attacks. The procedure in the design work should therefore comprise the following steps:

1. Establish the basic prerequisites!

2. Choose construction material and suitable surface treatment or other corrosion protection!

3. Carry out the design work proper!

L2.2 Establishment of basic prerequisites

The calculated life of the construction, the mechanical stresses it will be subjected to, how easily accessible it will be for maintenance and repair, etc. will evidently influence in a high degree both the choice of material, of surface treatments and/or of other corrosion protection methods, and the design work proper. The following questions give an idea of view-points of vital importance in this context:

1. Where is the construction to be used?
2. How long life is required?
3. Will the construction be accessible for maintenance?
4. Can stoppage or closing down be tolerated?
5. How corrosive is the environment?
6. Which type of corrosion may be expected?
7. Is there a risk of corrosion fatigue or stress corrosion cracking?
8. Are the conditions extreme: high temperature, high pressure, high flow velocity, etc. ?

For constructions in the atmosphere, the geographical location gives essential indications as to how seriously the corrosion problem has to be taken. It is of deciding importance whether the climate is rural, marine or urban. The worst corrosion problems will be found within or in the vicinity of chemical and metallurgical industries. The corrosivity of the environment deserves a more thorough study, however. Quite often, condensing moisture will have to be considered. The corrosivity of the environment may be greatly increased by the acidity and salt content of liquids, e.g. recycled cooling waters, or by the content of dust and highly corrosive gases, such as SO_2, SO_3, Cl_2 and HCl, in the atmosphere. Spillage of various corrosive liquids on a construction may often increase corrosion problems. Lubricating oils, gasolene and other petroleum products seldom cause corrosion directly, but will often damage conventional paints and lacquers and may therefore cause corrosion indirectly. Organic liquids containing halogen, e.g. chlorinated hydrocarbons, cause severe corrosion on light metals and their alloys, however.

L2.3 Choice of surface treatment or other corrosion protection

Most constructions require some sort of surface treatment both for aesthetic reasons and as a protection against corrosion. The designer should know at least the outlines of this surface treatment. This means that he should know the answers to the following questions:

1. Will the construction be painted, asphalted, rubber-coated or metallized?
2. Will the construction be accessible for maintenance, and is maintenance possible with the surface treatment chosen?
3. How long a life for the surface coating is assumed?
4. Is there a free choice as regards pre-cleaning method, mode of application and drying time of the coating?
5. Will special tolerances or margins have to be considered?
6. Is the use of cathodic protection or inhibitors an alternative to a protective coating?

L2.4 Design principles with regard to corrosion

The illustrations of this chapter give a number of examples valid for the design of both machines and buildings. Some of the most important general rules, illustrated by the figures, are collected below.

L24.1 Simplify the forms!

The simpler (rounder) the form that can be given to a construction, the greater are the chances that a good corrosion protection may be provided. The more angles, corners, edges and internal surfaces a construction contains, the more difficult is the practical realisation of surface treatment. In addition, a complicated construction has a larger surface, subjected to the corrosive medium. Tube-formed profiles are particularly easy to paint and to maintain and they usually give the minimum surface area. They are therefore a good alternative to the more common profiles, such as L, T and U, and particularly for framework constructions which are usually very difficult to maintain by painting or other surface treatment.

L24.2 Avoid residual moisture!

It is usually true that no corrosion occurs without the presence of moisture. One of the main tasks of the designer will therefore be to make sure that his construction is protected from moisture as much as possible. Profiles should be arranged in such a way that moisture is not retained, and, furthermore, so that the construction can be properly

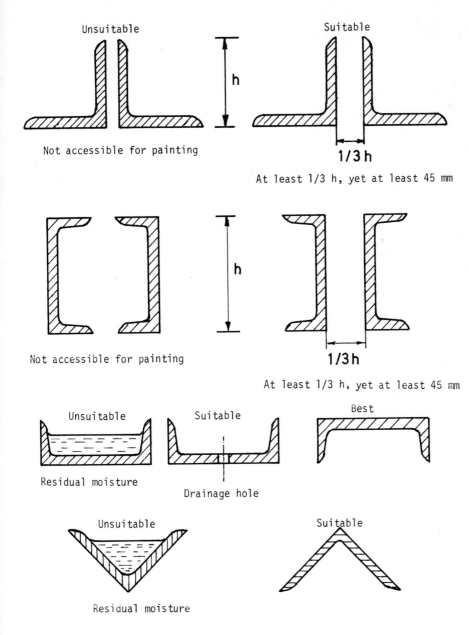

Fig. L1. Suitable and unsuitable arrangement of profiles.

painted and maintained (Fig. L1). Storage containers should be so designed that they can be completely emptied and cleaned (Fig. L2) and so that moisture will not collect below them (Figs.L3, L4). Supporting steel poles should be placed on concrete foundations (Fig. L5).

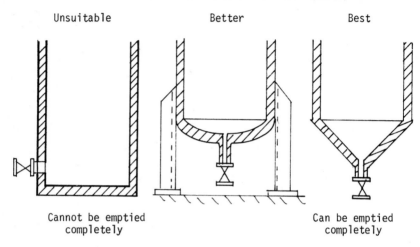

Fig. L2. Storage containers should be so designed that they can be completely emptied and easily cleaned.

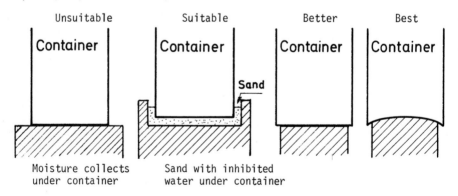

Fig. L3. Design of concrete foundations for containers.

Sheet roofs must have sufficient slope to allow a rapid drainage of rain-water. For a single-folded sheet roof the slope should be at least 1:4, whereas for a double-folded roof a slope of 1:10 or 1:30 may be sufficient.

Condensed moisture formed at the contact of a hot gas and a cold

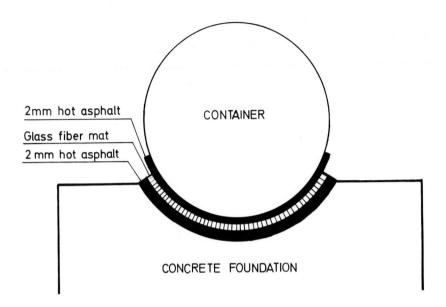

Fig. L4. Proper design of concrete foundation for a cylindrical container.

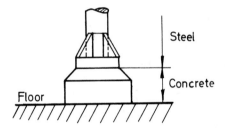

Fig. L5. Proper design of supporting pole. The bottom plate should always be placed on a concrete foundation above the floor.

metal surface is often a great problem. This is particularly so because the condensing moisture is usually not pure water, but rather aggressive solutions which condense much earlier (have a higher dew-point). Common examples are sulphuric acid and sulphurous acid that condense from combustion gases or flue gases from metallurgical plants. Corrosion problems caused by condensing moisture can usually be solved in a satisfactory manner only at the design or construction stage. Common solutions are

144

double-walled gas ducts or chimneys, but the choice of such a working temperature that condensation does not occur may sometimes be the best and most economical means. In connection with condensation, it should also be observed that many heat insulation materials contain dissolvable salts, usually chlorides and sulphates. Condensed moisture dissolves these salts and they may then be enriched on the wall of the insulated object, which may lead to surprisingly rapid attacks even if the wall consists of high-alloyed steels. Provisions should be made for draining off condensed moisture (Fig. L6). Condensation may sometimes be avoided by proper heat insulation (Fig. L7).

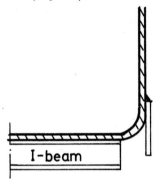

I-beam

Fig. L6. Draining off condensed moisture.

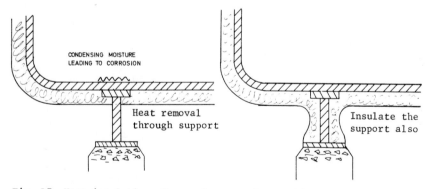

CONDENSING MOISTURE
LEADING TO CORROSION

Heat removal
through support

Insulate the
support also

Fig. L7. Heat insulation of reaction vessel or tubing for moist gases.

Profiled beams turned the wrong way (see Fig. L8) and partly closed spaces (see Fig. L9) should be provided with drainage holes. In

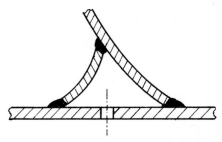

Fig. L8. Weakly sloping beam with web stiffeners where water and dirt have collected and caused rusting. Drainage holes should have been provided. Courtesy: K. Fr. Trägårdh, Swedish Power Administration.

Fig. L9. Partly closed spaces should be provided with drainage holes.

closed constructions, any drainage holes should be placed in such a way that the construction also receives a proper ventilation. In order to avoid residual moisture, ventilation is usually just as important as drainage. Drainage and ventilation openings should furthermore be made so wide that they are not plugged by dirt which may instead cause an accumulation of water and have an adverse effect. Ventilation openings may also be used for spraying in rust preventives, e.g. in cars.

Narrow crevices should be avoided in constructions if at all possible (See Figure L10).

Fig. L10. Avoid nooks and narrow crevices which collect dirt and are difficult to protect by coatings.

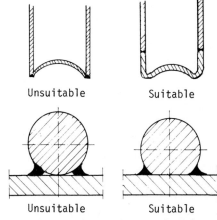

146

If they have to occur they should be caulked, preferably with rust protective sealing agents (red lead putty, zinc chromate putty, cf. Fig. L11)
or they should be seam-welded.

Fig. L11. Atmospheric crevice
corrosion of a log shoot in
Northern Sweden. The crevices
should have been sealed with
red lead putty prior to painting. Courtesy: K. Fr. Trägårdh,
Swedish Power Administration.

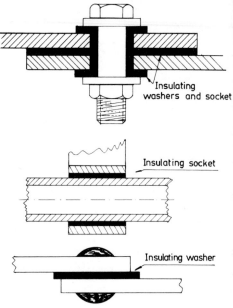

Fig. L12. Dissimilar metals may be separated by electrically insulating materials
to prevent galvanic corrosion.

L24.3 Consider the risk for galvanic corrosion!

For galvanic effects to occur, the following conditions must be fulfilled:

1. The metals must have a sufficient potential difference.
2. The metals must be in direct contact with each other.
3. Both metals must be in contact with the same electrolyte solution.
4. The solution must contain dissolved oxygen (or acid) for the maintenance of the cathode process.

It is the task of the designer to make sure that at least one of these
conditions is not fulfilled. If possible, different metals and alloys should
not be jointed and particularly not if they are situated far from each other
in the galvanic series of electrode potentials. Normally, galvanic effects
may be expected if the potential difference surpasses 50 mV.

The most common method to prevent galvanic corrosion is to interpose an

electrical insulator between the two metals (Fig. L12). A great many organic materials are at the disposal of the designer for this purpose, but
almost all of them are easily damaged by the application of high contact
pressures and are therefore not quite safe. Above all, the insulating
materials must not be porous since they may then absorb moisture and cause
crevice corrosion. Glued joints between various metals are very favourable
in this respect. Inorganic materials may also be used but usually they are
too brittle. Sometimes the best procedure is to introduce a middle piece,
which may be oversized and easily exchangeable or which has an intermediate
potential (Fig. L13). Examples of the latter case are zinc or aluminium
washers between steel bolts and light metals, lead joints between gutters
of copper and galvanized steel and brass sleeves between steel and copper
tubes.

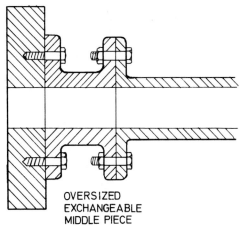

OVERSIZED
EXCHANGEABLE
MIDDLE PIECE

Fig. L13. Exchangeable middle piece for joining different
metals.

In order to prevent the direct contact between metallic materials
and a surrounding solution, a dependable anti-corrosion paint system is
used which will keep the galvanic corrosion at an acceptable level. It is
most important to paint the noble member of the galvanic couple. Painting
only the baser metal may aggravate the situation, since it may lead to pitting in pores in the coating.

If dissolved atmospheric oxygen is excluded, very little galvanic
corrosion will occur in spite of the existence of galvanic cells, since

the latter cannot work without a substance that maintains the cathode process. In closed water systems, even metals far from each other in the galvanic series, such as carbon steel and copper, may be safely joined if contact with the atmosphere is excluded. In the presence of oxygen, different metals in the construction should preferably be placed far from each other in order to increase the electrolytic resistance of the galvanic cell.

L24.4 Be particularly careful with joints and junctions!

The joining of various materials may cause the following effects of importance from a corrosion point of view:

   a) the creation of crevices,pockets and hollow spaces
   b) the creation of heterogeneous micro-structures (in welding and soldering)
   c) the occurrence of galvanic effects if different materials are joined.

A general principle for joints is that the dangerous combination small anode - large cathode must be avoided. Instead, the favourable combination small cathode - large anode should be deliberately created. In this way, the joint will be cathodically protected. Nuts, bolts, screws, welds and solders should therefore be more noble than the joined members of the construction (Fig. L14).

L244.1 Welding

Welding is the industrially most important method for the joining of metals. From a corrosion point of view and generally said, the welding processes making butt joints possible are to be preferred to those where lap joints are used, since the latter will often cause the formation of an abundance of crevices, pockets and hollow spaces. For most constructional steels and for the major part of the low-alloyed steels, most welding processes are acceptable from a corrosion point of view, provided that the welded joint has been made in a proper manner and that the correct filler material has been chosen. Light metals, high-alloyed steels and more exotic metals and alloys, on the other hand, often require a more selective choice of welding method. In these cases the MIG (metal-inert-gas) or TIG (tungsten-inert-gas) processes are often used because they give a high quality weld. Sometimes other processes also will give a good result.

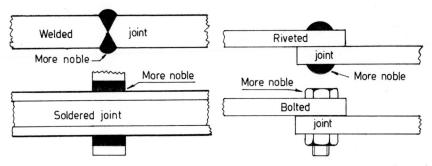

Fig. L14. The material of a joint should always be more noble than that of the joined members.

It is quite common that the filler material used for fusion welding has a composition which deviates somewhat from that of the basic material. The filler metal must be applicable for comparatively large groups of similar steels. This means that a certain and not always negligible potential difference is to be expected between the weld metal and the basic material. The usually very rapid cooling process in welding may also result in such potential differences, due to the differences in heat treatment between weld metal and basic material that occur in this way.

By the selection of a filler material that is somewhat more noble than the basic material (a choice that is often caused by other aspects of welding technology), the favourable combination small cathode - large anode is obtained. In this way many problems are eliminated, particularly in electrolytes of high conductivity. Sometimes, a preferential attack is observed in the heat affected zone, however. This has been found to be particularly true for steels containing active sulphide inclusions according to chapter B above. Such attacks should not be confused with the common cases of intergranular corrosion and pitting due to carbide precipitation and chromium depletion along grain boundaries in the outer parts of the heat affected zone along welds in stainless chromium or chromium nickel steels (see chapter G above). Welding of stainless steels should not be carried out with acetylene gas, however, since there is then a considerable risk for intergranular corrosion due to carburization and carbide precipitation. Welding stresses always influence the corrosion characteristics more or less (Fig. L15).

150

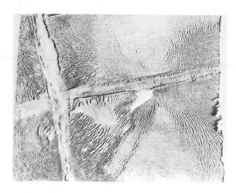

Fig. L15. General corrosion of
acid-proof 18 Cr-11 Ni-2.5 Mo
steel in a solution containing
H_2SO_4 and SO_2 at 40ºC. The special
appearance reflects welding stresses which have locally accelerated
the corrosion attack. Courtesy:
S. Henriksson, Avesta Jernverks AB.

From a corrosion point of view butt welds are preferred to fillet
welds or the kinds of welded joints that are a result of old riveting
philosophy (Cf. Fig. L16). Intermittent welds are unsuitable both from
a mechanical and from a corrosion point of view. Continuous welds are
more expensive but offer such advantages that they are to be preferred
(Fig. L17).

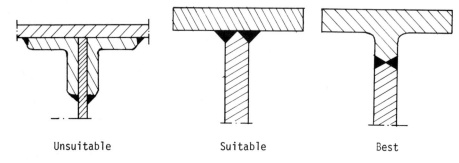

Unsuitable   Suitable   Best

Fig. L16. Unsuitable and suitable design of welded joints.

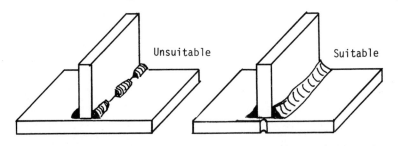

Fig. L17. Continuous welds are to be preferred to intermittent ones.

Welds should always be even and wellshaped, without pockets and crevices. The welds should always be cleaned so that slag and spatter are removed. In welding together plates of different thickness, the surplus part of the thicker plate should be placed and worked on that side of the wall where the environment is least corrosive. Likewise, the smaller side of a weld should be turned towards the corrosive medium (Fig. L18).

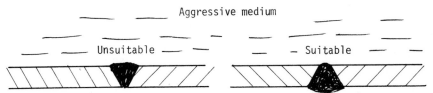

Fig. L18. The smaller side of the weld should be turned towards the aggressive medium.

L244.2 Soldering

Soldering with soft or hard solder in most cases gives considerable differences in potential between the basic and the filler material. Intermetallic compounds may also be formed, particularly in hard soldering with copper-containing solder. Most fluxing agents used in soldering give aggressive solutions of high conductivity with moisture, and may thus cause corrosion attacks later, particularly on light metals and their alloys.

From a purely constructional point of view, soldered joints do not constitute any serious corrosion problem. Crevices and pockets are usually well filled by the solder which, in most cases, has quite a good fluidity and good wetting properties. The heat treatment effects are usually also less serious than in welding due to normally low melting points of solders and negligible melting of the basic materials. Soldered joints are almost invariably designed on the principle small cathode/large anode since the solder is usually more noble than the basic material.

L244.3 Threaded, riveted and screwed joints

These give many chances for the formation of narrow crevices and small nooks. Cold-worked surfaces, such as rivets and threads also corrode faster than do hot-worked metal surfaces. In joining different materials soldering with a noble solder is usually to prefer to threading (See Fig. L19). For constructions that are dismantled relatively often and in which screwed joints are therefore used, the threads should be kept lubricated with rust-preventing grease. The threads may also be treated with a zinc

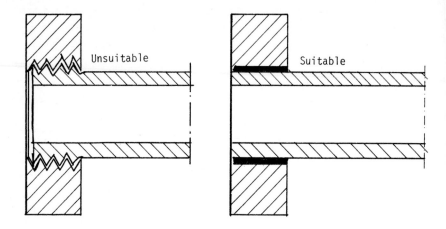

Fig. L19. Soldering is to be preferred to threading.

chromate primer before assembly. Both bolt and nut should preferably be galvanized (Fig. L20).

Fig. L20. Both bolt and nut should be galvanized.

Fig. L21. A stud should not be allowed to protrude inside the wall since this may lead to deposit or erosion corrosion.

In riveted joints the contact surfaces should be protected against corrosion before assemblage. In connecting tubes etc. to a tank, flanged studs are to be preferred to threading. Tube connections etc. should not be placed on different parts of the tank. It is better to concentrate them in one plac

preferably in a blind flange which may easily be exchanged if it has
rusted. A stud should not be allowed to protrude on the inside of the
wall since this may lead to localized corrosion around the connection
(Cf. Fig. L21).

L244.4 Glueing

Glueing as an industrial method for joining metals is increasing
strongly in importance. From a corrosion point of view, it has the
great advantage of giving automatically an electrically insulated
joint which means that galvanic corrosion is excluded. For constructions
in strongly corrosive environments the method is of limited applicability,
however. The choice of glue material and cleaning of metal surfaces before application of the glue is of the greatest importance. Hot-setting bi-
or multicomponent glues usually give the best joints considering both
mechanical strength and corrosion properties. The cleaning problem is
usually solved by sand blasting or pickling.

L24.5 Take into consideration dimensional changes due to corrosion!

Decrease of the thickness of the metal due to corrosion may cause
a proportionally larger decrease of the fatigue strength. Therefore,
constructions subjected to high dynamical stresses should be protected more carefully against corrosion so that their dimensions are not
changed noticeably. In constructions with lower stresses a certain decrease of the wall thickness may sometimes be allowed and is then compensated by a thicker original material. This is particularly true if
the construction is difficult or impossible to maintain, e.g. in the
soil, and if an applied surface protection does not have sufficient
durability.

Corrosion products often have a considerably larger volume than
the metal from which they are formed. In constructions with riveted
or bolted joints, a corrosion attack in the jointed surfaces may cause
such a large increase of volume and subsequent mechanical stress that
the metal is deformed between the rivets or bolts or that the latter
burst.These and similar constructions require particularly careful
corrosion protection. Cf. Figs. L22-L23.

154

Fig. L22. Glass wall of balcony,
destroyed by rusting of its frame of
steel profiles. The latter should
have been galvanized before painting.
Courtesy: K. Fr. Trägårdh, Swedish
Power Administration.

Fig. L23. Bursting effect of rust.
Ornament of copper on a frame of
steel tubing. Rust formed on the
steel has caused the copper to crack.
Courtesy: O. Nygren, Swedish Corrosion Institute.

L24.6 Take into consideration dimensional changes caused by protective
     coatings!

Metallic or other protective coatings may increase the wall thickness
and other dimensions of the original materials so that prescribed tolerances
or margins may no longer be maintained.

L24.7 Give directions for fabrication and care!

Fabrication, use and care of the finished construction should also be
considered from a corrosion point of view already at the drawing table.
Even if the designer is not directly responsible for these stages he may
contribute very actively to a decrease of corrosion damage also in these
respects. The designer should therefore give on his drawings, specifications
for fabrication with complete directions regarding working, materials handling, heat treatment, welding method, filler metal, tempering liquids, cutting fluids, etc. Regarding operations, the designer should provide working instructions of such a wording that even technically unskilled person-
nel may understand their meaning and contribute to keep corrosion damage
at a low level.

M. CORROSION PROTECTION BY CHANGE IN THE CORROSIVE MEDIUM

M.1 Removal of corrosive constituents

Examples of such measures are:

a) elimination of oxygen from water by evacuation, by saturation with nitrogen or by the addition of oxygen scavengers, such as sulphite or hydrazine

b) elimination of acid from water by neutralization, e.g. by the addition of lime

c) elimination of salts from water by ion-exchangers

d) elimination of water from air by dehumidification, e.g. using porous bags with silica gel in wrappings, in instruments and in other small closed spaces

e) lowering of the relative humidity of surrounding air by an increase in temperature, e.g. 6-7°C above the outer temperature in storage premises

f) elimination of solid particles from water or from air by filtration, smoke gas filtration etc.

Hydrazine is generally used to remove dissolved atmospheric oxygen in boiler water. Hydrazine is not a corrosion inhibitor from the electrochemical point of view, but is often designated as such in practice. Hydrazine reduces oxygen according to the reaction

$$N_2H_4 + O_2 \rightarrow N_2 + 2H_2O .$$

Hydrazine may, however, also oxidize and reduce itself to nitrogen and ammonia according to:

$$3N_2H_4 \rightarrow N_2 + 4NH_3 .$$

156

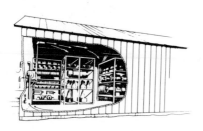

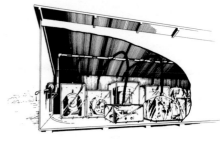

Fig. M1. Dehumidification of whole storeroom. Air-drier to the left. Air is partly recirculated.
Courtesy: Munters' Torkar AB, Sweden.

Fig. M2. Dehumidification of casings around stored objects. No circulation of air.
Courtesy: Munters' Torkar AB, Sweden.

Fig. M3. Storage of military equipment in dehumidified plastic tent. Air-drier to the left. Courtesy: L. Lund, Norsk Sivilforsvar.

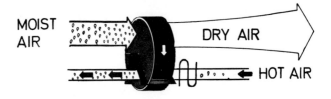

Fig. M4. Principle of rotary air-drier. Moisture in fresh air is absorbed by LiCl, bound on asbestos. The filter is regenerated by blowing hot air in the opposite direction for a certain sector of the rotation.

The latter reaction leads to an alkalization of the water along with the removal of oxygen. It is cheaper to carry out the alkalization with ammonia, however.

The use of hydrazine (usually available as a 15 % aqueous solution) usually gives good results in circulating boiler water. A dense and protective magnetite layer is formed, which ennobles the steel about 100 mV. The maintenance of a concentration of about 100 mg N_2H_4/l may be considered as safe.

Dehumidification of air as a measure against atmospheric corrosion of goods under storage may be used either to dehumidify the storeroom (Fig. M1) or special casings around stored objects (Figs. M2, M3). Hence, dry air from a dehumidification aggregate is supplied to machinery etc., enclosed in a casing or box of, for instance, plastic foil. Rotary airdriers, based on, for example, asbestos containing lithium chloride, are available (Cf. Fig. M4).

Storage of military equipment in dehumidified, dry air is an important application of this method. Other applications are the internal dehumidification of ships and of steel bridges.

M.2 Addition of corrosion-retarding substances (inhibitors)

Inhibitors are substances that in corrosion in moist environments are added to the corrosive medium to lower the corrosion rate by retarding the anode process and/or the cathode process. An anodic inhibitor increases the anode polarization and hence moves the corrosion potential in the positive direction, whereas a cathodic inhibitor in the corresponding manner displaces the corrosion potential in negative direction. With so-called mixed inhibitors, the potential change is smaller and its direction is determined by the relative size of the anodic and cathodic effects (Fig. M5).

M2.1 Anodic inhibitors

Anodic inhibitors are, as a rule, anions which thus migrate to anode surfaces and which in favourable cases passivate the latter, often in conjunction with dissolved oxygen. In the class of anodic inhibitors we find a number of important inorganic inhibitors, such as orthophosphate, silicate, nitrite and chromate and also benzoate. Non-oxidizing inhibitors are effective only in conjunction with dissolved oxygen.

158

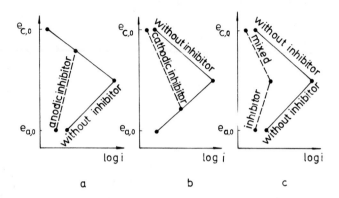

Fig. M5. Action of corrosion inhibitors.
a) Anodic inhibitors. Examples: Chromate, nitrite, orthophosphate, silicate, benzoate.
b) Cathodic inhibitors. Examples: $Ca(HCO_3)_2$, $ZnSO_4$, polyphosphate, As^{3+}, Sb^{3+} (on iron), Hg (on zinc).
c) Mixed inhibitors. Examples: Organic inhibitors, containing nitrogen and/or sulphur.

Although the anodic inhibitors are very effective and widely used, they usually have an undesirable property: if the content of inhibitor is or gradually becomes so low that it does not suffice to cover all the surface of the metal acting as an anode, the dangerous combination small anode and large cathode is obtained, which may lead to pitting. In such cases the inhibitor may do more harm than good. Anodic inhibitors are therefore often denoted as "dangerous". Benzoate seems to be an exception since insufficient inhibitor concentration just leads to general corrosion.

M21.1 Orthophosphates

Addition of orthophosphates (e.g. disodium phosphate) to water raises alkalinity but also contributes effectively in the formation of protective films if the water has a sufficient calcium hardness. These protective films seem to consist mainly of calcium carbonate plus iron oxides and only a small proportion of phosphates. This explains why phosphate addition alone is of little value in very soft waters if it is not combined with lime addition.

M21.2 Silicate

Sodium silicates of a composition, roughly corresponding to $Na_2O, 2SiO_2$ are used as inhibitors in water. They act partly as alkalizers, partly as anodic inhibitors. Their inhibitor effect seems to be connected with colloidal anions of the type $(m\ SiO_2, n\ SiO_3)^{2n-}$, formed by hydrolysis in aqueous solutions. These anions probably migrate electrophoretically towards anode surfaces. As with the phosphates, good protective films are formed only with a given content of soluble calcium salts in the water.

M21.3 Nitrite

While orthophosphates and silicates exert their protective action in conjunction with the calcium hardness of water, there are other inorganic inhibitors that act totally on their own and which are therefore effective even in very soft waters. Among these we find the important oxidizing inhibitors nitrite and chromate.

Nitrite seems to act by oxidizing the corrosion products to compounds with higher valency states which as a rule have lower solubility and therefore form protective films more easily. The corrosion potential of the metal is displaced in positive direction. Nitrite is usually mixed with other inhibitors, such as benzoate and phosphate. Nitrite alone is used in so-called cutting oils, i.e. emulsions of oil in water used as coolants in turning and milling and also in rinse waters to prevent rusting during drying.

M21.4 Chromate

Some chromates (such as Na_2CrO_4 or K_2CrO_4) are oxidizing inhibitors whose action partly consists in an oxidation of corrosion products to less soluble form. In addition, these inhibitors form a constituent part of the passivating films, which contain chromates as well as Cr_2O_3. Chromates are very effective inhibitors which in water afford good protection to many metals including steel and copper.

M21.5 Benzoate

Anions of many organic acids have inhibitive action. The oxidation products of linseed oil belong to this group. Of a number of organic acids tried as inhibitors, benzoic acid in the form of sodium benzoate has proved

to be the most suitable. Benzoate is not an oxidizer. In accordance
with its character of anion, it is usually classed among the anodic inhibitors. Despite this, it is not considered as dangerous, since too small
a concentration has no detrimental effect. Relatively high concentrations
of this inhibitor are necessary, however, in order to obtain a substantial
effect. Sodium benzoate, along with sodium nitrite,is often used as an im-
pregnant for paper wrappings intended for the protection of machinery
parts etc. against moisture in   transport.

M21.6 Required concentration of inhibitors

1 g/l may be given as a practical value for the concentration of inhibitors. Sodium benzoate requires a higher concentration, 10-15 g/l, to
give sufficient effect, however. Cf. also Fig. M6.

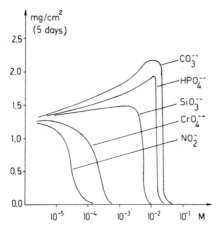

Fig. M6. Weight loss of carbon steel
in water at room temperature as function of additions of sodium salts of
inhibiting anions. For each ion, a
certain critical concentration is
needed for protection. This critical
concentration is raised by an increase
of temperature and by the presence of
chloride ions.

M2.2 Cathodic inhibitors

Cathodic inhibitors are, as a rule, cations which thus migrate towards
cathode surfaces where they are precipitated chemically or electrochemically
and block (isolate) these surfaces. One example is afforded by the retarding
action of As^{3+} and Sb^{3+} on the dissolution of iron in acids. There are probably formed electrically non-conducting coatings of elementary As or Sb,
which counteract hydrogen evolution. Other examples are afforded by the
natural content of calcium hydrogen carbonate in hard waters and by in-
tentionally added zinc sulphate. These substances react with cathodically
formed alkali to give sparingly soluble compounds ($CaCO_3$ and $Zn(OH)_2$
respectively) and hence protective films.

M22.1 Lime

It is an old experience that hard waters are less corrosive than soft waters. This is due to the deposition from hard waters of protective films of $CaCO_3$ + rust. Soft waters may therefore be improved from a corrosion point of view by a careful addition of lime, e.g. by allowing the water to pass through a filter with slaked lime or calcined dolomite. Since the lime is present in solution as cations which migrate to and are precipitated as carbonate on the alkaline cathode surfaces in the corrosion cells, it is a cathodic inhibitor and hence not dangerous. It is of particular value as a complement to additions of phosphate or silicate.

M22.2 Polyphosphates

The common additions to boiler water containing polyphosphates (trade names Calgon and Micromet) are also classed among the cathodic inhibitors. It is characteristic of the polyphosphates that they form large colloidal cations, particularly in the presence of calcium, e.g. of the type $(Na_5CaP_6O_{18})_n^{n+}$. These large cations migrate towards the cathodes in the corrosion cells where they are discharged and form relatively thick coatings. The water should have a certain content of calcium hardness for the polyphosphates to be effective as inhibitors. A ratio Ca/Na as 1/5 is suitable. Composite sodium calcium polymetaphosphates are therefore often used. Due to their ability to form complexes with calcium, the polyphosphates are added to hard waters in order to prevent also the formation of thick carbonate scales on heat transmitting surfaces.

M2.3 Double-acting organic inhibitors (adsorption inhibitors)

Organic corrosion inhibitors are usually of the same type as pickling inhibitors, used in the pickling of metals in acids, or as crystal growth inhibitors (brighteners) used in electroplating. Most of them contain nitrogen or sulphur or both. Since they are adsorbed all over the metal surface they are, as a rule, double-acting, i.e. they simultaneously retard both the anode and the cathode process.

The following groups of active substances of this type may be distinguished:

1. Compounds containing nitrogen, such as organic nitrites and amines.
2. Compounds containing sulphur as HS^- or S^{2-} or in a ring system.

3. Compounds containing both sulphur and nitrogen, particularly substituted thiocarbamides.

The adsorption of amines depends on the strength of the bond amine-
metal and on the solubility of the amine. The strength of the amine-metal
bond is due to the high density of electrons of the nitrogen atom and the
capacity of these electrons to form co-ordinate bonds. The inhibitor
power of the aliphatic amines increases in the following sequence:

$$NH_3 < RNH_2 < R_2NH < R_3N$$

if R is ethyl-, propyl-, butyl- or amyl-. If a fourth alkyl group is introduced, the inhibition effect is reduced strongly.

Inhibitors containing sulphur are usually more effective than nitrogen
compounds since sulphur is a still better electron donor than nitrogen, i.e.
it has a greater tendency to form co-ordinate bonds, leading to adsorption.
The inhibitive effect often increases with molecular weight. For a series
of sulphur inhibitors (thiols and sulphides) the inhibition effect increases in the order:

   methyl < ethyl < propyl < butyl < amyl.

M2.4 Mixtures of inhibitors

Just as several of the inhibitors mentioned above become fully effective only in conjunction with dissolved oxygen or with calcium salts,
it is found that a simultaneous addition of two inhibitors may result in
a considerably increased effect and also eliminate the risk for pitting
at small inhibitor concentrations.

Such inhibitor mixtures often consist of one oxidizing agent, such as
nitrate or chromate, and one non-oxidizing but precipitating, such as orthophosphate or silicate. Examples of such inhibitor mixtures are nitrite +
benzoate, which is the most frequent and effective inhibitor for automo-
bile radiators, and chromate + orthophosphate, which is quite effective
even in salt water. In other cases, the mixture consists of one cathodic
and one anodic inhibitor, e.g. polyphosphate + chromate.

M2.5 Vapour phase inhibitors

In order to prevent atmospheric corrosion in closed spaces such as in
parcels during storage and transport, it is possible to use volatile, so-
called vapour phase inhibitors (VPI or VCI, from Volatile Corrosion In-

hibitor). These inhibitors consist of aliphatic and cyclic amines and nitrites with a high vapour pressure. Examples are dicyclohexylammonium nitrite and -carbonate. Paper impregnated with vapour phase inhibitors is often used for anti-corrosive wrappings. Volatile inhibitors are also used in compressors and condensers.

Even for this type of inhibitor, the electrochemical theory of corrosion seems to be in good agreement with experimental facts, the protective action consisting in a retardation of the anodic or cathodic processes. In many cases the result seems to be passivation.

M2.6 Inhibitors soluble in oil

Objects or constructions of metals that are lubricated or protected with oil or grease often need a more effective protection against corrosion attacks. An inhibitor is then added to the oil or grease. Examples where this is useful are motor lubricants, hydraulic oils, circulating lubricant oils, most lubricant greases and so-called temporary rust preventives. Inhibitors used in oil may be oxidizing inhibitors (passivators) or adsorption inhibitors, sometimes both types together.

Examples of oxidizing inhibitors are sodium nitrite and lithium nitrite which as the solid salts may be finely dispersed in grease, and, furthermore, certain organic nitrites and chromates. The largest group of inhibitors in oil are adsorption inhibitors, often of the type organic nitrogen or sulphur compounds according to M2.3 above. Hence, amines are an important group of oil-soluble inhibitors. They may be used either uncombined or as salts of the lower carbonic acids. The most important type of oil-soluble inhibitors, is that of the sulphonates, obtained by sulphonating petroleum.

Literature

Bregman, J I, Corrosion Inhibitors, Macmillan, New York 1963.

N. CORROSION PROTECTION BY CHANGE OF THE ELECTRODE POTENTIAL METAL/CORROSIVE MEDIUM

N.1 Electrochemical (cathodic and anodic)corrosion protection

Since the corrosion of metals in moist environments is of an electrochemical nature it lies close at hand to try to stop corrosion by electrochemical means. Electrochemical methods for corrosion protection involve a change of the electrode potential of the metal in order to prevent or, at least, diminish its dissolution. Electrochemical corrosion protection is divided in cathodic protection and anodic protection, according as the electrode potential is displaced in negative or positive direction. Cathodic protection is by far the most important of the two methods.

The principles of cathodic and anodic protection may be illustrated by means of a potential-pH diagram such as is shown in figure N1 for iron in sulphate solutions. The iron content of the solution has been assumed to be 10^{-3}-molar (50 ppm), a reasonable value for technical electrolytes. Consider now a specimen of carbon steel, immersed in 1-molar sulphuric acid. It will pass into solution with hydrogen evolution. The corrosion potential of the specimen will lie somewhere between the equilibrium potentials corresponding to a hydrogen electrode and an iron electrode for prevailing concentrations.

According to the diagram, there are two ways to prevent corrosion by a potential change. By applying a cathodic current, the potential of the steel specimen may be displaced down into the immunity range where the metal is the thermodynamically stable state. It is also possible, however, to stop corrosion by increasing the electrode potential of the specimen up into the passivity range in which a higher oxide of iron is the stable phase. It is assumed, furthermore, that this oxide is obtained as a thin, dense and ad-

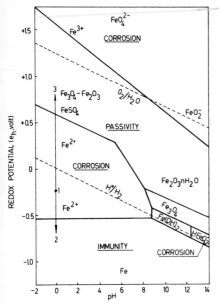

Fig. N1. Potential-pH diagram for iron in sulphate solutions. Iron conc. 10^{-3} mole/l. $25^\circ C$. 1. Unprotected, corroding specimen. 2. Cathodically protected specimen. 3. Anodically protected specimen.

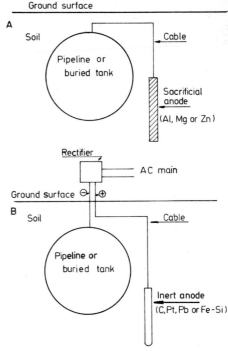

Fig. N2. Principle of cathodic protection with
A) sacrificial anode
B) impressed current

hering film. The protective film is a semi-conductor with small ionic conductivity and as soon as it has been formed a very small current is needed to maintain the steel in the passive state. In principle, it is thus possible to handle moderately diluted sulphuric acid in an apparatus of carbon steel if an outer current, cathodic or anodic, is applied.

N. 2 Cathodic protection

N2.1 Importance and sub-division

Cathodic protection means that the corroding object is coupled as a cathode in an electrochemical cell. The electrode potential of the metal is then displaced in negative direction to a value below its steady state corrosion potential in the solution in question. Its dissolution is thereby totally prevented (complete cathodic protection) or at least counteracted (incomplete cathodic protection). Instead, there occurs hydrogen evolution or oxygen reduction at a rate corresponding to the current passing. Cathodic protection is divided into galvanic and electrolytic cathodic protection according to the following scheme:

A. Galvanic cathodic protection: The corroding object is made the cathode of a galvanic cell, the anode of which is a baser metal (Mg, Zn, Al), and which by being sacrificed protects a valuable construction, e.g. of steel. The sacrificial anode metal may be applied:
a) as a coating on the basic metal (most important example: galvanized steel)
b) as dispersed anode plates, with or without current regulation.

B. Electrolytic cathodic protection: The corroding object is made the cathode of an electrolytic cell which is supplied with direct current from an outer current source (rectifier). The auxiliary anode of this cell is usually insoluble (Pt, Pb, C, Ni), but may sometimes be soluble (Fe, Al). The electrolytic method of cathodic protection may be controlled
a) by regulating the current via the applied cell voltage
b) by regulating the cathode potential by means of a potentiostat.

Fig. N2 illustrates the two methods of cathodic protection.

N2.2 Anode materials

In the galvanic method of cathodic protection, the corroding object is directly connected to a less noble metal, which then forms a sacrificial anode in a galvanic cell, the cathode of which is the object to be protected. Anode materials for the protection of steel are Mg, Zn and Al or often alloys of these metals with each other or with Ca. For the protection of copper, sacrificial anodes of carbon steel may be used. Even coating a metal with a less noble one (steel with a zinc coating) is an example of galvanic cathodic protection. The starting point for judging the relative protective action of the metals is their position in the galvanic series of corrosion potentials (see table E1).

Finding suitable materials for so-called insoluble anodes for electrolytic cathodic protection involves considerable difficulties. No material is completely insoluble if it is connected as an anode in an electrolytic cell. The standard material for chloride solutions is graphite whereas for sulphate solutions alloys of lead with antimony and/or silver are used. Newer types of permanent anodes consist of titanium, coated with thin layers of platinum metal or ruthenium oxide.

N2.3 Current and potential criteria

Figure N3 depicts cathodic protection for hydrogen-evolving corrosion. The state corresponding to complete cathodic protection is obtained if the

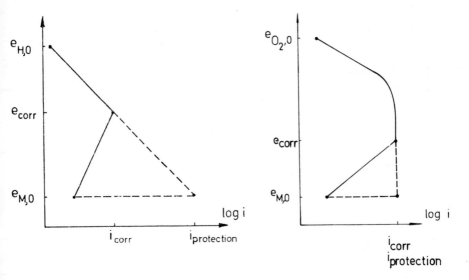

Fig. N3. Cathodic protection in the case of hydrogen-evolving corrosion.

Fig. N4. Cathodic protection in the case of oxygen-consuming corrosion.

cathodic polarization curve is extrapolated down to the equilibrium potential of the metal. The diagram shows that this requires a protective current which is considerably larger than the corrosion current. The hydrogen evolution will be quite considerable and may result in the scaling off of protective coatings.

Figure N4 represents cathodic protection in oxygen-consuming corrosion at the limiting current density. In this case, the protective current is theoretically the same as the corrosion current. In practice it is sufficient for this type of corrosion if the protective current is about 20 % higher than the corrosion current. Average values for neutral solutions at room temperature are: for bare steel 100 mA/m^2, for covered steel 5 mA/m^2, for aluminium 10 mA/m^2, and for anodized aluminium 0.01 mA/m^2. In strongly acid solutions or at higher temperature current densities many times higher may be required.

Both from a theoretical and from a practical point of view it is usually preferable to use the electrode potential of the metal rather than the current density as a criterion of cathodic protection. Empirically, it has been found that a good cathodic protection for carbon steel in sea water is obtained at an electrode potential of -0.85 V versus the $CuSO_4$/Cu-electrode, corresponding to -0.78 V versus SCE and -0.53 V versus NHE. This corresponds fairly well to the equilibrium potential of iron in a dilute Fe^{2+}-solution (about 0.001 M). The corrosion potential (see table E1) is about -0.40 V versus NHE.

N2.4 Combination of an electrically insulating coating and cathodic protection

It is usually advantageous to combine cathodic protection with an electrically insulating coating, such as paint.   The protective current will then be concentrated to defects in the insulating coating. This means a good distribution of current on the metal surface which on bare metal constructions involves difficulties. The current required and hence the electric installation will be small and easy to handle. The combination of an insulating coating and cathodic protection is often the most economic method of protection for the following reasons. If cathodic protection is applied, small defects and damages occurring in the coating may be tolerated whereas otherwise it would have to be completely dense to be protective. An absolutely tight coating will, however, cost much more in production and maintenance than a coating covering, say, 99 % of the surface. The cost of cathodic protection, on the other hand, may be considered to vary linearly with the exposed area of the metal. The minimum cost for a combined protection method is shown schematically in figure N5.

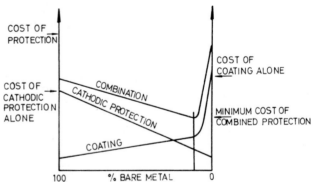

Fig. N5. Diagram, schematically showing the minimum of costs attained by a combination of an insulating coating and cathodic protection.

Cathodic protection is therefore usually combined with some sort of protective coating, such as paint   (e.g. on ships), tape impregnated with asphalt or plastic (e.g. on pipelines) or vitreous enamels or glass (e.g. in water heaters and in chemical reaction vessels).

N2.5 Applications

Ships' hulls are normally protected against rusting by several coatings of anti-corrosive paint. Considerable savings in maintenance costs can be made, however, by applying in addition cathodic protection on the parts of the hull below the water line. Usually, a galvanic cathodic protection is used in this case with sacrificial anodes of magnesium, zinc or aluminium, which via steel bands are welded to the hull. At the stern, the anodes are placed more closely since the corrosion attacks are highest there due to the proximity of the propeller, which partly exerts a stirring action, creating turbulent flow, and partly forms a galvanic couple with the hull. For larger vessels and for marine units electrolytic cathodic protection is sometimes used with insoluble anodes of, for instance, platinized titanium (Fig. N6). These are usually placed on the hull but electrically insulated from it. Sometimes just one anode is used, trailing in an insulated cable at a considerable distance behind the vessel. Even floating docks, pontoon bridges, piers, wave breakers and bridge foundations of steel are objects suitable for cathodic protection in sea water. Cathodic protection, preferably with zinc or aluminium anodes is also used in the oil tanks of tankers. During the voyage to the oil port, certain of these tanks are filled with a ballast of sea water which is strongly corrosive on the tank walls.

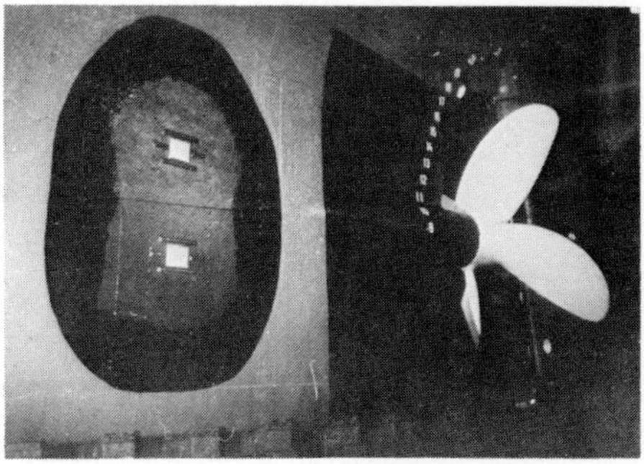

Fig. N6. Two anodes of platinized titanium, placed close to the propeller of a ship, provided with cathodic protection by means of impressed current. Note insulating coating around anodes. Courtesy: F. Klingenberg, Skarpenord A/S, Oslo.

Cathodic protection is also very widely applied for metal constructions immersed in the soil. This is particularly true for gas, oil and water pipe lines of cast iron and steel, for lead-sheathed electric cables and for fuel tanks, buried in the soil. The latter may be cathodically protected on the inside also (Fig. N7).

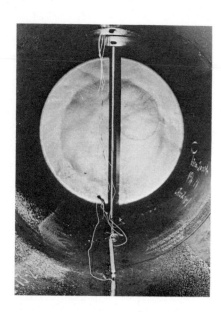

Fig. N7. Internal cathodic protection of oil tank by sacrificial
magnesium anodes. Cables connect
the anodes electrically to top of
tank. Courtesy: O. Nygren, Swedish
Corrosion Institute.

Fig. N8. Platinized titanium anode
for cathodic protection of cooling
system of atomic reactor by impressed
current. Protective casing of PVC.
Connection between cable and anode
totally moulded in plastic (rectangular field). Courtesy: O. Nygren,
Swedish Corrosion Institute.

A pipe-line can be protected with galvanic anodes which should be buried
sufficiently deep in order to stay in moist soil. Each anode is surrounded by
a bag with "backfill", e.g. a mixture of clay, gypsum and sodium sulphate.
In this way, a zone with good electric conductivity is created in the immedia
surrounding of the anode. The ohmic potential drop between anode and cathode
is mainly localized to this region in which the current density is high. In
cathodic protection of a well insulated pipe-line or cable sheath, the distance between anodes may be of the order of magnitude of a mile. It may be
still higher in very dry regions (deserts).

Cathodic protection is also used in various civil engineering applications. Steel piles under buildings in particularly corrosive soil, e.g. old
sea bottom, are sometimes cathodically protected. Cathodic protection may
also be used for the steel wires in pipe-lines of pre-stressed concrete

in water and soil.

Cooling systems are often cathodically protected, particularly if brackish or salt water is used as cooling medium (Fig. N8). Tube coolers usually consist of tubes and tube plates of a copper alloy, while the water boxes at the ends are made from steel or cast iron. The ferrous parts are very subject to corrosion, i.a. by affording galvanic protection for the copper alloy parts. Attempts to reduce the corrosion of the end boxes by some kind of coating often lead to worse results due to local attack in pores in the insulating coating. If sacrificial anodes of zinc are applied, both water box and tube plates may be protected, however.

N.3 Anodic protection

N3.1 Limitation and subdivision

Anodic corrosion protection implies that the object to be protected is coupled as an anode in a galvanic or usually an electrolytic cell. The electrode potential of the metal is then displaced in a positive direction. For many metals this might accelerate the corrosion by anodic dissolution of the metal. Anodic protection is therefore in principle applicable only to metals which show chemical passivity. Furthermore, the composition of the corrosive solution must favour passivation. Anodic protection cannot, therefore, be used in the presence of high concentrations of activating anions, as in chloride solutions. Higher concentrations of other anions, e.g. sulphate ions present in the same solution may, however, displace the chloride ions from the metal surface. Hence, 18/8 steel may be anodically protected in 30 % H_2SO_4 + 1 % NaCl.

Anodic protection may also be subdivided into galvanic and electrolytic according to the following scheme:

1. Galvanic anodic protection: Noble metals (Pt, Pd, Ag, Cu) are applied as alloying additions (forming local cathodes in the corrosion process) or as surface coatings on passivating metals (stainless steel, Ti, Ta, Zr).

2. Electrolytic anodic protection: Direct current from an outer source is supplied via an auxiliary cathode and the electrode potential of the protected object (the anode) is regulated by means of a potentiostat.

N3.2 Anodic protection by alloying or coating with a more noble metal

Galvanic anodic protection is obtained by putting the object to be protected in contact with a more noble metal which thus is made the

cathode in a corrosion cell. In most cases, this is a sure means to raise
the corrosion velocity (note   for example the effect of impurities on the
dissolution rate of zinc in acids). If the basic metal can be passivated,
however, and if the electrolyte furthermore favours passivation, contact
with a more noble metal may promote passivation still further. The noble
metal acts by raising the electrode potential of the basic metal so that
it is raised into and stays in the passivity range.

In stainless steels, alloying additions of 0.1 % Pd or 1 % Cu bring
about a strong reduction of the corrosion rate in sulphuric acid solutions
(Fig. N9). The same effect may be obtained by a thin coating (1 µm) of a

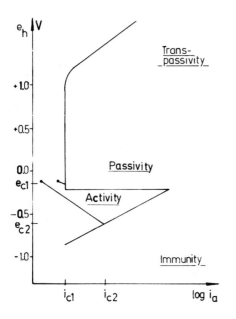

Fig. N9. Schematic anode and cath
polarization curves of stainless
steel, also showing corrosion
potential and corrosion current
with (e_{c1}, i_{c1}) and without
(e_{c2}, i_{c2}) addition of noble
metals, acting as local cathodes
for hydrogen evolution. High exchange c.d. and low hydrogen over
voltage of local cathodes make
the cathode curve intersect the
anode curve in the passivity rang
instead of the activity range.

noble metal on the stainless steel or by the addition of small amounts
of copper or silver salts to the acid (Fig. N10). An addition of copper
to stainless and acid-proof steels also reduces their sensitivity towards
pitting in chloride solutions (Cf. page 88).

N3.3 Anodic protection by means of an external electric tension

Electrolytic anodic protection is obtained by applying an external
electric tension between the protected object as an anode and an auxiliary
electrode as cathode. A reference electrode is also required. Between the
latter and the object (the anode) a potentiostat is connected which reacts

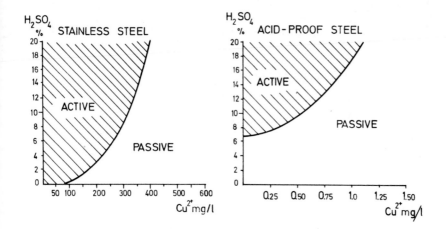

Fig. N10. Protective effect on stainless (18Cr 9Ni) and acid-proof (18Cr 12Ni 3Mo) steel of an addition of copper sulphate to sulphuric acid.

to the potential difference between these electrodes and by regulating the current keeps this potential difference constant at a suitable value so that the object remains in the passive state all the time.

The stainless and acid-proof steels, important materials of construction for chemical apparatus, are in principle well suited for anodic protection. The same is true of apparatus of carbon steel for handling alkaline sulphide solutions (e.g. sulphate cellulose digesters) or concentrated sulphuric acid (sulphonation plants) and, furthermore, chemical apparatus made of titanium.

Literature

Morgan, J H, Cathodic Protection, MacMillan, New York 1960.

O. CORROSION PROTECTION BY MEANS OF SURFACE COATINGS

0.1 Pretreatment of metal surfaces before the application of surface coating

Before the application of various types of protective coatings on metal surfaces, it is as a rule necessary to clean the surface very carefully in order to remove both dirt, such as grease and salts, and oxides, such as mill scale and rust. In addition, the surface must be given a surface finish, suitable as a basis for the intended type of coating. This pretreatment is of particular importance in electrodeposition and in applying vitreous enamels. The most stringent claims are met with in electroplating from acid baths, but even in ordinary rust preventive painting the cleaning and pretreatment of the surface is often the most important step in the whole process.

The pretreatment is usually carried out in two steps. One step aims at removing organic substances such as oil and grease, whereas the object of the other step is to remove inorganic substances such as mill scale, rust and other corrosion products and also to give the surface a suitable finish. The two pretreatment steps may, according to circumstances, be repeated several times and in different orders.

Washing and degreasing is necessary before all coating methods and usually also before pickling; sometimes even before sandblasting. It should be observed that different types of grease and oil, according to their chemical nature, necessitate different methods for degreasing. Mineral oils and greases (hydrocarbons, like vaseline etc.) may be removed with organic solvents, while for the fatty oils and fats (e.g. lanoline) and also for some waxes, saponification of the esters of the fatty acids in alkaline solution is to be preferred. A satisfactorily degreased metal surface is characterized by its complete wetting with water and absence of dry spots on drainage (waterbreak test).

Mechanical pretreatment methods usually involve a certain change in the roughness of the metal surface since more or less metal is removed. Grinding may be used both to give a detail its final shape and also to produce a certain surface finish. If a particularly fine surface is required, the grinding is usually followed by polishing which is mostly carried out mechanically but may also be done by bright pickling or anodic polishing. The latter processes are usually carried out on a previously etched surface. A certain amount of grinding and polishing is also obtained by tumbling. Blast cleaning is the most efficient method to remove thick scale and heavy rust and gives a surface finish suitable for metal spraying and also for painting and phosphatizing. Acid pickling is also used to remove mill scale and rust from metal surfaces.

01.1 Degreasing

011.1 Organic degreasing

In organic degreasing, volatile organic solvents are used, usually hydrocarbons, e.g. white spirit, or chlorinated hydrocarbons, e.g. trichloroethylene. Both have serious drawbacks: The former are flammable and the latter are poisonous.

The degreasing may be carried out by dipping the objects in a tank containing the solvent or by brushing them with a brush dipped in the solvent. A more efficient method consists in circulating the solvent with a pump and spraying it against the objects through a nozzle. During the circulation of the solvent, suspended material and water present may be removed.

In degreasing with condensing vapours, Fig. 01, the solvent, usually trichloroethylene, is boiled in a tank of stainless steel, its vapour, which at the boiling point, $87^{0}C$, is 4.5 times heavier than air, being condensed on the cold work-piece introduced into the vapour phase. Greasy impurities on the surface are removed by the pure condensed solvent until the metal object has assumed the temperature of the vapour. Perchloroethylene (tetrachloroethylene, $CCl_2 = CCl_2$, boiling point $121^{0}C$) is also used for the same purpose. Its high boiling point makes easy degreasing of thin objects which in trichlorethylene assume the temperature of the vapour too quickly. It should be observed that salts which are insoluble in organic solvents may still be present on the metal surface after organic degreasing and may later cause underfilm and filiform corrosion under organic coatings.

011.2 Alkaline degreasing

Alkaline degreasing is carried out in an aqueous solution, containing a cleaning agent, such as soap or a synthetic surfactant, and alkali, such as alkali phosphate or alkali silicate. Simultaneous mechanical treatment of the surface by brushing or spraying and also increased temperature are favourable. It is also possible to utilize the mechanical effect of electro- lytic gas evolution (electrolytic cleaning). Alkaline degreasing leads to the cleanest surfaces and is often used as the final step, e.g. immediately before electroplating.

011.3 Emulsion cleaning

Emulsion cleaning is a sort of combination of the previous two methods, involving the use of an emulsion of an organic solvent in an aqueous soap solution. The main constituent in this type of cleaning agent is the organic solvent, usually a hydrocarbon mixture (white spirit). To this base is added the emulsifier which is usually a soap, e.g. potassium oleate, that emulsifies the organic solvent when the liquid is mixed with water during the cleaning process. As a rule, a higher alcohol or a surfactant is also added to give a stabilizing action. The objects are dipped into the mixture of organic solvent and emulsifier and are then sprayed with water which results in an oil-in-water emulsion and the surface is cleaned.

011.4 Steam degreasing

Steam degreasing is carried out by means of steam containing small amounts of some cleaning agent and which under high pressure is blown against the surface to be cleaned. Steam degreasing may be used with ad- vantage for rinsing after emulsion degreasing and after removing of paint by alkali before repainting. It is often used for cleaning particularly large objects, railway cars and the like.

01.2 Removal of mill scale and rust and creation of a desired surface finish

Mill scale and rust are insoluble in liquids used for degreasing and usually adhere so strongly to the steel surface that they are not carried away with the solvent like dust and other loose dirt. Rust and other sur- face oxides may be removed and the surface may be given a suitable evenness in the following ways:

Fig. 01. Continuous vapour degreasing.
A conveyor carries the objects through
the vapour of an organic solvent, con-
tained and heated in the lower part
of the apparatus.
Courtesy: KIAB Apparater AB, Karlstad.

Fig. 02. Flame-cleaning of steel.
An acetylene-oxygen burner is
moved across the surface. Mill
scale peels off due to higher
thermal expansion than the steel.
Courtesy: AGA AB, Sweden.

012.1 Mechanically

a) through hammering, scraping, wire-brushing and grinding, which operations may be carried out manually or mechanically,

b) by pneumatic blasting, in which process dry or wet silica sand or steel
   sand is blown against the metal surface by means of compressed air. If
   the sand is suspended in water, the latter should contain inhibitors
   (e.g. phosphate + nitrite, or phosphate + chromate) in order to prevent re-rusting of the cleaned surface,

c) by centrifugal blasting (sling-cleaning), in which process steel shot
   or small steel balls are slung against the metal by a rotating blade
   wheel (wheel-abrator),

d) by tumbling, by which it is possible to clean, deburr, round off sharp
   edges and corners and improve in general the surface finish of small
   mass-produced details by rolling them together with a suitable grinding

agent in a rotating drum. The tumbling may be carried out as wet or dry
tumbling. In a variation of this process, the objects are instead vibrat-
ed together with the grinding material,

e) by polishing, in which process bright and reflecting metal surfaces are
obtained by letting fine-grained polishing agents on a soft support slide
over the surface of the object, usually with rotation. As a rule, the
polishing agent is dispersed in a suitable polishing wax which later
must be removed very carefully by degreasing.

012.2 Thermally

a) by flame-cleaning

In this method a special acetylene-oxygen burner is moved across the
steel surface at a certain angle. Mill scale and rust are loosened, organic
impurities are burnt away and the surface is dried out. Flame-cleaning is
followed by wire-brushing for removing oxides detached by the thermal
treatment. Painting may take place on the still hot steel surface. This
method is particularly suitable for large constructions (Fig. 02).

b) by induction heating

This method is suitable for steel bands, rods and tubes. They are
heated to about $175^{\circ}C$ by passage through an electric induction aggregate
and then cooled with a spray of cold water so that the mill scale peels
off.

012.3 Chemically by pickling

Pickling of steel is carried out by immersing the objects in an
aqueous solution of sulphuric, hydrochloric or phosphoric acid. Mill scale
and rust are dissolved, or at least dislodged, from the basic metal, partly
due to hydrogen evolution under the oxide layers.

On heating soft steel to between 575 and $1370^{\circ}C$ there is formed on
the steel surface an oxide scale which consists of three well defined
layers, see Fig. 03 and compare Fig. K2, page 122. Closest to the metal,
a layer of wüstite is formed which has the approximate composition FeO.
Outside this layer there is formed a magnetite layer (Fe_3O_4) and outermost
a thin layer of hematite (Fe_2O_3). On rapid cooling, the wüstite layer is
hardly changed and the steel becomes hard to pickle. The same is true if
the steel is rolled below $575^{\circ}C$, in which case no wüstite layer will
be formed. On slow cooling of a hot-rolled steel the wüstite layer is partly decomposed into magnetite and finely dispersed metallic iron. During

pickling, acid penetrates through pores and cracks in the insoluble layers of ferric oxide and magnetite and attacks the wüstite layer. The attack is rapid due to the formation of small galvanic cells with iron particles as anodes, acid as electrolyte and magnetite as a cathode, on which there occurs hydrogen evolution contributing to the dislodgement of oxide. Since not only iron but also magnetite and the pickling acid are good electrical conductors, the ohmic potential drops will be small and the pickling rate will depend upon the rate with which acid can penetrate the oxide layers.

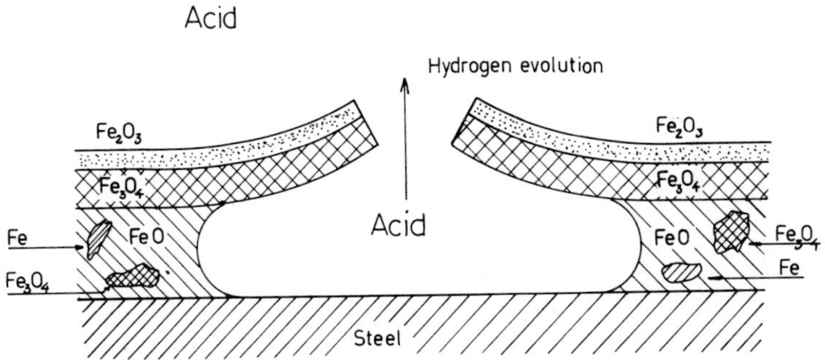

Fig. 03. Pickling of steel plate, rolled at high temperature ($>575^{\circ}$C) and then slowly cooled. Partly decomposed wüstite layer next to the steel.

While the main part of the evolved hydrogen escapes in molecular form, part of it diffuses as hydrogen atoms into the metal and causes hydrogen embrittlement. In carbon steel the embrittlement is often of a temporary nature and may disappear in a few days due to the diffusion of hydrogen out of the steel. Gentle heating facilitates this process. In alloyed steels, however, the embrittlement often becomes permanent.

By the addition of pickling inhibitors, so-called restrainers, to the acid, the attack on the steel is diminished and the consumption of both acid and steel is reduced. Remarkably enough, hydrogen embrittlement is often increased by the use of pickling inhibitors in spite of the smaller total hydrogen evolution, and may become permanent due to an adsorbed inhibitor film which prevents the escape of hydrogen from the steel.

By connecting the object to be pickled as anode or cathode in the pickling bath (electrolytic pickling), a strong stirring action is obtained on the metal surface and both time and temperature for the operation can be reduced. Acid consumption is not reduced thereby. Electrolytic pickling involves certain disadvantages, however, such as increased hydrogen embrittlement on cathodic pickling.

Bright and reflecting metal surfaces may be created even by chemical
or electro-chemical means. The metal is immersed for a short time in a
concentrated solution of strong acids (bright pickling) or it is connected
as an anode (anodic polishing) in a concentrated electrolyte solution,
often containing phosphoric acid. Most chemical and electrolytic polishing is
done under conditions corresponding to an anodic limiting current density
and is related to mechanical passivity according to E5.1. A diffusion
layer is formed, saturated with respect to a salt of the metal, and solid
salt is precipitated in scratches and pits in the metal surface. This results in a preferential dissolution of protruding parts and hence a polishing effect.

01.3 Rust grades for steel surfaces and preparation grades prior to pro-
     tective coating

A Swedish Standard (SIS 055900) has been prescribed that specifies
a four-degree scale of rusting, and a quality scale for the preparation of
steel surfaces with the specified rust grades, prior to protective painting.

The Standard refers to
surfaces of hot-rolled steel with four rust grades (A,B, C and D),
the same surfaces without preparation (St 0), and prepared by manual scraping and wire-brushing according to a three-grade quality scale (St 1, St 2
and St 3),
the same surfaces unprepared (Sa 0), and prepared by blast cleaning according to a four -grade quality scale (Sa 1, Sa 2, Sa $2^1/_2$ and Sa 3).

The grades may be described as follows:

Rust grades
A: Steel surface covered completely with adherent mill scale and with little
if any rust.
B: Steel surface which has begun to rust and from which the mill scale has
begun to flake.
C: Steel surface where the mill scale has rusted away or from which it can
be scraped, but with little pitting visible to the naked eye.
D: Steel surface where the mill scale has rusted away and where pitting is
visible to the naked eye.

Preparation grades. Manual scraping and wire-brushing
It is assumed that the steel surface has been cleaned of dirt and grease,
and that the heavier layers of rust have been removed by chipping.
St 0: No preparation of surface.
St 1: Light wire-brushing. The brush is moved with light pressure back and
forth over the surface so that every part is brushed twice.

St 2: Thorough scraping (with hard-metal scraper) and wire-brushing. Strong pressure is applied to the scraper so that loose scale, rust and dirt are removed. The surface is then wire-brushed vigorously. Loosened material should be removed during the operation so that the result can be checked. After dusting, the surface should have a faint metallic sheen.

St 3: Extremely thorough scraping (with hard-metal scraper) and wire-brushing. Surface preparation as for St 2, but the scraping is performed first in one direction and then at right angles. After dusting, the surface should have a pronounced metallic sheen.

Preparation grades. Blast cleaning

It is assumed that the steel surface has been cleaned of dirt and grease,

and that the heavier layers of rust have been removed by chipping.

Sa 0: No preparation of surface.

Sa 1: Light blast cleaning. The jet is passed rapidly over the surface so that loose mill scale, rust and foreign matter are removed.

Sa 2: Thorough blast cleaning. The jet is passed over the surface long enough to remove all mill scale and rust and practically all foreign matter. After dusting, the surface should be greyish in colour.

Sa $2^1/2$: Very careful blast cleaning. The blast cleaning is maintained long enough to ensure that mill scale, rust and foreign matter are removed so thoroughly that any residues of these appear only as slight shadows or discolourations on the surface.

Sa 3: Blast cleaning to white metal. The jet is passed over the surface long enough to remove all mill scale, rust and foreign matter. After dusting, the surface should have a uniform metallic colour.

For the preparation grades St 2, St 3, Sa 2, Sa $2^1/2$ and Sa 3, dust is removed with a vacuum cleaner, with clean and dry compressed air or with a clean brush.

0.2 Metallic surface coatings

02.1 Review of various methods for metallizing (application of metallic surface coatings)

021.1 Mechanical methods

To this group we count mechanical plating (rolling of a metal foil onto a basic metal) and spraying of molten metal such as Al or Zn. Painting with zinc or aluminium dust paint that gives an essentially metallic coating, may also be included in this group.

021.2 Physical methods

0212.1 High temperature methods, involving surface alloying

If the metallizing is carried out at a high temperature, surface

alloys are formed by diffusion. In this category we find hot-dipping in
in baths of molten Zn, Pb, Sn or Al and tumbling at a high temperature
in a powder of the coating metal, mixed with a suitable fluxing agent.
Special tumbling methods are sherardizing (coating of steel with zinc) and
calorizing (coating of steel with aluminium). A carbon steel surface may
also be coated with stainless steel by welding.

0212.2 Low temperature methods, not involving surface alloying

In other procedures, relying on condensation of the coating metal on
the cold basic metal, surface alloys are not formed and the bonding to the
basic metal is mainly mechanical. Examples in this group are vacuum sublimation and electric arc sublimation (cathode sputtering).

021.3 Chemical methods

0213.1 High temperature methods, involving surface alloying

In these methods the object (A, e.g. steel) is introduced into a
smelt or vapour of a chemical compound, often a chloride, of the coating
metal (B, e.g. Cr). The coating metal may be deposited according to:

    a) exchange: $A + BCl_2 \rightarrow B + ACl_2$

    b) chemical reduction: $BCl_2 + H_2 \rightarrow B + 2HCl$

    c) thermal dissociation: $BCl_2 \rightarrow B + Cl_2$.

In all these cases the coating metal B will be more or less alloyed
with the basic metal A.

0213.2 Low temperature methods, not involving surface alloying

In this category we find metallizing by:

    a) Electrodeposition (electroplating)

    b) Chemical reduction (e.g. silver plating with silver nitrate and
       formaldehyde, chemical nickel plating by reduction with hypophos-
       phite)

    c) Cementation, involving the reduction of a more noble metal from one
       of its salts by the less noble basic metal.

02.2 Purely shielding metal coatings more noble than the basic metal

Metallic coatings more noble than carbon steel are, for instance, Cu,
Ni, Cr, Pb, Sn and Ag. In soft waters, even Al is more noble than steel.
Above $60^{\circ}C$, Zn also becomes more noble than steel due to the formation of a
zinc/zinc-oxide electrode.

Coatings of metals more noble than the basic metal should be completely
dense. If there are pores or scratches, the dangerous combination small
anode - large cathode is formed which may result in pitting attacks. Metal
coatings more noble than the basic metal are also called cathodic (Cf. Fig.04)

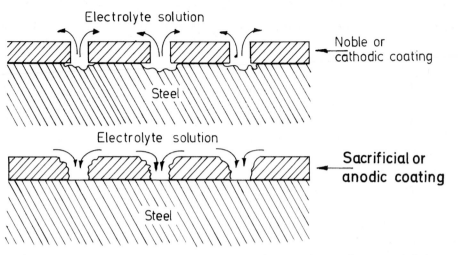

Fig. O4. Sketch of current flow at defects in a noble and in a sacrificial coating on steel.

The most important protective metal coating within this group is electrolytic nickel plate on steel. The steel is sometimes first electro-plated with Cu, since a) copper is cheaper than nickel,b) copper is easier to polish than steel, and c) a copper coating is more easily obtained without pores. From improved modern nickel baths it is possible to plate quite dense nickel layers directly onto steel, however. These are more resistant to corrosion than the copper-nickel layers, particularly in industrial atmospheres.

For bright nickel coatings, a so-called duplex nickel plate is often used, consisting of a basic layer of semi-matt nickel, deposited from a bath containing certain levelling addition agents, and a top layer of bright nickel, obtained from a nickel bath containing other addition agents, so-called brighteners (crystal growth inhibitors, as a rule organic sub-stances, often of the same type as those used as corrosion and pickling inhibitors). The use of two different nickel layers diminishes the pro-bability for penetrating pores (pits), formed by hydrogen bubbles, adhering to the cathode during the electrodeposition process. The bright nickel layer is, furthermore, less noble than the semi-matt nickel layer and there-fore exerts a cathodically protective action in existing pores. It is ge-nerally true that the corrodibility of nickel layers, as of other electro-deposited metal coatings, increases with the content of co-deposited addition agents in the layer.

Out of doors, nickel plate is tarnished fairly rapidly by oxidation. Nickel electroplate for atmospheric use is therefore electrolytically covered with a very thin coating of chromium, which maintains brightness but which does not substantially increase the protective effect. This is the wellknown chrome-plate on cars, the main part (35-50 μm) of which thus consists of nickel and just a very small part (0.3-0.5 μm) of chromium. The thin chromium coating, which is more noble than the nickel layer, is never quite dense. As a matter of fact, a greater number of micro-cracks or micro-pores in the chromium coating seem to be of advantage since the larger anode surface results in a slower penetration of the nickel layer. Micro-porous chromium may be obtained by co-deposition from the bright nickel bath of small, suspended non-conductive particles, e.g. $BaSO_4$, into the bright nickel layer.

Thick layers of chromium, electroplated directly on steel, are used as a protection against wear and are termed hard chromium plate. Important applications are found in printing practice (e.g. the printing of paper currency). The piston rings of combustion engines are also often hard chromium plated.

Nickel coatings may also be obtained by chemical or current-less nickel plating. Nickel may be deposited from aqueous solutions of its salts by reduction with sodium hypophosphite, $NaPH_2O_2$. The deposited nickel layer is amorphous but crystallizes on heating to above 400^oC. The layer will contain about 7-9 % phosphorus , deriving from occluded nickel phosphide. In a similar process, borohydrides are used as reducing agents. The nickel layer will then contain boron.

02.3 Shielding metal coatings, also affording cathodic protection

023.1 Purely metallic coatings

A coating of a metal, less noble than the basic metal, apart from a shielding effect also affords cathodic protection by acting as a sacrificial anode in relation to the basic metal. Such coatings are therefore called anodic, see Fig. 04. Due to cathodic protection in pores or scratches such coatings need not be absolutely dense. Examples of metal coatings which are anodic in relation to steel are,above all,zinc and also cadmium. In environments containing chloride ions aluminium coatings also are anodic to steel. Sprayed aluminium layers are always less noble than steel. Tin, as a rule, is more noble than steel but may be less noble than steel on the inside of tin cans, probably due to the formation of complex tin ions containing organic acids.

The practically most important application of anodic metallic coatings is zinc-coated steel. The zinc-coating operation may be carried out in several different ways. Single construction elements are zinc-coated by electroplating or by dipping in molten zinc. Larger objects, such as whole constructions may be zinc-coated by spraying with molten zinc or by painting with zinc-rich paint. The last-mentioned two methods are considerably more expensive than the first two.

The protective power of electrolytic zinc-coatings is often increased still further by a subsequent chromatizing. Preferably, zinc-coated steel for use in the atmosphere should be painted. The zinc surface must then be pretreated in a suitable way in order to neutralize its alkaline character. This may be done by means of an etch (wash) primer or by phosphatizing or chromatizing. The zinc is then painted with a paint, not sensitive to alkali.

In the zinc-coating of steel by hot-dipping, usually referred to as galvanizing, a carefully cleaned steel object is dipped into a bath of molten zinc. A fluxing agent is used to dissolve oxides formed on the steel surface between cleaning and galvanizing and hence facilitate the reaction between iron and zinc. Depending on the way in which the fluxing agent is applied, various hot-dipping methods are referred to as dry hot-dipping and wet hot-dipping.

In dry hot-dipping, the cleaned object is dipped in a flux solution, consisting of zinc chloride and ammonium chloride, dissolved in water and is then dried in a drying oven before immersion in the zinc bath.

In wet hot-dipping, the cleaned object is directly immersed in the zinc bath, on the surface of which there is a molten layer of flux, consisting of zinc chloride and ammonium chloride even in this case. The bath surface is partitioned in two parts by a vertical steel plate. One part has a layer of flux on the surface, whereas the other is free. The objects are dipped into the bath through the flux layer and are removed through the part free of flux. Galvanizing by hot-dipping is normally carried out at a temperature of $450-460^{0}$ in the zinc bath.

Two special modes of zinc-coating by hot-dipping are continuous galvanizing of steel band according to the Sendzimir method and so-called Sherardizing.

In the Sendzimir method, the steel band is pre-treated in the gas phase. It is first carried through an annealing furnace with oxidizing atmosphere for burning away carbonaceous impurities (e.g. grease, carbon particles after pickling) and is then passed through an annealing furnace with an atmosphere of cracked ammonia which reduces surface oxides and fulfils the same task as oxide-dissolving flux in other methods. The band is then carried further through a zinc bath, and finally it is cooled, straightened and cut. The method gives a thin zinc layer.

Sherardizing is a tumbling procedure for coating small articles with zinc. The objects are charged in an annealing furnace together with zinc powder. The furnace is rotated and heated to a temperature just below the melting point of zinc and is kept there for about an hour. The method gives a thin, well-adhering layer.

Zinc-coating by hot-dipping costs about the same as a first class anti-corrosive painting but it lasts longer. A zinc layer of usual thickness, 80-125 μm, on a steel construction in a rural environment has a life of at least 40 years.

In zinc-coating by spraying, zinc in the form of a wire or a powder is fed into an acetylene-oxygen flame where the zinc melts and is thrown as fine droplets towards the steel surface by means of compressed air. With the zinc in wire form the melting can also be carried out by electric heating.

In similar ways, steel may be coated with aluminium by hot-dipping, by tumbling or by spraying, but not by electroplating. Aluminized steel is a very suitable material for silencers and exhaust pipes on cars and also for other flue and smoke-gas systems, also under reducing conditions, e.g. sulphurous gases in which alloyed steels often fail.

023.2 Zinc-rich paints

A coating of zinc affording cathodic protection may also be formed by painting a steel surface with a zinc-rich primer. The paint must have a very high content of zinc dust, corresponding to about 95 % of the dry film, so that the zinc particles are in electric contact partly with each other and partly with the basic metal which must be very clean, e.g. sand-blasted. In the long run, zinc oxide is formed which acts as a cathodic inhibitor (cf. M2.2 above).

The binder of a zinc-rich paint may be organic(epoxide or phenolic

resin) or inorganic (lead silicate) or both (ethyl silicate). Zinc-rich
paints afford very good protection against corrosion under atmospheric
conditions and may be used without a top coat. They are often used for re-
pairing surfaces, previously zinc-coated by hot-dipping or spraying. They
also constitute a common type of so-called shop primers (see below). The
type with the widest use is the zinc-lead silicate combination; like other
paints containing lead it has the ability to neutralize sulphates and, to
some extent, chloride ions.

0.3 Inorganic, non-metallic coatings

03.1 Purely shielding coatings

031.1 Vitreous enamels

Vitreous enamel is a glassy substance formed by: glass former, flux,
stabilizers, opaque agents and colour pigments. The glass former consists
mainly of silica sand (SiO_2) and borax ($Na_2B_4O_7$), and the flux of potassium
and sodium oxide. Stabilizers for obtaining better chemical resistance are
calcium oxide and aluminium oxide. The opaque agents usually consist of
titanium dioxide and zirconium dioxide which are insoluble in the glass.
The colour pigments are coloured metal oxides.

The chemicals are smelted together at 1200-1300°C and the molten mass
is granulated and cooled in water. This granulate is finely milled in ball
mills together with water, clay and sodium silicate to a viscous, not se-
dimenting dispersion which, by dipping or spraying, may be applied on the
carefully cleaned object. The coating is first dried at a temperature of
about 125°C and then burnt at 500-850°C for 4-10 minutes, depending on the
kind and thickness of the basic metal. The enamel, which is partly molten
in this process, is strongly bonded to the basic metal and forms a shining
surface.

Vitreous enamel has good resistance towards alkali (not too strong),
acids (with the exception of hydrofluoric acid), boiling water and water
vapour and various organic solvents and also towards heat (up to 600°C).
It furthermore shows good colour permanence, is electrically insulating, is
free from taste and odour and has a good resistance towards wear.
The great weakness of enamel is its brittleness so that even a slight deformation of the metallic support leads to flaking off (spalling).

Steels, as a basis for enamelling, should preferably be low carbon
special steels or at least unkilled steels which have a pure surface layer
low in carbon. Aluminium killed steels cause a serious defect, so-called

fish-eyes. This is a spontaneous spalling of the enamel which in certain
cases does not appear until after one or two months. It seems to be connected with a collection of hydrogen or methane under the enamel layer.

Apart from enamelling of jewelry and ornamental objects, enamelling
of the non-ferrous metals has been practically applied mainly on aluminium,
particularly in the building industry. The enamel surface can be obtained
bright or mat and it may be pigmented to a practically unlimited choice
of permanent colours. Enamelled aluminium thus allows greater freedom in
the choice of colour for architectural purposes than does anodized material
(see below).

031.2 Oxide films

A metal may sometimes be protected by forming on it a mechanically
passivating oxide film. One example is the so-called black-oxidation of
steel in caustic containing an oxidation agent. The result is a black-
brown oxide layer, consisting of magnetite (Fe_3O_4), which is a suitable
basis for rust preventing oils and greases. As a protection for the uranium
fuel rods in atomic reactors, a zirconium alloy (Zircaloy) containing 1.5 %
Sn and about 0.1 % Fe, Cr and Ni is often used. The zirconium alloy in its
turn is protected by means of a dense black layer of ZrO_2 formed on it by
controlled oxidation in steam.

On certain metals, particularly Al, thick oxide layers may also be
generated by electrolytic processes. The process is called anodizing since
the metal objects are connected as anodes in an electrolytic bath of suitabl
composition. The anodic oxide film formed is porous and can therefore easily
be dyed. The protective value of the anodized film is increased by so-called
sealing, which involves a treatment in hot water, preferably containing some
inhibitor, such as potassium chromate. Even Mg, Zn, Zr and Ti may be anodize
in a similar manner.

Anodizing of aluminium and aluminium alloys for the formation of protective surface coatings involves a strengthening of the natural oxide film
with which aluminium is always coated in contact with air. The aluminium
object is connected as anode in a suitable electrolyte, usually an aqueous
solution of sulphuric acid or chromic acid, whereas the cathode consists
of lead. The electrodes are connected to a direct current source. Oxygen
is evolved at the anode (the aluminium object) and reacts to form a layer
of mainly aluminium oxide, insoluble in acids.

Since the oxide film formed in anodizing is built up from the metallic base, the latter will be consumed while the oxide layer grows in thickness. The oxide layer occupies a larger volume than the metal from which it was formed, however, and the result is a dimensional increase with about 1/3rd of the film thickness.

Data for anodizing processes

	Electrolyte concentration %	Temperature °C	Cell voltage V	Current density A/dm^2	Anodizing time mins.	Film thickness µm
Chromic acid process	3-10	ca 40	10-50[a]	0.1-0.3	20-60	1-8
Sulphuric acid process	20	< 20	12-24	1.2-2.0	10-60	5-30

a = increased successively

After anodizing in sulphuric acid, the film is sealed in hot water or in an aqueous solution, e.g. potassium chromate solution, at 95-100°C for 30 minutes. The sulphuric acid method is considerably less expensive than the chromic acid method, both in chemicals and in electric energy. Objects with cavities and crevices, e.g. riveted joints, cannot be anodized in sulphuric acid, since remaining electrolyte residues in such places will give rise to corrosion. In the chromic acid process there is no such risk because of the corrosion inhibiting properties of chromic acid. Objects for anodizing should never contain parts of heavy metals since these are strongly attacked in the anodizing process.

Anodized films from chromic acid baths are usually not sealed but they have better corrosion resistance than unsealed films from a sulphuric acid bath; these on the other hand are usually sealed and then afford still better protection. Films from the sulphuric acid bath are, as a rule, lighter and more decorative and also better suited for subsequent dyeing than the grey to yellow-grey films from chromic acid baths. The former films are, furthermore, hard and brittle, whereas the latter films are relatively soft and elastic.

03.2 Shielding coatings with inhibitive action
032.1 Phosphating (phosphatizing) films

Phosphating (phosphatizing) of steel is usually carried out in phosphoric acid solutions containing acid phosphates of zinc or manganese. The solution is applied by dipping or spraying. The steel is attacked by the acid with the formation of iron phosphates which are strongly bonded to the metal surface and also act as nuclei of crystallization for sparingly soluble manganese or zinc phosphates. The latter are precipitated due to a pH increase at the metal surface. The phosphating process is accelerated by the addition to the phosphating bath of oxidation agents (so-called accelerators), such as nitrates or chlorates. Nitrate is preferable since it is reduced to nitrite which later on exerts an inhibitive action. The pre-treatment of a steel surface before phosphating is acid pickling if the phosphate layer is going to be lacquered but preferably sandblasting if the phosphate film is going to form a basis for oil or grease.

The thickness of the phosphate film is usually 2-3 μm and may vary within the limits 1-10 μm. It has a crystalline structure, it is brittle and stands only little strain without bursting. Its appearance is mat, the colour is grey to brown in different shades of darkness. Phosphate films have a good adherence and are somewhat porous and therefore form an excellent basis for paints, lacquers and rust-preventing oils and greases. The protective value of a phosphate film alone is insufficient. Phosphatizing is also used to reduce friction in cold drawing operations.

So-called thin or light phosphating is carried out in weakly acid alkali phosphate baths. These have such a low acid content that they can at the same time contain detergents and hence serve as degreasing baths. These phosphate films consist of Fe(III)-phosphate and Fe_2O_3, are very thin, 0.1-0.2 μm, finely crystalline and very hard.

To afford better protection against corrosion, all phosphating films should be given a final rinse in a dilute solution of chromic acid and then be carefully dried. If lacquering is carried out electrophoretically (see below), drying is superfluous, however.

Phosphating of non-ferrous metals does not differ in principle from phosphating of steels. There is formed on the metal surface a coating of zinc or manganese phosphate. Phosphating is excellent for zinc and cadmium, gives good results on aluminium and can also be used on magnesium.

032.2 Chromating (chromatizing) films

Chromating is a process resembling phosphating and often used as a passivating treatment after phosphating. It is not used alone on steel but on light metals and on zinc and on cadmium. Chromating processes are rapid, cheap and easily carried out. They all involve an oxidizing treatment of the metal surface in a bath containing chromic acid or chromates and accelerating anions. There are formed layers containing chromates and chromium oxide. Depending on the conditions of formation (increasing acid concentration) these layers may be green, yellow or colourless. The layers are usually very thin, 0.5 µm, have a gel structure and are very dense. The adherence is very good and the films form an excellent basis for painting. They have little resistance towards abrasion but if the layers are damaged at some spot they have a certain power of self-healing since the chromates are not quite insoluble so that diffusion from the surrounding areas leads to a measure of passivation of the exposed surface.

Aluminium is, as a rule, chromated in acid baths, containing chromic and sulphuric acids and sometimes fluoride ions as accelerators. They work rapidly, require a treatment time of only a few minutes and give a film thickness of only .01-.05 µm. Due to their good properties, these chromate films have a very wide application, particularly as a basis for painting. They are widely used as a cheaper substitute for anodizing, where the latter treatment is avoided due to high cost or special difficulties, such as in constructions containing other metals also.

Zinc and cadmium are chromated in solutions containing chromic, nitric and sulphuric acid. Electrodeposited zinc coatings on steel are also often chromated.

0.4 Organic coatings

Coating of metal surfaces with organic materials, particularly paints and lacquers, is by far the most important of all methods for corrosion prevention and probably accounts for about half of all costs spent on anti-corrosive measures.

04.1 Some fundamental concepts of paint and lacquer technology

041.1 Binder, pigment and solvent

Characteristic of paints and lacquers is that the material is applied on a substrate in liquid condition and is then subjected to a drying process.

The liquid product is then transformed to a solid, coherent and adherent material, termed layer, film, coat or coating of paint or lacquer. The final coating usually consists of or contains a substantial proportion of polymeric organic substances, forming a gel.

The following three main components may usually be distinguished in paints and lacquers: 1) binder, 2) pigment, 3) volatile solvents and thinners.

The binder is responsible for the coherence within the paint film and for its adherence to the substrate or support base. In some cases, the binder itself is brittle and has a bad adherence. This can be remedied by the addition of so-called plasticizers. The plasticizer must not be volatile but must remain in the paint film after drying.

The pigment is primarily responsible for colour and hiding power, but it plays an important part also for the consistency, the hardness and the strength of the paint film. The pigment in anti-corrosive primers should have inhibitive or otherwise rust preventing properties. In top paints for anti-corrosive purposes, the pigment used often consists of flake-like particles which greatly increase the diffusion path for oxygen and water.

A solvent is used if the binder is a solid substance at ordinary temperature, as is the case with resins and glue-like substances. In oil paints, containing an oil of low viscosity, there is no need for a solvent. The solvent is of importance not only for the applicability of the paint but it affects also its adherence and other properties. The fluid mixture of binder, solvents etc. is called the medium or vehicle as it maintains the pigment in the dispersed state.

Diluent or "thinner" is a volatile liquid that is added to the paint to reduce its viscosity before application. In many cases the same liquid may function as both solvent and diluent.

Of the paint components mentioned, the binder is the most important. The nature of the binder is deciding for the type and properties of the paint products which are therefore often sub-divided and denoted according to the character of the binder (See Table 01).

Paint is a product for surface coating, containing pigment in addition to binder, binder solution or binder emulsion. An oil paint contains a drying oil as main binder. In latex paints, the binder is an emulsion of certain polymerizates, such as poly(vinyl acetate), poly(styrene-butadiene) and acrylic resins in water.

Lacquer is a product for surface coating in which the binder consists of an organic film-forming substance, often dissolved in a solvent. The film-forming substance may be a natural or synthetic resin, a polymerized or in some other way chemically modified drying oil, cellulose esters or ethers, chlorinated rubber, a bituminous substance or a combination of substances of these types. The solvents are, as a rule, volatile organic liquids. There are also lacquers, containing binders soluble in water, however.

The term lacquer is usually reserved for coatings obtained by physical drying, whereas a varnish contains a drying oil and thus is dried by oxidation. A pigmented coating obtained by curing at ordinary or elevated temperature is sometimes referred to as enamel or enamel paint. Such organic enamels should be clearly distinguished from the vitreous or glassy enamels dealt with above, which are inorganic coatings burnt at a very high temperature. The term enamel should therefore be avoided in the paint field.

A melt coating is a material for surface treatment applied as a powder or as a melt by powder-spraying, flame-spraying or by dip-coating.

041.2 Consistency, drying and adherence

Like other types of surface treatments of metals, painting or lacquering has a twofold function: Partly to protect the surface against corrosion attacks and other outer damage , partly to give the object a pleasant appearance. In order to fulfil these functions the paint,etc.,must have a suitable consistency and fluidity corresponding to the way of application - brushing, spraying, dipping, etc. Furthermore, the drying process must proceed in an appropriate manner and result in good adherence to the substrate.

The consistency of a paint, etc., is primarily dependent on the viscosity of the constituent liquid components, on the amount and character of pigment and on the temperature. In hot spraying of paint, it is possible to use considerably smaller amounts of diluent than in cold spraying.

The drying process may take place by physical drying (physical film formation) and chemical drying (chemical film formation); see   Table 01. Physical drying consists of evaporation of volatile solvents and diluents or dispersion media or, in melt coatings, of solidification of the binder.

TABLE 01. Subdivision of organic coatings after binder and drying process.

---

1. PHYSICAL DRYING

a) Evaporation of solvent

Coating type	Binder	Solvent	Diluent[x]
Cellulose lacquer	Cellulose nitrate	Esters, ketones, glycol ethers	Alcohols, aromatic hydro-carbons, white spirit
Spirit varnish	Shellac, copal, novolac	Ethanol	-
Chlorinated rubber lacquer	Chlorinated rubber	Xylene, esters	White spirit
Asphalt lacquer	Asphalt	White spirit, turpentine	-
Vinyl lacquer	PVCA	Ketones, esters, trichloroethylene	Aromatic hydro-carbons

b) Evaporation of dispersion medium

Coating type	Binder	Dispersion medium
Latex paint	PVA, acrylic resin, poly(styrene-buta-diene)	Water
PVC coating	PVC	Ketone, xylene, white spirit (organosol)

c) Solidification of molten polymer

Polyethylene coating	Polyethylene	-
Nylon coating	Nylon	-
PVC coating	PVC	Plasticizer (plastisol)
Epoxide coating	Epoxide resin	-

2. CHEMICAL DRYING

a) Oxidative drying

Coating type	Binder	Solvent	Diluent
Oil paint	Drying oil	-	Turpentine, white spirit
Alkyd paint, air-drying	Linseed oil alkyd	White spirit	-

---

[x] Often referred to as "thinner"

Table 01 (continued).

---

b) Cold-curing (polymerization at room temperature)

Coating type	Binder	Solvent	Diluent
Carbamide lacquer	Carbamide resin	Aromatic hydro-carbons, butanol	–
Polyester lacquer	Glycol male-inate, glycol fumarate etc.	Styrene	–
Epoxide lacquer, amino-cured	Epoxide resin	Esters	–
Urethane lacquer	Polyurethanes	Aromatic hydro-carbons, esters	–

c) Stove-curing (polymerization at elevated temperature)

Coating type	Binder	Solvent	
Alkyd lacquer, stoving	Alkyd-carbamide Alkyd-melamine	Aromatic hydro-carbons	White spirit
Epoxide lacquer, stoving	Epoxide resin+ phenolic or amino-resin	Esters	
Acrylic lacquer, stoving	Acrylic resin	Styrene	Butanol

The molecules of the binder then approach each other so closely that the weak inter-molecular attraction forces, active only within a short distance, may come into play. A film formed by physical drying is therefore soluble in solvents which can penetrate between the molecules of the binder, e.g., the original lacquer solvent.

Chemical drying, on the other hand, involves a chemical reaction by which the molecules of the binder are united by covalent bonds that are not broken by solvents. Linseed oil and other drying oils react with atmospheric oxygen, which forms bridges between the oil molecules. Covalent bonds are also formed in the so-called curing (hardening, setting) of coatings, which involves a polymerization, polycondensation or polyaddition in the coating and takes place at an ordinary temperature in so-called cold-curing lacquers but at an elevated temperature ($100\text{-}200^{0}$C) in so-called stoving or baking coatings.

Mechanical adhesion occurs mainly on uneven and porous surfaces on which the paint may be sucked into porosities by capillary forces and where the dried film is attached onto microscopic, obliquely protruding points (Fig. 05). It is possible to obtain good adhesion on even a completely non-porous, polished and bright metal surface, however. In this case _specific adhesion_ occurs due to inter-molecular attraction forces between the film molecules and the substrate. Polar groups in the binder such as carboxyl, hydroxyl, carbonyl, amide and nitrate play an important part for specific adhesion. In some cases, as with etch or wash primers, there are formed even stronger truly chemical bonds between the coating and the substrate.

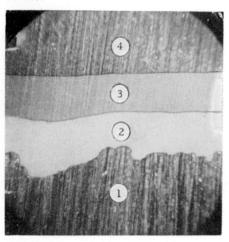

Fig. 05. Ground cross section of paint films on steel surface. 200X. 1 = sand-blasted steel, preparation grade Sa 3. 2 = = primer, consisting of red lead urethane alkyd paint, 3 = topcoat, consisting of iron oxide alkyd paint. 4 = moulding resin. Courtesy: S. Berg, AB Alfort & Cronholm.

The adhesion of organic coatings to metallic surfaces may be considerably improved by applying a suitable undercoat. Phosphating of steel, anodizing of aluminium and chromating of light metals in general result in inorganic undercoats which are themselves strongly bonded to the metal surface and on which, due to their porosity, paint films are strongly fixed by mechanical adhesion.

A paint film has a higher coefficient of thermal expansion than the metallic base. If the coating is not sufficiently elastic, such high shearing stresses between the coating and the base may occur that the coating peels off. Binders that are rich in oil and said to be long, give more elastic coatings than those containing mainly resins and only a little oil, and which are said to be short.

04.2 Polymer materials in organic coatings

042.1 Chain polymers and crosslinked polymers

Most binders in paints, lacquers and varnishes are polymer substances
which in the drying process are transformed to high polymers. While the
monomolecular unpolymerized starting material is called monomer, the term
"mer" denotes the periodically recurring unit in a polymer, which is hence
a macromolecule, formed by mers.

According to their structure, polymers may be divided into two main
groups:
1. chain polymers: polymers in which the mers are bonded to each other
   in chains, which may be linear or branched
2. network polymers: polymers in which the mers are bonded to each other
   in a three-dimensional network.

Due to the free rotation of a single bond, a chain polymer has a
certain elasticity. Under the influence of a straining force, the usually
curved molecules are straightened out. The elasticity increases with the
chain length. A polymer with a straight, unbranched chain is more elastic
than a chain polymer with branches (branched polymer). With increasing
chain length the viscosity of a solution of the polymer also increases.
A viscous lacquer need not therefore result in a thick film. Certain thermoplastic chain polymers, such as PVC, polyethylene and nylon have such long
chains that they are not soluble in ordinary lacquer solvents and they cannot therefore be applied as lacquer solutions. In lacquer films, formed from
chain polymers by evaporation of a solvent (physical drying), the polymer
molecules are kept together by weak intermolecular forces. Such a film is
therefore soluble in certain organic solvents, e.g. the original lacquer
solvent.

A network or crosslinked polymer may be formed if chain molecules are
joined to each other by covalent bonds in bridges. The denser these bridges
lie in the three-dimensional network, the harder and less elastic is the
material. These crosslinks cannot be broken up by solvents or by the supply
of small amounts of kinetic energy, that is by an increase of temperature
within reasonable limits. A network polymer is therefore insoluble and
unmeltable. Curing (hardening, setting) of so-called convertible coatings
at an ordinary or elevated temperature involves a transformation of a soluble,
thermoplastic chain polymer to an insoluble, thermosetting network polymer.

TABLE 02. Examples of thermoplastics, thermosets and elastics.

Chemical name	Trivial or trade name	Chemical formula of mer (sometimes approximate)	Approximate highest temperature of use
Thermoplastics			
Poly(vinyl chloride)	PVC	CH_2CHCl	70^oC (hard)
Poly(vinylidene chloride)	-	CH_2CCl_2	100^oC
Co-polymer of vinylidene chloride and acrylonitrile	Saran	-	-
Poly(vinyl acetate)	PVA	$CH_2CHOOCCH_3$	-
Polystyrene	PS	$CH_2CHC_6H_5$	70^oC
Poly(vinyl butyral)	PVB	$(CH_2CHO)_2CHC_3H_7$	45^oC
Poly(methyl methacrylate)	Perspex, Lucite	$CH_2CCH_3OOCCH_3$	90^oC
HD Polyethylene (hard)	PE	CH_2	110^oC
LD Polyethylene (soft)	PE	CH_2	90^oC
Polytetrafluoroethylene	Teflon	CF_2	250^oC
Poly(hexamethyleneadipamide)	6,6-nylon	$CO(CH_2)_4CONH(CH_2)_6NH$	125^oC
Poly(caprolactam)	6-nylon (Perlon)	$NH(CH_2)_5CO$	130^oC
Polyacetal (polyoxymethylene)	Delrin	CH_2O	120^oC
Polypropylene	PP	CH_2CHCH_3	130^oC
Poly(ethylene terephthalate)	Terylene	$COC_6H_4COOCH_2CH_2O$	180^oC
Phenol-formaldehyde resin (excess of phenol)	Novolac	$C_6H_3OHCH_2$	-
Thermosets			
Phenol-formaldehyde resin (excess of formaldehyde)	Bakelite, resole	$C_6H_2OH(CH_2)_2$	150^oC
Carbamide-formaldehyde resin	Carbamide resin	$CH_2NHCONH$	80^oC

Table 02 (continued).

Chemical name	Trivial or trade name	Chemical formula of mer (sometimes approximate)	Approximate highest temperature of use
Cyanamide-formaldehyde resin	Melamine resin	$NCNCH_2CH_2OR$	$100^\circ C$
Alkyd resins (e.g. poly(glycerolphthalate-linoleate))	Alkyd	$(CH_2O)_2CHRC_6H_4(CO)_2$ (R=fatty acid chain)	$175^\circ C$
Epoxide resin	Araldite Epicote	$(C_6H_4O)_2C(CH_3)_2CH_2CHOHCH_2$	$80^\circ C$
Polyurethane (poly(carbamide acid-esters))	Urethane resin	$R(NHCOO)_2R_1$	$90^\circ C$
Polysiloxane	Silicone	$SiO(CH_3)_2$	$350^\circ C$

Elastics

Polyisoprene	Natural rubber	$CH_2CH=CCH_3CH_2$	
Polybutadiene	Buna	$CH_2CH=CHCH_2$	
Poly(styrene-butadiene)	Buna S	$CH_2 \cdot CHC_6H_5 \cdot CH_2CH=CHCH_2$	
Poly(chlorobutadiene)	Neoprene	$CH_2CCl=CHCH_2$	
Chlorosulphonated polyethylene	Hypalon	$(CHCl)_{12} \cdot (CH_2)_{72}CHSO_2Cl$	

042.2 Thermoplastics, thermosets and rubbers

Practically all organic binders in paints, lacquers and varnishes, possibly with the exception of drying oils, may be referred to as resins or, after drying, plastics. Plastics may be defined as materials consisting of, or containing as characteristic components, polymeric organic substances and which in some stage of their treatment are plastically workable to end products that are usually solid.

According to their mode of formation, the plastics may be subdivided in those formed by polymerization, polycondensation and polyaddition or by the modification of natural products, such as cellulose and rubber. According to their properties plastics may be classified as thermoplastics, thermosets and elastics.

As their name implies, the thermoplastics consist of linear or branched chain polymers, not crosslinked to each other. Thermosets harden during their first moulding to crosslinked polymers with a well developed network structure. They do not become plastic again upon heating. On very strong heating they are decomposed by the breaking of chemical bonds.

Elastics (rubbers) are substances that at the temperature of their use are usually rather soft. In elastics, the local freedom of motion of chain segments is maintained, but flow, that is the sliding of whole molecules along each other, is prevented. This is connected with a weak network structure of elastically stretching crosslinks. If the degree of crosslinking is increased, hard materials are obtained, e.g. hard rubber (ebonite, vulcanite) by adding 30 % sulphur to rubber. The borderline between thermosets and elastics is therefore not sharp.

Table 02 shows that thermoplastics and elastics are often polymerizates of molecules of the same kind, whereas thermosets are often polycondensates, formed from different molecules by giving off water or some other small molecule. Examples of polyaddition, i.e. addition of monomers without emitting small molecules, are found in the formation of polyurethanes from glycol and isocyanates.

As well as binders in paints, lacquers and varnishes, the polymer materials are used for corrosion prevention even in the form of claddings, which are made by glueing foils or plates of the material to the metallic substrate. Although the plastics are usually more resistant to chemicals than construction steels, they are also attacked in different ways. Depending on the character of the plastic and the surrounding corrosive medium, the attack may take the form of hydrolysis (particularly of ester and ether groups), oxidation (particularly of double bonds), swelling (e.g. rubber in organic solvents) or of stress-cracking (e.g. of ethylene and acrylic plastics).

The plastic materials are in general quite resistant, however, towards aqueous solutions of non-oxidizing acids, salts and alkalis. The thermosets have good resistance also towards organic solvents, in which the thermoplastics tend to swell. Saran shows good resistance towards oil, however, and may therefore be used, as an alternative to amino-cured epoxide coatings, for the internal corrosion protection of oil tanks.

042.3 Organosols_and_plastisols

Many polymerizates, e.g. poly(vinylchloride), are insoluble in organic solvents, and cannot therefore be applied as paints or lacquers. This limitation in the use of high polymer substances for surface coatings has been overcome by using a dispersion of the polymer. The disperse phase may, in some cases, amount to 40-50 % without increasing the viscosity of the dispersion unduly. Three types of such dispersions are used for surface coatings:

1. Latex paints, in which polymerizates, e.g. PVA, poly(styrene-butadiene) or acrylic resin are dispersed in water as a dispersion medium (OW-emulsion). This type has gained wide use, although less often for metals.

2. Organosols, in which the polymerizate is dispersed in a suitable mixture of volatile organic liquids. The mixture should contain both polar and non-polar components. Good consistency and fluidity requires a small diameter of the dispersed particles of the polymerizate, about 0.1 μm. It is therefore necessary to control this quantity closely. This is accomplished by using certain carefully determined proportions of the polar and non-polar liquids. The organosols do not give a coherent film after evaporation of the volatile liquid but a layer of discrete particles. To obtain a dense and strong film it is necessary to heat the layer for a few minutes to sintering at 150-180°C.

3. Plastisols, in which the polymerizate is dispersed in a plasticizer. These mixtures do not contain volatile constituents. The difficulty in the preparation of a plastisol is to select the most suitable plasticizer for the actual binder. The plasticizer should in itself have a sufficiently low viscosity and should not have any dissolving or swelling effect on the binder. Preferably, the plasticizer should be reactive, i.e. polymerizable. Plastisols are applied by dipping or with a putty knife. Even in this case, it is necessary to heat the layer so that the discrete particles merge to form a continuous film.

04.3 Shielding organic coatings_with inhibitive_action

043.1 Anti-corrosive_primers

As shielding organic coatings with inhibitive action we may count ordinary oil paints, containing drying oils, such as linseed oil. It is known that the oxidation products of linseed oil, such as cinnamic and pelargonic acid, exert an inhibitive action in the same way as benzoic acid.

But above all we find in this group primers containing pigments acting as passivators or anodic inhibitors. To act in this way the pigment must have a certain suitable solubility, about 0.1-1 g/l. Water that penetrates the coating will form a saturated solution of the inhibitor which passivates the metal and in this way exerts a certain distant action at defects in the coating. Examples of such inhibiting pigments are red lead, calcium plumbate, lead cyanamide, zinc chromate, calcium and zinc molybdates. Sometimes, the inhibiting substances seem to consist of soaps formed from basic pigments and linseed oil.

0431.1 Basic linseed oil paint

Water loses its corrosive properties after contact with paints, prepared by mixing basic pigments with linseed oil. White lead (basic lead carbonate or sulphate), litharge (lead oxide) and zinc oxide are examples of such pigments. In the absence of linseed oil, these pigments do not give the water an inhibitive effect, which must therefore be ascribed to products (metal soaps) formed by a reaction of the linseed oil and the pigments.

0431.2 Red lead paint

The oldest and, for steel, still most widely used pigment in anti-corrosive primers is red lead, Pb_3O_4, which structurally consists of a double oxide of Pb(II) and Pb(IV). Most red lead pigments contain, in addition, about 6 % free PbO. The corrosion preventing effect seems to be due partly to the inhibitive action of Pb(IV), partly to the formation of lead soaps from lead oxides and degradation products (acids) of linseed oil, which normally constitutes the binder in red lead paints. These lead soaps are tough, elastic, strongly adherent and also water repellent. Red lead paint based on linseed oil therefore gives good results even on steel surfaces that are not completely free from rust, e.g. wire -brushed but not sandblasted surfaces. Any sulphate or chloride ions in the rust are, furthermore, bound as $PbSO_4$ and $PbCl_2$.

Due to the risk of lead poisoning, red lead paint should not be sprayed without extensive precautions. Red lead paint is obviously not suitable for painting less noble metals, such as Zn, Al and Mg, partly

because the lead oxides may be reduced to metallic lead, partly because
the linseed oil tends to be saponified by a base and basic metal surface.
The alkali sensitivity of the red lead linseed oil paints also make them
unsuitable in connection with cathodic protection, e.g. on ships. In the
form of putty, red lead is often used for caulking of joints in order to
avoid crevice corrosion.

0431.3 Zinc chromate paint

Of the anodic corrosion inhibitors previously referred to, chromates
are used as pigments in anticorrosive primers. The chromate ion has inhibitive properties in neutral and alkaline solutions. The effect may be
described as a reaction in which iron is oxidized to hydrated oxide, while
the chromate is reduced to hydrated chromium oxide. This gives a passivating film on the metal surface. In acid environments, there is the risk that
the hydrated oxides are not precipitated. It has, accordingly, been found
that chromate primers are not effective in industrial atmospheres with a
high content of acid products.

While alkali chromates have such a high solubility that they would
soon be leached out of a paint film, lead chromate which is of importance
as colour-giving pigment (chrome yellow), has a too low solubility, about
10^{-4} g/l, to exert a sufficient inhibitor action. A suitable solubility is
found with certain zinc chromates, such as basic zinc chromate, K_2CrO_4,
$3ZnCrO_4$, $Zn(OH)_2$, $2H_2O$, with the solubility 1.1 g CrO_3/l and zinc tetrahydroxidechromate, $ZnCrO_4$, $4Zn(OH)_2$, with the solubility 0.02 g CrO_3
/l, which are therefore used in some anti-corrosive primers. These primers
usually contain synthetic resins, such as alkyd resins as binders. Alkyd
paints with zinc chromate pigment have a much shorter drying time than red
lead paints and the films become harder. Their efficiency is more dependent
on the pre-treatment of the painted surface than is the case with red lead
paints, however. Some other binders have been tried with good results, e.g.
phenolic resins. In contrast to red lead paints, zinc chromate paints
are well suited for zinc and light metals, too, and for putty and jointing
material for these metals.

0431.4 Wash primers and shop primers

Along with poly(vinyl butyral) and phosphoric acid, zinc tetrahydroxide
chromate is a constituent also in so-called etch or wash primers, which are

a sort of compromise between anti-corrosive primers and phosphating solutions and which can be used on steel as well as on light metals.

A wash primer may be prepared from its various constituents in two different ways. The components are either all mixed together from the beginning or delivered as a two-can paint to be mixed immediately before application. The table below gives a typical example of a wash primer of a two-pack type (the figures denote weight parts).

Solution A	Solution B
7.2 poly(vinyl butyral)	3.6 phosphoric acid (85 %)
6.9 zinc tetrahydroxidechromate	3.2 water
1.1 talcum	13.2 isopropanol
48.7 isopropanol	
16.1 butanol	
80.0	20.0

The two-pack types have the advantage that a reactive mixture is applied on the metal surface. After reaction with the metal, a strongly adhering and almost neutral film is obtained. A substantial drawback is that the mixture thickens rather quickly which usually precludes application by dipping. The primer must be used within a short time, e.g. 8 hours, after it has been mixed.

The one-pack type, on the other hand, may be stored for months. In wash primers of this type, chromium(III)phosphate is substituted for zinc chromate. This gives poorer adherence and inferior film properties.

Another type of etching primer is pigmented with iron oxide in addition to zinc tetrahydroxidechromate. This increases its resistance towards abrasion considerably. This type is used as so-called shop primer or prefabrication primer in the manufacturing industries as a temporary protection against corrosion of semimanufactured goods, which are later to be painted or lacquered. Before this is done, the surface has to be cleaned (degreased) again. Before a top coat is applied, the shop primer should be coated with an ordinary anti-corrosive primer such as zinc chromate primer. Other, non-etching primers, such as zinc or aluminium dust paints, are also used as shop primers. One requirement of all shop primers is that they should allow welding.

043.2 Oils, greases and waxes with inhibitor additions

Oils, greases and waxes with the addition of suitable corrosion inhibitors are used to protect metal surfaces against corrosion during storage
and transport. They are often referred to as temporary rust preventives.
Agents of this type are used for the temporary rust preventive treatment
of cars.

The temporary rust preventives may be divided into anti-rust liquids,
which contain an evaporating solvent, anti-rust oils and anti-rust greases,
whose properties are evident from their designations, hot dipping anti-rust
agents, which are based on waxes and asphalt, and finally anti-rust emulsions, which contain or may be diluted with water before application.

The temporary rust preventives are often used in cases where a combination of a lubrication and a temporary rust protection is required.
One important characteristic of agents of this type is that they can be
removed by organic solvents. A great many mixtures of this type appear on
the market under various trade names.

In the temporary and periodical rust preventive treatment of cars,
the anti-rust agent is sprayed by means of a high pressure "airless" pistol
through specially drilled holes into existing cavities and inner spaces in
the car body. Some of the holes are later plugged up while others are left
open for ventilation and drainage in order to prevent the accumulation of
moisture due to rain, washing or temperature variations. A similar treatment with a rust preventive agent and a suitable underseal compound is
carried out on the chassis and in the wheel housings of the car. This
treatment should be carried out once every year.

04.4 Topcoats

An anti-rust paint system usually consists of a primer with special
corrosion preventing properties and a topcoat. One task of the topcoat
may be to protect the primer, e.g. red lead primers, which are sensitive
to the influence of the atmosphere. An ideal coating system would be absolutely impenetrable and possess perfect adherence and coherence. The
topcoat should reduce the rate of transfer for water vapour, oxygen and
other corrosive agents to the primer. Moisture and also oxygen penetrate
paint films relatively rapidly, however. Pigmentation, particularly with
flake-like particles as of iron oxide, aluminium or stainless steel, in-

creases the diffusion path for the corrosive gas   and hence decreases its rate of transfer through the film.

Organic coatings, which may often be considered as semipermeable membranes, are not so impenetrable to water and oxygen that they can control corrosion by preventing these substances from reaching the metal surface. Their barrier action rather consists in preventing corrosive salts and solid particles from reaching the metal surface. In this way, a high electrolyte resistance is also maintained which counteracts ionic migration and hence the flow of corrosion currents.

Even unpigmented lacquers and varnishes have a considerable protective effect. Iron oxide paint, whose pigment does not exert any inhibitive action, affords good protection against corrosion as long as the paint film is continuous and undamaged. If, however, the paint film deteriorates at some spot, corrosive agents rapidly reach the metal surface and start corrosion.

The following table shows the main components of three topcoats which in long term field tests have shown good results in anti-rust painting of steel in the atmosphere.

Paint notation	Pigment	Binder
Micaceous iron oxide paint	Micaceous iron oxide + Al-powder	Linseed oil
White lead paint	White lead (+Al-powder)	Linseed oil
Iron oxide alkyd paint	Red iron oxide	Long alkyd

The ability of a topcoat to resist the deteriorating influence of the atmosphere is primarily a function of the binder. Alkyds are better in this respect than the drying oils. For coatings subjected to special strain, e.g. under water or in chemical factories, binders with a particularly high resistance towards water and chemicals are available, e.g. chlorinated rubber, vinyl resins, acrylic resins, epoxide resins, urethanes, and so on.

In the surface treatment of metals with anti-corrosive paints, it is of great importance that a sufficient total coating thickness is obtained. There is a clear relation between the thickness and the life of a coating (according to certain tests direct proportionality). Each coat must not be made too thick, however, with regard to complete drying and the risk of skinning. For oil paints, each coat should not be thicker than 40 μm and should be completely dry before the next coat is applied. Since the climate plays the dominating role for the strength of rust attacks, the total coating thickness and hence the number of individual coats should be adjusted according to the climate. In marine and industrial atmospheres, it is economic to apply two coats of primer and two coats of top paint. In rural environments, on the other hand, it is usually sufficient with one coat of primer and one topcoat.

04.5 Methods for the application of organic coatings

The most widely used methods for application of organic coatings are brushing, spraying, roller painting and dipping and two types of electro-coating, viz. electrodeposition and electrostatic spraying of paint.

Brushing is the oldest and best known method for the application of paint. If the paint has a low fluidity, brushing may result in considerable variations in the coating thickness (brush strokes) which are, however, equalized if several coats are applied. On surfaces that are not quite clean, brushing is the best method. Rust and dust on the metal surface are then dispersed in the paint instead of staying under the paint film and causing under-rusting.

Spraying of paint is usually carried out by means of compressed air. It gives very even films if it is carried out correctly. If the paint is warmed it is possible to spray it without adding thinners. Such hot spraying of paint gives a film about 50 % thicker than spraying at an ordinary temperature.

A new form of spray painting is the so-called airless spraying. The paint is then thrown out of a spray pistol towards the object with a very high pressure (ca 125 kp/cm^2) but without the presence of compressed air. Due to good penetration into irregularities in the metal surface, the airless spraying is a good substitute for brush painting. Whereas in conventional spraying with compressed air (Fig. 06) there is a considerable recoil of paint droplets from the object, this effect is almost eliminated in airless spraying (Fig. 07).

A special mode of spray painting is the so-called electrostatic spraying, in which the spray aggregate is at a very high negative electric tension (-50.000 V) relative to the object which is earthed. The paint is

Fig. 06. Conventional spraying of
paint (on internal surface).
Strong recoil of paint.
Courtesy: AB Brdr.Michaelsen, Malmö.

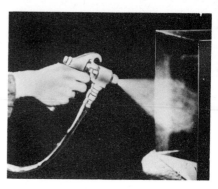

Fig. 07. Airless spraying of paint
(on internal surface). Little recoil
of paint.
Courtesy: AB Brdr.Michaelsen, Malmö.

Fig. 08. Sketch of automatic
equipment for powder-spraying
of polymer coatings.
1. Aggregate
2. Spray pistol
3. High voltage rod
4. Object to be coated
5. Earthed conveyor
6. High voltage cable
7. Powder recovery ramp
8. Powder recovery
9. Ventilator
10. Return air.

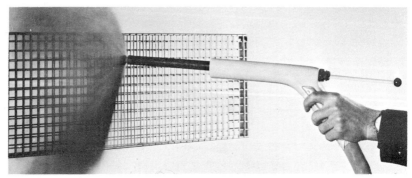

Fig. 09. Manual powder spraying of grill screen.
Courtesy: Universal Electronics AB, Sweden.

finely dispersed in the spraying aggregate, usually by mechanical means. The small paint droplets are negatively charged by electrons, migrate in the electric field and deposit on the object. The paint spreads even to the back of small articles, but not, due to a Faraday cage effect, to crevices and internal surfaces as is the case in the electrodeposition of paint (see below). The method is also used for the spraying of powder (PVC, epoxide etc.) which is then sintered to a continuous coating. Electrostatic spraying is based on the same principle as the wellknown electrostatic flue gas cleaning.

Roller painting is a rapid method for coating large, relatively flat surfaces, even wire netting fences. Since there is some difficulty with complete wetting of the surface, brushing is to be preferred for the first primer coat, even if the following coats are applied by roller.

Dip painting is carried out by simply dipping the objects in the paint and let the excess drain off. Special paints suited for the method are used and give quite even layers. This mode of application is best suited for small articles which have to be coated both inside and outside. Great cleanliness has to be observed in order not to contaminate the paint in the dipping tank.

Electrodeposition of paint may be considered as a special mode of dip painting. The article to be coated is immersed for a short time as an anode in an aqueous electrolyte solution in which the paint is emulsified as negatively charged colloidal drops which migrate in the electric field and are deposited on the article. The method gives quite even and dense coatings, both on edges and corners and on internal surfaces, since the coating has a high electric resistance and therefore forces the current to still uncovered areas.

Other methods for paint application used on a large industrial scale, e.g. for the coating of semi-manufactured goods, such as steel sheet, are coil coating, which is carried out in a sort of roller mill, curtain coating, in which method the articles are carried through a curtain of paint, generated by spray nozzles, and flow coating which is carried out in a similar way in a special tunnel.

Thermoplastic insoluble materials, such as PVC, polyethylene and nylon are applied by powder spraying, dip coating in powder or flame spraying and a subsequent melting or sintering of the resultant powder layer.

04.6 Degrees of rusting and of paint protection efficiency

In order to estimate the ability of a paint to hinder the appearance and spreading of rust on a painted steel surface, a series of ten photographs is used, defining partly the degree of rusting from Re 0 (no rust) to Re 9 (the entire surface coated with rust) and partly the degree of paint protection efficiency (earlier called paint value) from 1 (the entire surface covered with rust) to 10 (no rust). The photographs, which are based on test panels painted with oil-based, air-drying anti-rust paint, are shown in the Swedish Standard SIS 185111, European scale of degree of rusting for ant corrosive paints, Stockholm 1964. The estimates are necessarily subjective (Fig. 010).

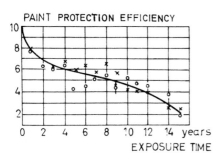

Fig.010. Estimation of the degree of paint protection efficiency by two observers, A (x) and B (o).

Fig.011. Steel bridge in Stockholm, painted in 1935 and not yet repainted. See text. Courtesy: L. Wallin, Swedish Institute of Steel Construction

04.7 Repainting

As well as in the first painting, the result of repainting is greatly dependent upon the care with which the pretreatment is carried out. Old paint may be removed mechanically by the same tools that are used in mechanical derusting. It is also possible to use burning with gas burners, blow lamps and electric burning devices. The paint film is heated until it starts to boil and the softened paint can be pushed away with a putty knife. The metal surface is then scraped and brushed in the usual way. Paints based on linseed oil, alkyds and other esters can be saponified by treatment with caustic or ammonia if they are applied on steel. Old paint may also be removed by special emulsifying agents, particularly methylene chloride, CH_2Cl_2. Stoving enamels are harder to remove but may sometimes be softened with cresols or chlorinated cresols.

A first-class anti-rust paint should last for at least 20 years, even in urban and marine atmospheres. That this can be accomplished is shown by one of the bridges in Stockholm, Västerbron, built in 1935. Its original paint coat was in very good condition after 35 years (Fig.011) and has only been touched up on certain parts, for aesthetic reasons mainly. The paint system on this bridge consists of two coats of red lead in linseed oil and two topcoats of micaceous iron oxide paint (Section 04.4 above). The pretreatment before painting consisted in washing, scraping and wire-brushing to preparation grade St 2 as per section 01.3 above. Blast cleaning was not used. The painting was carried out and controlled very carefully.

Literature

Burns, R M & Bradley, W W, Protective Coatings for Metals, Reinhold Publ. Corp., New York 1967.

P. CORROSION TESTING

P.1 Different types of corrosion tests

P1.1 Classification of corrosion tests

Corrosion testing may be carried out by means of laboratory tests (I) or service tests (II).

I. Laboratory tests may be sub-divided into

A. Model experiments, i.e., long-time tests without acceleration, in which service conditions in actual plants are simulated in a small model apparatus in the laboratory. Such tests are carried out in order to provide a basis for the selection of the most suitable material or method of protection for a certain process or application. Model experiments are preferred to service tests for the following reasons:

a) in order not to cause operational disturbances in industrial processes or other technical applications

b) because test conditions are more easily controlled and maintained and test results more safely evaluated in a small model apparatus than in an actual plant in which unintentional variations in service conditions often make the results uncertain.

B. Accelerated short-time tests, in which one or several corrosion factors are intensified in order to make the corrosion attack proceed faster than under actual service conditions. Accelerated short-time tests are carried out according to carefully specified directions and are used mainly in quality control of metallic materials or of protective coatings for such materials. They may also serve as a first orientation regarding possible applications in the development of new materials or coatings. The value of an accelerated short-time test should always be ascertained after comparison with long-time tests, i.e., service tests or model experiments, carried out under service conditions.

II. Service tests may be sub-divided into

A. Plant tests, carried out in actual technical plants and used for the selection of the most suitable material or method of protection for a certain process or application. Model experiments in the laboratory may often with advantage be substituted for plant tests.

B. Field tests, aiming at finding the most suitable material or method of protection for applications in natural environments (atmosphere, soil or water) and at estimating its probable life. While model experiments in the laboratory may sometimes be used instead of field tests in water, this is rarely the case for atmosphere and soil exposure conditions.

Pl.2 Long-time laboratory tests

Instead of carrying out tests in an actual plant, it is usually better to use a small model apparatus in which the conditions of the plant are closely simulated and in which small test specimens, suitable for weighing, are introduced. Although this may be considered as a laboratory test it is not subject to the unreliability of accelerated laboratory tests. In fact, long-time laboratory tests in a model apparatus are often more reliable than actual service test in an industrial plant. Laboratory tests have the important advantage that test conditions may be much more easily controlled, observed and maintained than in plant tests. The latter therefore usually give a much larger variation in test results than closely controlled laboratory tests. In laboratory tests in a model apparatus the results are more easily obtained by various observations and measurements, by weighing of the specimens, by analysis of the corrosive medium etc. Fig. Pl shows a sketch of a model apparatus used to test inhibitors for domestic central heating systems.

Closely controlled laboratory tests may sometimes also be used with advantage instead of field tests. One example is provided by the general corrosion of various types of carbon steels and low-alloyed steels in natural waters, which is now known to be governed by oxygen diffusion. In the former half of this century, long-time field tests lasting for decades were carried out in order to find out how different types of steel, cast iron etc., behaved in sea water. The results were then variable and contradictory. Sometimes one material was the better, sometimes another. The situation could be clarified only after careful laboratory tests had shown that general corrosion in water is governed by the amount of dissolved atmospheric oxygen transported to the metal surface in unit time but is independent, within certain limits, of the type of iron or steel used. In the long-time field tests, the results were influenced by accidental variations in the distance to the water surface, in flow conditions, in temperature, etc.

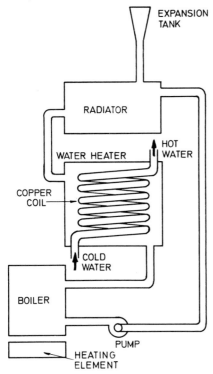

Fig. Pl. Laboratory model of central heating system with water heater used in testing corrosion inhibitors for circulating boiler water. Steel and copper specimens were inserted in the water heater and were taken out for weighing after each experiment.

Pl.3 Accelerated laboratory tests

In accelerated laboratory tests, one or more corrosion factors are intensified so that the corrosion process takes place more rapidly. The result is therefore obtained after a shorter time of testing that may be counted in weeks, days, hours or even minutes. It is usually not possible, on the basis of such accelerated short-time tests, to make any prediction regarding the life of the material or coating in any naturally occurring, less aggressive environment. At best, one can hope to obtain a correct sequence of the materials or coatings in the tests. The result of an accelerated test is often the more unreliable the higher the degree of acceleration and the shorter the testing period. This is particularly true if the test environment deviates in its chemical composition from that in the corresponding practical case. It is often necessary to strike some sort of compromise between a reliable test result and a short testing time.

It is obvious, that in the development of new corrosion-resistant materials and coatings and other methods for surface protection, it is not possible to resort immediately to long-time model or plant tests and still less so to field tests. In the beginning, it is necessary to use accelerated laboratory tests. These should be used and applied in such a way, however, that the results have the highest possible relevance for the practical application.

A fundamental principle in the choice of short-time tests in the laboratory is that the corrosion environment in its nature, that is in its qualitative chemical composition, should be the same as in the corresponding practical case. An attempt is made to produce a certain acceleration of the corrosion process by a change in degree, that is by intensifying some dominating environmental factor such as moisture, temperature or the concentration of a certain corrosive agent.

The most important methods of accelerating a corrosion test consist in increasing the relative humidity and temperature in the testing procedure, in using salt spray, if the purpose is to simulate marine atmospheric conditions or sea water, or in adding high contents of sulphur dioxide if the purpose is to intensify the corrosion in industrial atmospheres for which a salt spray test often gives misleading results. The ability of atmospheric oxygen to maintain the cathode process in corrosion reactions is sometimes strengthened by the addition of oxidizing agents. Dissolution of protective films at low pH values is sometimes accelerated by the addition of acetic acid, whereas an ammoniacal atmosphere may be imitated by using an ammonia solution. The oxidizing action of a corrosive medium may sometimes be strengthened by applying a certain constant anodic current density or, which is in principle more correct, a constant potential more noble than the natural corrosion potential.

It is of prime importance that the type of corrosion in an accelerated corrosion test is the same as in the corresponding practical case. There is obviously little value in rapid tests with small test plates if the dominating effect there is an attack on the edges of the plates that is not encountered in practice. Insulation of the edges of small test plates by means of wax or lacquer is a common method to circumvent this difficulty.

If laboratory testing results only in general attack while in the corresponding natural corrosion case pitting or stress corrosion cracking occurs, the accelerated test is yet valueless.

But even if such pitfalls have been avoided and it has been possible to find an accelerated test which gives an attack of the same character as under natural field or plant conditions, one can seldom hope to establish any given acceleration factor. Much would, of course, be gained by an acceleration of, for instance, 100 times, e.g. that a 2 years field or plant test is reduced to one week s laboratory testing. What should be definitely required from an accelerated short-time test, however, is that the relative corrosion rates of various materials or coatings, or the relative efficiency of the various corrosion protection methods investigated, should be about the same as in a long-time service test. If this has once been established by comparison with long-time tests, the accelerated test method can obviously be used with some safety in other similar cases.

The reliability of results from short-time testing in the laboratory is often inversely proportional to the degree of acceleration used. Certain devices used for corrosion testing seem to have been "invented" rather than developed on the basis of practical experience. Although accelerated tests are of great value in development work and in materials control, all important conclusions must be based on confirmation from long-time tests either in model experiments in the laboratory or in field or plant tests. As there is no general corrosion protection method applicable under all conditions, there does not exist and cannot exist any general short-time test giving reliable results for all the various corrosion conditions occurring in practice. We must accept we have to work with a great many short-time tests, each of them worked out due to experience gained in comparison with practical long-time tests in a special corrosion environment.

P1.4 Service tests

Field tests in nature or tests in industrial plants mean that the test material is subjected to the practically occurring natural corrosion environments. Such tests are always particularly valuable and sometimes indispensable. There is hardly any possibility to simulate in the laboratory the conditions to which a metal specimen is subjected in natural exposure in the soil, for instance. The naturally occurring formation of protective films on zinc, aluminium and slow-rusting steels in the atmosphere is also very difficult to simulate in the laboratory.

For corrosion testing in the atmosphere small test plates are used which are individually suspended either vertically or at an angle of 30° to 45° towards the horizontal plane (Fig. P2). They are placed in parallel

Fig. P2. Field test station for atmospheric corrosion testing on West coast of Sweden. Courtesy: O. Nygren, Swedish Corrosion Institute.

and facing the direction that is assumed to give the highest corrosion rate, e.g. towards the sea, towards an industrial area or towards the sun. Particular attention must be devoted to the suspension of specimens during the corrosion tests, since undesirable effects may otherwise be obtained due to galvanic or crevice corrosion. The test plates or specimens should be electrically insulated from surrounding metallic materials and should be point-wise supported by glass, porcelain, teflon or some other inert and non-absorbing material (Fig. P3). The specimens should furthermore be positioned in such a way that corrosion products are not transferred from

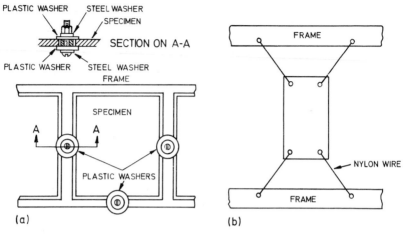

Fig. P3. Arrangements for support of outdoor exposure test panels.

one panel to another. For galvanic corrosion tests in the atmosphere, e.g. between light metals and stainless steel, ASTM has recommended a special system of circular test plates pressed against each other but with a certain part of the surface freely exposed (Fig. P4).

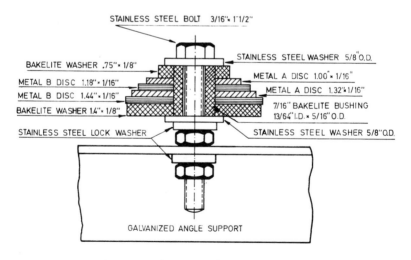

Fig. P4. Atmospheric galvanic test assembly.

Service tests in industrial plants are carried out by introducing small test specimens in the actual environment. Such plant tests may cause disturbances in the operation of the plant, e.g. in the testing of various inhibitors, and the result may also be unreliable due to shut-downs and stoppages and other unexpected variations of the test conditions.

P.2 Variation of corrosion velocity with time

It is often of great practical interest to elucidate the dependence of corrosion rate on time. The corrosion rate is usually highest in the beginning of an exposure. Later, it often declines due to the accumulation of more or less protective corrosion products on the metal surface. In favourable cases, the metal loss or film thickness increases parabolically rather than linearly with time. Extrapolation of corrosion rates obtained in short-time tests to longer times often gives too high values, there-fore. With some test methods, such as the resistance-wire method (see paragraph P5.7 below) or in the continuous weighing of specimens in oxida-tion experiments, the corrosion-time relationship is directly obtained. In most cases, however, corrosion rates are determined as weight losses. It is then necessary to remove the more or less protective corrosion pro-ducts from the surface before weighing. It would then be meaningless to expose the specimens again. In order to obtain the corrosion-time relation-ship in such cases, it is therefore necessary to use a great many specimens and take them out of the test successively for cleaning and weighing. If, for instance, 15 specimens are exposed at the same time, 3 may be removed after 1, 2, 4, 8 and 16 units of time, respectively. The time unit may be day, week, month or year, depending upon corrosion rate. In atmospheric corrosion tests, it is of particular importance that all specimens to be compared are put out at the same time, since the life of a specimen is often strongly dependent on its initial corrosion rate and therefore on the season during which it is first exposed. It should also be observed that the climate is generally becoming more corrosive due to increasing air pollution.

P.3 Characterization of test materials

Irrespective if short-time or long-time tests, if service or laboratory experiments are used for corrosion testing, there are certain general rules which must be adhered to. One such rule involves sufficiently accurate characterization of the composition, structure, surface condition and stress condition of test materials, i.a., in order to obtain reproducibl results if the testing has to be repeated. A complete chemical analysis alone is not sufficient to characterize a metallic material. It is also necessary to know in detail the structure and stress condition of the metal or alloy. It should also be known which phases appear in the metalli material, if metallic or non-metallic precipitates or inclusions occur, the grain size, etc. This characterization from a structural point of view is primarily given by an accurate statement of heat treatment and cold work of the sample. At higher degrees of accuracy in the characterization, these statements should be supplemented with michrophotographs and a description of the structure.

It is furthermore of great importance that the surface of the specimens is produced in a reproducible manner. The surface preparation is sometimes a natural stage in making the specimens, namely in investigations of protective coatings, but even on test specimens with unprotected metal surfaces preliminary cleaning and surface preparation should be carried out with the same accuracy. It is particularly important to remove any surface rust, millscale, grease, etc., and to produce as homogeneous and reproducible a surface as possible, by sandblasting or by pickling and, perhaps, by polishing. The surface condition, such as the degree of polishing, is of particular importance on passivating metals, such as stain less steels.

Sharp edges and corners often constitute the starting points for local corrosion and may therefore give rise to misleading results. Edges should therefore be ground in order to remove burrs and in order to obtain rounded corners and edges on which paint films etc. will attain sufficient thicknes

It is also very important to clean all test specimens before testing by degreasing. The specimen may be considered as sufficiently clean if it is completely wetted by water without forming dry patches on drainage (the so-called water-break test). After such a test the specimens should be rinsed in alcohol or acetone and be dried in a dessicator before they are weighed. Thereafter, they should not be handled with bare fingers.

Special attention must be paid to tests designed for corrosion types influenced by mechanical factors, such as stress corrosion cracking, corrosion fatigue and hydrogen embrittlement. In such specimens, internal stresses may appear as a result of heat treatment and cold-working. For more practical technological tests such internal stresses in, for instance, loop test bars may be sufficient, particularly if a great number of test specimens are used in order to equalize statistically accidental variations in stress condition. It is usually better, however, to apply some controlled outer mechanical tensile stress which should be static in the case of stress corrosion cracking and hydrogen embrittlement,but cyclic,that is varying between two extreme values, in the case of corrosion fatigue. For accurate tests with corrosion cracking in the laboratory, a uni-axial tensile stress produced in a wire or a test bar is to be preferred, due to higher reproducibility.Unevenness in the surface of such specimens, whether initial or a consequence of local corrosive attack, may act as do notches. This is particularly true for corrosion fatigue. Figs. P5 and P6 show two devices for testing the sensitivity of steels towards corrosion cracking. The specimens may be polarized, anodically or cathodically.

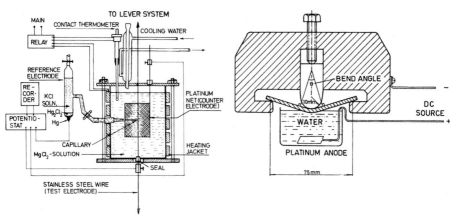

Fig. P5. Schematic view of test cell for potentiostatic testing of sensitivity of stainless steel towards SCC. Test solution: 45 % MgCl$_2$ soln. at 140°C.

Fig. P6. Bending test device for testing the sensitivity of high strength steels towards hydrogen embrittlement.

It is also necessary to carry out special corrosion tests on welded specimens if welded joints occur in the envisaged construction. Welds deviate from the basic material in several respects: composition, heat treatment, structure and stress condition. Corrosion testing of welded specimens

may serve to elucidate the resistance to corrosion of the welding seam.
They may also serve to test the sensitivity to corrosion of the heat-
affected zone of the basic material along the weld which may be influenced
by changes of slag inclusions, precipitates, structure and stresses caused
by the welding process.

P.4 Control of experimental conditions in laboratory tests

While the corrosive environment and its fluctuations in field tests
are fixed by atmospheric and other natural conditions and in plant tests
by normally occurring operation conditions, it is necessary, on the other
hand, to pay special attention to the nature and maintenance of the artificially created conditions prevailing in laboratory tests.

P4.1 Composition of test solution

The composition of the corrosive medium must be controlled, even with
respect to unintentional impurities. Analytically pure chemicals often
have a different effect than the technically polluted solutions encountered in practice. Although 3 % NaCl solution is sometimes used in order to
simulate sea water, it must be observed that the two solutions behave
quite differently. The other salts, particularly magnesium chloride and
calcium chloride, occurring in sea water exert a considerable influence
since cathodically produced alkali causes them to precipitate as sparingly
soluble hydroxides or carbonates which subsequently retard the corrosion
process. The corrosion rate, particularly after a long testing time is
therefore several times higher in the 3 % sodium chloride solution than
in sea water. It is inconvenient to carry out a laboratory test in natural
sea water which has to be transported a long way, stored etc., and which
may not have a constant composition due to accidental circumstances. It is
therefore generally customary to carry out laboratory tests aiming at
testing corrosion in sea water in an artificially produced sea water of
accurately stated analysis. This will give a far more reproducible environment than water taken directly from the sea.

The concentration of salt or acid in a corrosive solution often plays
a great role. It is far from always true that corrosion velocity increases
with concentration. Increasing ion pair formation, association etc. with
increasing concentration of the electrolyte may actually decrease the
concentration of an ion active in corrosion reactions. It is well known

that the strong acids in concentrated form are usually less corrosive than their somewhat diluted solutions. Regarding salt solutions, their conductivity increases with salt concentration. At the same time, however, the solubility and diffusivity of dissolved oxygen decrease and the tendency towards precipitation of protective coatings increases. The net result is that the corrosion rate reaches a maximum at a certain concentration and then declines quite rapidly at high concentrations (Cf. Fig. F11, p. 93).

P4.2 Aeration of test solution

Since corrosion in neutral media occurs only if dissolved atmospheric oxygen is available for the cathode process, it is obviously very important in corrosion experiments in the laboratory to control the aeration of the test solution very carefully. If the corrosive medium is an aqueous solution in which specimens are immersed, it should be kept saturated with air or oxygen by means of bubbling gas through it. This also contributes to uniform experimental conditions by the resultant stirring, which reduces temperature and concentration differences.

If it is of interest to study various degrees of aeration it is usually better to vary the oxygen content of the bubbled gas than its quantity. In a similar way, corrosion in deaerated solutions is studied by bubbling nitrogen or argon through the test solution. Hydrogen, a reducing agent which affects the corrosion potential, cannot be considered as an inert gas. A particularly efficient aeration of the corrosive solution is obtained in various kinds of laboratory apparatus (salt spray cabinets, aerosol apparatus, weatherometers, etc.) in which the corrosive solution is finely dispersed by means of a spray nozzle or a centrifuge.

P4.3 Temperature of test solution

The influence of the temperature of the corrosive medium on corrosion velocity is complicated since temperature affects several other corrosion factors, such as oxygen solubility, pH, oxide film formation, condensation of moisture etc. in various directions. It is thus not permissible to extrapolate corrosion velocities over large temperature intervals. Corrosion velocity often shows a complicated dependence upon temperature. In aqueous solutions, it usually reaches a maximum around $80^{\circ}C$. In wet flue gases, corrosion is often at a minimum around $100^{\circ}C$, then reaches a maximum just below the dew point of sulphuric acid around $130^{\circ}C$ and then passes through a minimum again before increasing at still higher temperatures.

The corrosive medium should be thermostatically controlled and should be kept at a temperature not far from that encountered in practice. In corrosion tests in aqueous solutions the temperature is sometimes kept constant by using a boiling solution. If the solution is not saturated, a reflux cooler has to be used in order to avoid concentration changes and hence a change of boiling point. Boiling should be avoided, however, in all cases where a close control of the content of the dissolved gases is desired. Many test results obtained in testing the sensitivity of stainless steel towards stress corrosion cracking in boiling magnesium chloride solution are probably uncertain because the oxygen content of the solution has not been under close control. If one desires to keep the oxygen content at practically nil, an inert gas should be blown into the reflux cooler.

P4.4 Volume of test solution

The volume of the solution used in corrosion testing constitutes a problem in laboratory tests where, for practical reasons, the volume has to be limited. Insufficient volume of the solution may lead to depletion of the corrosive component or to an increase of the concentration of corrosion products in the solution which may influence the results in one way or other. Sometimes, a minimum volume of 50 ml test solution per square centimetre of test area is prescribed. If the test solution is rapidly consumed it has to be periodically renewed.

P4.5 Flow velocity of test solution

The flow velocity of the test solution is another important factor influencing corrosion velocity. As a rule, the corrosion rate increases with increased flow velocity and the type of corrosion is changed from general to erosion corrosion and finally to cavitation corrosion. In order to investigate the influence of flow rate on corrosion, it is necessary to use an apparatus with well-defined flow conditions. Furthermore, it is often desirable to use a setup that resembles the actual practical case. An apparatus which fulfils these requirements consists of tubing through which the corrosive liquid is circulated by means of a pump. Such a plant is relatively simple and safe in operation. In order to make evaluation of the test results possible, the tubing must consist of small pieces tightly and evenly jointed to each other. In this way even galvanic effects may be studied.

Rotating cylinders and rotating circular discs are often used in studying the influence of flow rate on corrosion velocity. The flow situation around such rotating bodies is relatively simple and may be treated by the mathematical methods of hydrodynamics. In order to reach high linear velocities by means of small rotating cylinders, extremely high rotation numbers are necessary, however. This results in very strong centrifugal forces, so that corrosion products may be hurled away from the surface, whereas eventual gas bubbles in the solution are pressed towards the mantle surface of the cylinder. By using large cylinders which entirely consist of the test material these problems are minimized but an accurate gravimetric measurement of the corrosion velocity is then no longer possible. With a large rotating cylinder of plastic with inlaid metal specimens in the cylinder mantle, on the other hand, centering becomes difficult, as does also the arrangement of electrical connections for the measurement of corrosion potential.

A test specimen in the shape of a rotating circular disc, involves the great advantage of giving corrosion velocity as a function of flow velocity in one single experiment. If the peripheral velocity is high enough there is obtained at a certain distance from the centre a transition from laminar to turbulent flow. As a rule, corrosion velocity then increases suddenly. The opposite may be true for passivating metals such as stainless steels and nickel alloys which more easily retain their passivity under turbulent conditions due to a more copious supply of oxygen. Experiments with rotating discs are of great value as a first orientation. It should be observed, however, that misleading effects may be obtained due to macrocells formed as a result of differing oxygen and metal ion concentration and hence differing potential at various distances from the rotation centre.

In an accurate study in the laboratory of the influence of the flow velocity of the corrosive medium on corrosion rate, it is much better to use an apparatus consisting of two concentric cylinders of perspex, for instance,in which the metal specimens are inlaid in the inner mantle surface of the outer cylinder (Fig. P7). The flow velocity is created by rotating the inner cylinder which drags along the test solution in the narrow slit between the two cylinders. This cylinder apparatus gives a flow picture (Couette flow) that is well defined, can be treated mathematically and allows the corrosion rate and corrosion potential to be easily measured.

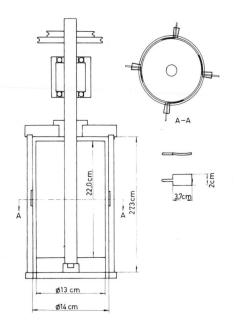

Fig. P7. Apparatus for the study of corrosion in flowing solutions, consisting of two concentric cylinders of plastic. The inner cylinder (of PVC) is rotated at a high speed, whereas test plates are inlaid in the inner mantle surface of the outer stationary cylinder (of perspex).

In attempting to simulate practical conditions involving relative motion between a metal and a corrosive solution, or in relating laboratory results to service conditions, it should be observed that the relevant variable is not the linear flow velocity but the Reynolds number $Re = u \cdot L/\nu$ where u equals linear flow velocity (cm/s), L equals a characteristic length, e.g. diameter, width of a slit (cm) and ν equals the kinematic viscosity of the solution (cm^2/s). At a certain critical value of Reynolds number there occurs a transition from laminar to turbulent flow (see Fig. F12). Since the Reynolds number contains the product of flow velocity and the characteristic length it is found. for example, that a model apparatus with smaller tube diameter than in the practical case can give a correct result only if the flow velocity is increased correspondingly.

P4.6 Exposure degree of specimens

In corrosion testing in aqueous solutions in the laboratory metal specimens may be totally, partially or intermittently immersed in the corrosive medium. Totally immersed samples that are to be compared should be suspended at the same depth below the surface of the solution. Small specimens suspended at various depths along a vertical line do not corrode in the same way as one single long specimen. In the latter case a macro-cell is formed due to differential aeration on a specimen of large dimensions.

Partially immersed samples are of particular value in studying water-line attack. They also give a hint of the relative corrosion rate in the solution itself and in the atmosphere above it.

Experiments with intermittently wetted specimens often resemble actual conditions more than those with completely or partially immersed specimens. The intermittent wetting may be carried out according to some predetermined cycle by alternately immersing and draining the specimen or by intermittently spraying the corrosive medium onto it in a special cabinet. The intermittent wetting of a sample with the test solution resembles natural conditions such as occur due to ebb and flow, flooding with sea water due to wave motion and wind, and intermittent rain.

If an intermittent immersion is carried out with such a high frequency that the specimen is never allowed to dry, the corrosion rate is often much higher than of continuously wetted samples, due to particularly efficient aeration in the intermittent wetting. If, on the other hand, the specimen is allowed to dry completely between wettings, the corrosion rate is often considerably reduced. When the surface of a metal specimen is continuously wetted, corrosion products (metal ions) are constantly removed from the metal surface. If the thin liquid film adhering to the metal surface after immersion is allowed to dry completely, the metal ion concentration will finally reach a value at which insoluble metal oxides or hydroxides are precipitated onto the metal surface and may form a film that exerts a protective action during the following immersion and so on. This is of importance for so-called weathering low-alloyed steels which are found to show their best properties if they are able to dry completely between wettings but which are little better than ordinary carbon steels if they are constantly wetted. Drying between periods of wetting is also of importance in washing machines. Many modern washing agents based on synthetic detergents exert a corrosive action on metal parts in washing machines, particularly copper and aluminium. If corrosion tests with such agents are carried out by constantly running the machine with the wash agent solution, the corrosion rate is found to be drastically higher than if the machine is emptied, rinsed and allowed to dry intermittently as is actually the case in practical operation.

P.5 Various methods for the evaluation of corrosion tests

P5.1 Visual observation of natural corrosion attacks

The simplest way to examine corrosion damage and to evaluate corrosion experiments is   direct visual observation with or without a magnifying lens or a microscope. This involves a qualitative statement whether the metal has corroded or not. It is usually also easy to see which type of corrosion oc-. curs, if it is general corrosion or some type of local attack. It is some- times useful to try some suitable colour indicator on the surface of the corroding or corroded metal, e.g. the ferroxyl indicator described previously In this way, small pits which have occurred in a nickel layer on a steel sur- face are made easily visible by the blue spots formed with this indicator by iron(II).

For visual evaluation of corrosion tests photographs of characteristic test plates are also of great value. Such photographs are used in the eva- luation of the degree of paint protection efficiency and the degree of rust- ing according to the Swedish Standard SIS 18 51 11 mentioned above (04.6), and also in the estimation of the rust grades and preparation grades of steel surfaces before surface treatment, according to SIS 05 59 00 (01.3).

The qualitative visual method may be made semi-quantitative by noting the number of corrosion spots or the corroded fraction of a given area, e.g. 1 dm^2. Even the time needed for the appearance of attacks of a certain character and size may be used for this purpose.

P5.2 Visual observation of accelerated corrosion tests

If a corrosion indicator is added to a corrosive solution which gives an intensified attack, weak points of the metal surface may be located easily. Thus a test solution containing sodium chloride and potassium cyano- ferrate (III)   may be used to locate pores in phosphate coatings on steel and also to study the tendency towards pitting of various stainless steels. In the latter case a potentiostatic determination of the pitting potential is a safer method.

In order to determine whether a stainless steel is sensitive towards intercrystalline corrosion, a sulphuric acid solution containing copper sulphate and copper turnings is used (the so-called Strauss´ test). For the same purpose, boiling   nitric acid may also be used (the so-called Huey test). For the determination of the sensitivity towards stress corrosion cracking of brass, a mercury nitrate solution containing 1 % free nitric acid is often used. In this way it is possible to determine rapidly whether the brass contains internal stresses which make it liable to stress corrosion cracking in media containing ammonia or amines or other similar nitrogen compounds. This accelerated test is so rapid that a specimen of cold worked brass, which is immersed in the solution, falls to pieces very quickly, sometimes even with the production of sound.

P5.3 Metallographic evaluation of corrosion tests

Another type of visual evaluation of corrosion tests is the microscopic study of polished and etched cross sections of corroded specimens. This method is of particular value in examining deeply penetrating corrosion attacks, such as pitting, intercrystalline corrosion, stress corrosion cracking, erosion corrosion, cavitation corrosion, etc. By such metallographic examination of etched cross sections, it is possible to decide, for instance, whether a stress corrosion crack is intercrystalline or transcrystalline.

P5.4 Evaluation of corrosion tests by chemical analysis

The most important forms of quantitative evaluation of corrosion tests involve applications of the methods of chemical analysis. The most widely used method is the recording of the weight loss of metal test specimens after corrosion products have been carefully removed chemically, with particular precautions not to cause a further attack on the metal. If the corrosion products adhere quantitatively to the metal as is often the case in high temperature oxidation, the amount of corrosion may also be determined as the weight increase of the test specimens. The analysis may also be carried out as a determination of the oxygen consumption or of the increase of the metal ion concentration in the corrosive solution. In some cases, finally, the amount of evolved hydrogen may be used as a measure of the corrosion in a test. These chemical methods of determining the corrosion rate have their main applications in the case of general corrosion leading to more or less even attack.

Before the determination of the weight loss of a corroded metal specimen, all corrosion products must be completely removed. This procedure must be carried out in such a way that the metal is not further attacked. Sometimes, loosely adhering corrosion products may be removed mechanically by rubbing the metal with a stiff brush or a rubber stopper and simultaneously

rinsing with water. Usually, however, some chemical or electrochemical method has to be used to dissolve the corrosion products. It is often suitable
to combine such a chemical treatment with a mechanical brushing of the specimen. Table P1 gives a review of different solutions and ways of treatment
for the removal of corrosion products from some common metals before weighing after corrosion tests. Some of the solutions used act by passivating
the metal whereas other are so mildly aggressive that they do not attack
the metal noticeably. If stronger and more aggressive acid solutions are
used, the attack on the metal may be reduced by means of corrosion inhibitors or cathodic protection. In the latter case the metal specimen is
put in contact with a piece of zinc or a cathodic current is applied from
an outer current source. Sometimes the combination of corrosion inhibitors
and cathodic protection is useful. Under all circumstances, a blank test
on a non-corroded metal specimen of the same size should be carried out
in order to find out whether the attack on the metal itself is negligible
or if perhaps a small correction should be applied.

In the case of very low corrosion velocities it is sometimes more
suitable to determine the increase of the metal ion concentration of a
corrosive solution rather than the weight loss of the metal specimen.
By employing sensitive methods of analysis, e.g. colourimetry, polarography
and atom absorption spectrophotometry, much higher sensitivity is obtained
than by using gravimetric methods. This makes it possible to determine
the corrosion in cooling systems in which the time of contact between
water and metal parts is very short, but in which the attack may never-
theless be considerable due to the large total amount of water passing
through the system. Other examples are the study of the corrosion of washing machines in detergent solutions and the internal corrosion of beer cans.

In particular cases it is more suitable to determine the corrosion
velocity by measuring the amount of evolved or consumed gas during the
test. In experiments on corrosion or pickling in acid, deaerated solutions
the collection of evolved hydrogen is a rapid, sensitive and accurate
method for determining the rate of attack on the metal (Fig. P8). In neutral
water or aqueous solutions in closed systems the decrease in oxygen concentration or the decrease of oxygen or air volume may be taken as a measure
of the amount of corrosion.

TABLE P1. Chemical and electrochemical methods for the removal of corrosion products from corroded metal specimens prior to weighing.

Metal	Solution	Conditions	Remarks
Carbon steel and cast iron	HCl, d. 1.16 Sb_2O_3, 20 g/l $SnCl_2$, 20 g/l	Room temp. 15-20 min.	Clarke's solution. Sb^{3+} acts as inhibitor. Sn^{2+} reduces Fe^{3+} to Fe^{2+}.
Carbon steel and cast iron	NaOH, 10-20 %	$60-100°C$, 5-10 min.	Contact with zinc or cathodic current ($1-10$ A/dm^2) reduces metal loss.
Stainless steel	HNO_3, 10-30 %	$20-60°C$, 5 min.	
Copper, nickel, stainless steel	H_2SO_4, 5 % + pickling inhibitor	$75°C$, 5 min. 10 A/dm^2	Cathodic protection.
Aluminium	HNO_3, conc. +CrO_3, 50 g/l	$20°C$, 5-10 min.	
Aluminium	H_3PO_4, 5 % + CrO_3, 2 %	$80-100°C$, 30 min. 1 A/dm^2	Cathodic protection
Aluminium	10 % I_2 in absolute C_2H_5OH	$50°C$, 10 hrs	Metal dissolves, oxide left
Magnesium	CrO_3, 200 g/l Ag_2CrO_4, 10 g/l $BaCrO_4$, 1 g/l	Boiling solution, 5 min.	Ag^+ removes Cl^- Ba^{2+} " SO_4^{2-} Dissolves conversion coatings also.
Magnesium	$(NH_4)_2CrO_4$, 100 g/l, pH 8-10	Room temp., 24 hrs, air agitation	Coatings not dissolved
Zinc, lead	NH_4-acetate, sat. soln	Room temp., 2 hrs	
Zinc	CrO_3, 200 g/l $BaCrO_4$, 1 g/l	$80°C$, 1 min.	

232

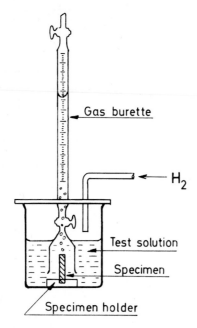

Gas burette

H₂

Fig. P8. Apparatus for measuring the
rate of hydrogen evolution corrosion
in deaerated solutions.

Test solution

Specimen

Specimen holder

P5.5 Evaluation of corrosion tests by thickness measurements

In some cases of far-reaching general corrosion, it is possible to
estimate the amount of wasted metal by thickness measurements rather than
by weighing. But even if weight losses are recorded they are often recalculated to thickness losses which are a more practical measure of the rate
of attack. Usual figures are in μm per year or per 10 years, inches per
year (ipy), mils per year (mpy) etc. Conversion factors between some common units of corrosion rate are given in Table P2. In the same way, the decrease of the thickness of protective metallic coatings may be estimated
by using instruments based on magnetic principles or the measurement of
eddy-currents or radio-active radiation.

With pitting attacks it is of little use to report the weight loss or
the average decrease in thickness of the metal. The important quantity to
measure in this case is the depth of the deepest pit. A common procedure
is to measure the depth of the 10 deepest pits on a given surface area,
say 1 dm² and report the maximum and average depths. The frequency, distribution and shape of the pits should also be noted. For wide pits, the depth
may be measured by a needle micrometer. The depth of very small pits may
be estimated by means of a microscope by focusing first on the uncorroded
metal surface and then on the bottom of the pits and reading the difference on the micrometer screw of the objective. It is customary to report

TABLE P2. Relations between some usual units for corrosion rate.

Given unit	Factor for recalculation to					
	mdd	g/m^2 · day	µm/year	mm/year	mpy	ipy
mg/dm^2 · day (mdd)	1	0.1	36.5/ρ	0.0365/ρ	1.44/ρ	0.00144/ρ
g/m^2 · day	10	1	365/ρ	0.365/ρ	14.4/ρ	0.0144/ρ
µm/year	0.0274 · ρ	0.00274 · ρ	1	0.001	0.0394	0.0000394
mm/year	27.4 · ρ	2.74 · ρ	1000	1	39.4	0.0394
mil/year (mpy)	0.696 · ρ	0.0696 · ρ	25.4	0.0254	1	0.001
inch/year (ipy)	696 · ρ	69.6 · ρ	25,400	25.4	1000	1

1 mil = 10^{-3} inch = 25.4 µm; 1 µm = 10^{-6} m = 10^{-3} mm

ρ = density of the metal, g/cm^3.

the ratio between deepest penetration and average one-sided thickness loss of the test specimen (Fig. P9). This ratio, which is called the pitting factor, is obviously a measure of the severity of the pitting attack.

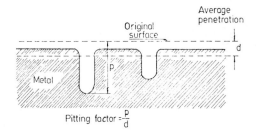

Fig. P9. The pitting factor is the ratio of deepest penetration (p) and average penetration (d).

P5.6 Mechanical evaluation of corrosion tests

For some special types of corrosion such as intercrystalline corrosion, selective corrosion, etc. the loss of metal is no good measure of the degree or amount of damage. In such cases, as in various cases of embrittlement, e.g. hydrogen embrittlement, mechanical methods are of great importance for an evaluation of the results of corrosion tests. Examples of such

measurements are tensile and compressional strength, the life of a specimen with a given load, bending and impact tests, hardness measurements
etc. according to current methods used in materials testing of metals. It
is important that such measurements are carried out on a sufficiently large
number of specimens and, furthermore, on   uncorroded specimens of the
same origin.

Mechanical test methods are also of great importance in connection
with the corrosion types that are directly influenced by mechanical factors
such   as   stress corrosion cracking, corrosion fatigue and fretting
oxidation. In these cases a suitably chosen mechanical load is an important
factor in the corrosion test itself.

P5.7 Electric evaluation of corrosion tests

A quantitative measurement of the corrosion rate of a uniformly corroding metal specimen, preferably in the form of a wire, may be carried
out conveniently and accurately by measuring its electric resistance during
the corrosion test. The corrosive medium may be either a liquid or a gas.
Since the resistance of the wire is inversely proportional to its cross sectional area, the resistance will increase according as the cross sectional
area is reduced by the corrosion or oxidation process. This method is useful
for the rapid testing of various metals and alloys in different solutions,
and also for the evaluation of suitable corrosion inhibitors. A pronounced
disadvantage with this method is, however, that pitting and other local
attacks are not adequately indicated. Devices for measuring corrosion
velocity according to this principle are commercially available.
Another electric evaluation method for corrosion tests is the study of
films of oxides or other corrosion products by means of capacitance
measurements. Such measurements give a measure of the pore-free, often
amorphous part of the film thickness.

P5.8 Electrochemical evaluation of corrosion tests

Since corrosion in moist environments is usually of an electrochemical
nature, electrochemical corrosion test methods are of particular interest.
Electrochemical measurements, above all the recording of polarization
curves, are of utmost importance in elucidating the mechanism of various
corrosion reactions. The kinetics of atmospheric corrosion have also
been clarified by electrochemical experiments on thin liquid films in a

controlled atmosphere. Even in practical corrosion testing, electrochemical methods find an ever-increasing application.

The mere measurement of corrosion potentials may provide valuable
information, although it is certainly true that there is no direct relationship between corrosion potential and corrosion velocity. In some
connections, however, the change of corrosion potential in one direction
or another may by experience be connected with an increase or a decrease
in corrosion rate. Hence the formation of passivating oxide films usually
results in a more noble corrosion potential whereas, on the other hand,
the breakthrough of a passivating film produces a potential change in the
negative direction. The measurement of corrosion potentials may likewise
be used to follow the formation of protective lime layers on steel in tap
water. The measurement of corrosion potentials is furthermore of great
importance in the evaluation and classification of corrosion inhibitors.

The most important electrochemical corrosion test methods, particularly some short-time tests for passivating metals and alloys, are based on
the recording of polarization curves, preferably determined by potentiostatic or potentiodynamic techniques. The application of an anodic current
or an anodic potential is used to intensify the corrosive environment.
Though galvanostatic methods, based on the application of a constant
anodic current, have been used extensively, potentiostatic methods, i.e.
the application of a constant anodic potential, are becoming more important
because they are sounder in principle.

P.6 Some applications of accelerated laboratory testing

P6.1 Testing at increased humidity and temperature in humidity cabinets
The aim in this case is to accelerate the corrosion by increasing
the atmospheric humidity above the critical value of 60-70 %. As a rule,
the temperature is also raised and is subjected to a cyclic change so that
condensation occurs intermittently on the metal specimen. The humidity
cabinet usually consists of a rectangular box with a tightly fitting cover
and with arrangements within it for suspending the specimens, for heating
the cabinet and for a sufficiently exposed water surface to keep the air
at the required relative humidity (see Fig. P10). If the cabinet is large
the air should be circulated and the apparatus should be automatic in
order to maintain constant conditions. In spite of this, identical specimens placed in different parts of the cabinet may give different results.

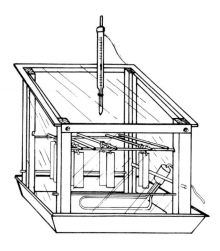

Fig. P10. Humidity cabinet for accelerated corrosion tests at elevated humidity and temperature.

For electrodeposited coatings of zinc and cadmium on steel, for example, a test is recommended which consists of 16 hours at 55°C and 95 % relative humidity followed by a condensation period of 5 hours at 30°C in the same cabinet.

P6.2 Testing in salt spray chambers

In so-called salt spray chambers, the corrosion test specimens are subjected to a mist of sodium chloride solution of a certain concentration and at a prescribed temperature. The test plates are suspended on a non-metallic support and in such a way that the corrosive liquid is not retained as drops. The corrosive solution is used just once and the test specimens may not dry during the test, although the salt spray may be intermittent. Testing times between 16 and 96 hours are usually used depending upon the type of metal or coating tested. The test is carried out in a chamber which is made from or lined with some corrosion resistant material, e.g. perspex (Fig. P11). Even the spraying device consist of some corrosion resistant material. Various types, shapes and sizes of salt spray chambers are used. Precautions should be taken so that the salt spray does not hit the specimens directly. In spite of this, the corrosion velocity is never quite the same in various parts of a salt spray cabinet. In order to compensate this variation, a number of specimens of the same kind are suspended in the chamber according to a certain system Even greater differences are obtained between different chambers. A sloping arrangement of the test plates is often to be preferred to the vertical arrangement indicated in Fig. P11.

Fig. P11. Example of salt spray chamber for accelerated corrosion testing.

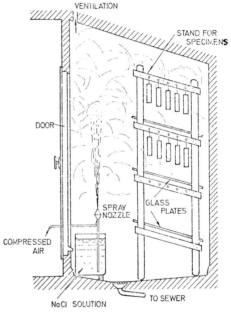

A common, commercially available form of the salt spray chamber is the so-called Aerosol Chamber (Fig. P12). In this apparatus, the salt mist (aerosol) is created not by a nozzle but by a special centrifuge in which sodium chloride solution is hurled against a lattice and finely dispersed. It would seem that a more even particle size (1-2 micrometres) in the aerosol is obtained in this way and therefore also more even and reproducible test conditions. The test solution contains just 0.5 g NaCl per litre. Different programmes are used to correspond to various corrosion environments. If the aerosol centrifuge is switched on and shut off at intervals of 30 minutes at room temperature, conditions are obtained which correspond to total immersion in 3 % sodium chloride solution with air bubbling. Due to more efficient aeration, the corrosion proceeds about five times as fast in the aerosol chamber . If the heat is switched on while the aerosol centrifuge is not working so that the temperature is made to vary between 30° and 40°C and the relative humidity between 50 % and 95 %, an accelerated test is obtained which corresponds to atmospheric corrosion in a marine climate.

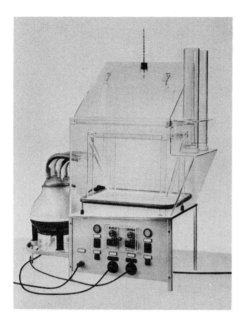

Fig. P12. Aerosol Chamber. The salt mist is produced in the centrifuge to the left. The chamber is constructed from Perspex. The lid rests in a waterlock and slopes so that condensing moisture will not drop down on the specimens but run off to the wall. The test specimens are hung on the rack inside the chamber. The two exhaust pipes to the right are filled with glass balls when the apparatus is in use.

While neutral sodium chloride solution in a spray chamber is of little value in testing chromium-nickel coatings on steel, an addition of acetic acid to the solution to a pH value of 3.2 to 3.5 will give results resembling those obtained under atmospheric corrosion of such coatings. A temperature of 35°C is maintained and the specimens are sprayed continuously for 8 to 72 hours. This "acetic acid salt spray" test (ACSS test) is described in ASTM B287-62 and in BS1224.

In another modification of the salt spray test, the test solution contains not only acetic acid but also copper chloride, corresponding to a concentration of 0.3 g $CuCl_2$, $2H_2O$ per litre. The temperature held in this case is 50°C. In this way the rate of attack is still further increased, particularly on nickel. This so-called CASS test (built up from the initials of the expression "copper accelerated acetic acid salt spray" test) is therefore still more accelerated than the ACSS test, referred to above; it also seems to have a wider applicability. 16 hours of CASS testing is stated to

correspond to one winter's exposure of chromium-plated car bumpers in a
metropolitan street. This means an acceleration of about 100 times. The
CASS test is described in ASTM B368-68 and in BS 1224.

P6.3 Testing by means of a salt-containing clay coating in a humidity cabinet (Corrodkote test)

In the testing of chromium-plated car parts, according to the so-called
Corrodkote test, a corroding coating (hence the designation) is used instead of a salt spray. The coating is prepared from a suspension of clay
in an aqueous solution containing chloride, ferric and copper ions. The
test has been developed as an accelerated test in order to simulate the
effect of road dirt on chromium plated car parts. The suspension consists
of 60 g of porcelain clay in 100 ml of a solution containing NH_4Cl (20 g/l),
$FeCl_3$, $6H_2O$ (3.3 g/l), and $Cu(NO_3)_2$, $3H_2O$ (0.7 g/l). This suspension is
brushed on the test plates. After the suspension has dried the test plates
are transferred to a humidity cabinet with a relative humidity of 90 %
at a temperature of 38^0C and are kept there for 20 hours. The coating is
then washed off and the specimens are examined. The test may be continued
with more cycles using a newly mixed suspension each time. The acceleration
of the corrosion produced by one cycle is about the same as in the CASS
test, i.e. about 100 times. The Corrodkote test is described in ASTM B380-65
and in BS1224.

P6.4 Testing in a humidity cabinet with an atmosphere containing sulphur dioxide

Whereas tests carried out in a chloride containing test environment
often give satisfactory results in comparison with marine corrosion conditions or with a corrosion environment dominated by road salts, they
show, on the other hand, a low correlation with corrosion in a typically
industrial atmosphere, dominated by a high content of sulphur dioxide.
For this purpose it is better to carry out the accelerated test in a moist
atmosphere, containing sulphur dioxide. An example of such a test is
illustrated in Fig. P13. Twelve or more specimens are suspended in a
vertical position in the condensing vapour above a dilute sulphur dioxide

240

solution at 45°C. The test vessel consists of a covered 5 litre beaker on an electric heating plate controlled by a thermostat. The beaker is

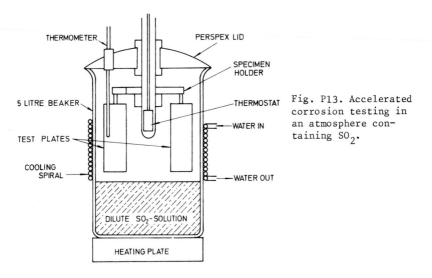

Fig. P13. Accelerated corrosion testing in an atmosphere containing SO_2.

furthermore surrounded by an outer cooling coil around its upper part. The beaker contains half a litre of distilled water to which is added daily 5 ml of a sulphur dioxide solution containing 3 grams of SO_2 per litre and obtained by diluting saturated sulphur dioxide solution 20 times. This addition of sulphur dioxide is made 5 days a week. Every 7th day the beaker is emptied and a new 5 day cycle with additions of sulphur dioxide is started. The cooling water is made to leave the coil at a temperature below 30°C so that condensation takes place in the upper part of the vessel. The positions of the specimens are changed every day in a specified manner.

A somewhat different procedure is used in the so-called Kesternich chamber, in which the test pieces are exposed to a humid atmosphere containing SO_2 for 8 h at an elevated temperature. The exposure is interrupted regularly and the specimens are allowed to dry. For details, see DIN 50018.

P6.5 Testing of paint films in a weatherometer

For accelerated corrosion testing of painted metal surfaces in the laboratory, a so-called weatherometer is widely used. This is a sort of climate machine in which painted test plates are exposed to moisture, heat, light, drying, freezing, etc., according to a given scheme. The apparatus,

Fig. P14, may consist of a low cylindrical container with 120 cm diameter
and provided with a cover through which a strong arc lamp and a fitting,
holding three spray nozzles above each other, are inserted. The test plates,
which may have the dimensions 15 cm x 7.5 cm, are placed in an almost vertical position on three levels, around the internal mantle surface of the
cylinder which is rotated every 20th minute. Since the water spray is di-
rected against a fairly small surface, wetting of the test plates occurs
intermittently and, meanwhile, the plates are dried up by the heat from the
arc lamp. The ultraviolet component of the light from the arc lamp contributes to the deterioration of paints in the same way as the same
light in nature.

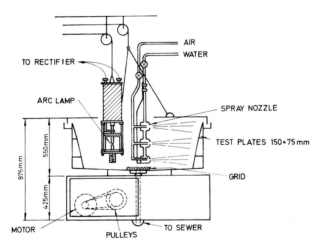

Fig. P14. Weatherometer (climate machine) for accelerated testing of paint
coatings.

P6.6 Electrochemical test methods

Of later years, accelerated electrochemical test methods have gained
increased importance. The main reason for this development is increasing
knowledge of the electrochemical mechanism of various types of corrosion.
The commercial production of electronic potentiostats, which for many of
the methods used are quite indispensable, has also been of great importance. Most of these electrochemical methods may be classified in
the following groups:

A. Recording of anodic and cathodic polarization curves

a. Polarization resistance method

For small polarizations, up to 20 mV from the corrosion potential, there is a linear relationship between the applied current I and polarization η. The slope of this straight line is

$$\frac{d\eta}{dI} = \pm \frac{b_a \cdot b_c}{2.3(b_a + b_c) \cdot i_{corr}}$$

where b_a and b_c are the slopes of the anodic and cathodic Tafel lines. An experimental determination of $\frac{d\eta}{dI}$ allows the calculation of i_{corr}. This method may be applied for the determination of corrosion velocity even for passive metals ($b_a = \infty$) or if the cathode reaction is governed by diffusion ($b_c = \infty$).

b. Extrapolation_of_Tafel_lines

For greater polarizations, η > 50 mV, corrosion velocity may be determined by extrapolation of the Tafel line for the anodic or cathodic reaction to the corrosion potential. The corrosion current may also be obtained directly from the point of intersection of the two Tafel lines.

c. The polarization_break_method

According to the so-called polarization break test the corrosion current i_{corr} is determined from the following equation

$$i_{corr} = \frac{I_a \cdot I_c}{I_a + I_c}$$

where I_a = the applied anodic current at which the cathodic reaction at the test electrode is negligible, which is reflected in a break on the anodic polarization curve corresponding to the transition from a linear to a logarithmic relation between η and I_a, and I_c = the corresponding applied cathodic current.

The methods referred to above are applicable only for general corrosion corresponding to an even current distribution on the test electrode and not if the corrosion current is concentrated to a few active areas, as in pitting or in stress corrosion cracking. The polarization curve methods have been applied for accelerated testing of general corrosion in water and in soil, for the evaluation and testing of corrosion inhibitors etc. A good correlation has been obtained with conventional test methods (weight loss determinations, analysis of test solutions). This is particularly true for the polarization resistance method. For the clever use of these methods a knowledge of the electrochemical properties of the system investigated is desirable.

B. Recording of anodic polarization curves for passivating metals

With the methods dealt with so far it is possible to work galvanosta-
tically (with variation of an applied current) as well as potentiostatically (with variation of an applied potential). Electrochemical methods for
the testing of passivating metals depend upon the use of a potentiostatic
technique, however. These methods are based on the recording of anodic
polarization curves of the type shown in Figs.E5 and G11.They are particularly useful for the development of new alloys, e.g. stainless steels and
for the determination of the influence of various alloying constituents
and impurities on the corrosion properties of such alloys. The current
peak at the passivation potential defines the tendency of the alloy to
become passive in a given corrosive medium, whereas the passivity current gives the corrosion velocity in the passive state. The passivation
potential and the transpassive potential define the limits of the passivity range. By recording anodic polarization curves of passive metals in
environments containing chloride ions or other activating ions, it is
furthermore possible to determine the pitting or breakthrough potentials.

For the recording of polarization curves it is possible to use a
potentiodynamic method with a continuous increase of the potential, or a
potentiostatic method with a stepwise increase of the potential. In both
cases the potential increase should be carried out slowly in order to obtain reproducible results.

C. Maintaining a constant anodic potential

This method has been found to be particularly suitable for accelerated
laboratory tests for intercrystalline and stress corrosion, but it has also
been used for testing corrosion inhibitors and metallic coatings. In intercrystalline corrosion, one or more structural constituents in the grain
boundaries are dissolved more rapidly than the body of the grain. This may
be utilized in potentiostatic testing by maintaining a potential at which the
less noble areas corrode at a high rate, whereas the general corrosion
of the main part of the grain is negligible. For testing the sensitivity of
austenitic stainless steels to intercrystalline corrosion, the test potential
is maintained in a potential range, +50 - +100 mV versus NHE, in which the
austenite matrix is passivated, whereas the chromium-depleted grain boundaries are still in the active state. A suitable electrolyte for such a
potentiostatic test is a 5 % sulphuric acid solution with an activating
addition of 0.01 % NH_4SCN. In this way it is possible to reduce the test-

ing time to 5 minutes, which means a considerable saving of time in comparison with the conventional Strauss test, using a solution of sulphuric acid and copper sulphate containing copper turnings, in which the testing time amounts to 25 to 100 hours. The reason is that in the Strauss test the redox potential of the solution is determined by the copper sulphate electrode, that is about +350 mV to the NHE. At this potential, all the test area is in the passive range in which there is just a small difference in corrosion velocity between areas of different chromium content.

Even in testing the sensitivity of materials to stress corrosion cracking a potentiostatic method may be used since anodic polarization is then a strongly accelerating factor. In testing the sensitivity of aluminium alloys to stress corrosion cracking, it is possible by using anodic polarization to cut down the testing time to about one thousandth in comparison with the conventional sodium chloride — hydrogen peroxide test. Application of an anodic potential also results in shorter testing times and more reproducible results in testing the sensitivity of austenitic stainless steels to stress corrosion cracking in boiling magnesium chloride solution.

For the testing of decorative chromium plate (copper—nickel—chromium or duplex nickel—chromium) a potentiostatic test method has been developed with the designation EC-test (electrolytic corrosion test). An anodic potential +300 mV relative the SCE is used in an electrolyte in which under these conditions the chromium layer is passive and the mat nickel layer is partly passivated, whereas the bright nickel layer and an eventual copper layer corrodes freely. Two minutes of anodic polarization in the EC-test is considered to correspond to one year´s exposure in a metropolitan area.

Literature

Champion, F A, Corrosion Testing Procedures, Chapman & Hall, London 1963.

Q. POTENTIAL-pH DIAGRAMS FOR SOME TECHNICALLY IMPORTANT METALS

The theoretical potential-pH diagrams described in chapter D constitute a convenient means to collect and represent equilibrium data for different metals and their compounds in the presence of water. In many cases, the theoretical potential-pH diagram fairly well represents the corrosion properties of the metal and also the extension of the passivity range. For certain decidedly passivated metals, however, the theoretical diagrams give a misleading picture of the corrosion properties of the metals by showing much smaller passivity ranges than those actually occurring in practice. If the theoretical diagrams are modified with regard to practical experience of the corrosion and passivity of metals in acid, alkaline and oxidizing media and of their behaviour on anodic polarization, empirical potential-pH diagrams are obtained which give a truer picture of the corrosion properties of the metals and which are therefore of greater practical value. In the following, such diagrams are presented for a number of technically important metals. The pH of a corrosive solution is usually easy to measure or estimate. The redox potential in the solution can be measured by means of a bright platinum electrode. The corrosion potential (mixed potential) which develops on a certain metal can also be easily measured relative to a calomel electrode, for instance. It is then possible to judge from the potential-pH diagram whether corrosion will occur or not.

Potential-pH diagrams for some metals in non-complexing solutions at 25°C are shown in the sequence:
1 Mg. 2 Al. 3 Ti. 4 Cr. 5 Fe. 6 Ni. 7 Cu. 8 Ag. 9 Zn. 10 Cd. 11 Sn. 12 Pb.

For the same metals, the corrosion properties in various environments are listed on the opposite page.

Empirical potential-pH diagrams may be constructed even for alloys. The corrosion properties of the stainless steels are fairly well represented by the potential-pH diagram for chromium.

246

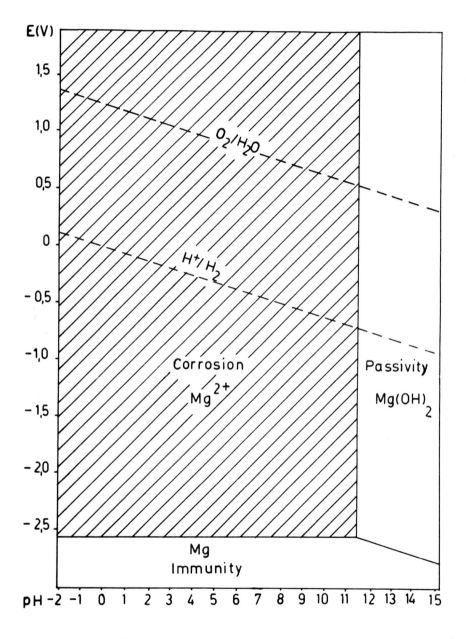

Fig. Q1. Potential-pH diagram for Magnesium.

Corrosion resistance of Magnesium in various environments

Resistant to   Not resistant to

Acid solutions

HF, conc. > 2 %   Inorganic acids except

Pure H_2CrO_4, free   those mentioned to the left.

from Cl^- and SO_4^{2-}-ions   Organic acids

Alkaline solutions

NaOH, KOH < $60^{o}C$ NaOH, KOH > $60^{o}C$

Concrete

NaClO, NH_4OH (conc.)

Salt solutions

Chromates, fluorides, nitrates,   Chlorides, bromides, iodides,

phosphates of Na, K, Ca, Ba, Mg, Al   sulphates, persulphates,

                                                   chlorates, hypochlorites.

                                                   Salts of heavy metals, dis-

                                                   placed by Mg

Gases

Some dry gases, e.g. Cl_2, I_2, NO, NO_2

F_2, Br_2, S_2, H_2S, SO_2 Alkyl halides

Dry freons   Moist freons

248

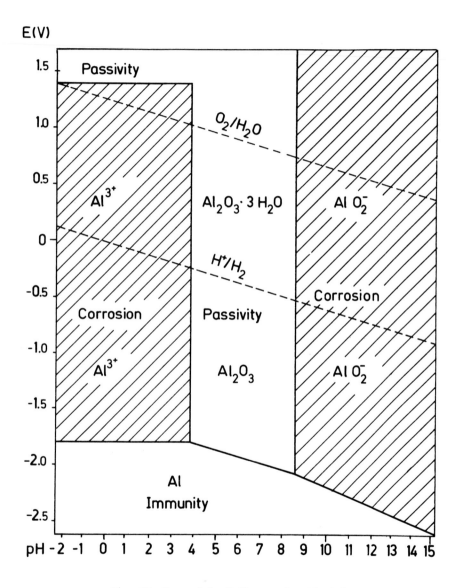

Fig. Q2. Potential-pH diagram for Aluminium.

Corrosion resistance of Aluminium in various environments

Resistant to   Not resistant to

Acid solutions

Acetic acid, room temp.   HCl, HBr, H_2SO_4, HF,

Citric   " ,   "   " $HClO_4$, H_3PO_4

Tartaric " ,   "   "   Formic acid

Boric   " ,   "   "   Trichloracetic

$HNO_3 > 80$ %, $< 50^\circ C$ Oxalic acid

Fatty acids

Alkaline solutions

$Ca(OH)_2$ (concrete)   LiOH, NaOH, KOH, $Ba(OH)_2$.

$NH_4OH > 10$ %, $< 50^\circ C$ $NH_4OH < 10$ %, Na_2S, NaCN

$(NH_4)_2S$, Na_2SiO_3

Salt solutions

Sulphates, nitrates, phosphates   Salts of heavy metals, e.g.

and acetates of NH_4, Na, K, Ca,   Hg, Sn, Cu, Ag, Pb, Co, Ni.

Ba, Mg, Mn, Zn, Cd, Al.

NaClO, inhibited with Na_2SO_3. $NaClO_4$, containing Cl^-.

$NaClO_4$ without Cl^-.   NaClO, $Ca(ClO_2)$.

$KMnO_4$, room temp., 1-10 %.

Gases

Most dry gases:

Br_2, $Cl_2 < 125^\circ C$, $F_2 < 230^\circ C$,   Moist SO_2, SO_3, Cl_2, HCl,

HCl, HBr, Ozone, S_2, SO_2, SO_3, NH_3 etc.

H_2S, CO_2, NO, NO_2, NH_3 CCl_4, CH_3Cl, CH_3Br

Freons, most chlorinated

hydrocarbons

250

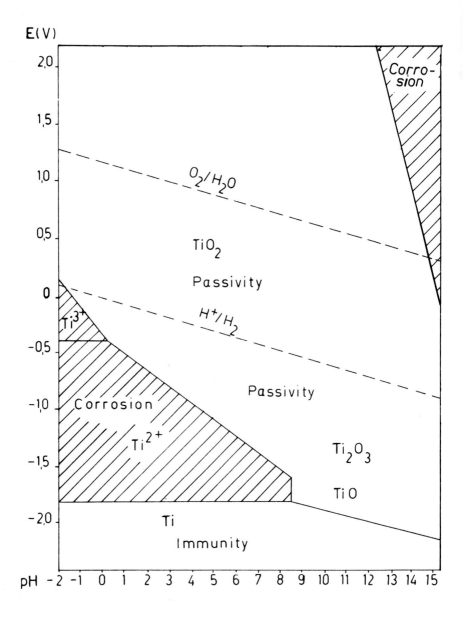

Fig. Q3. Potential–pH diagram for Titanium.

Corrosion resistance of Titanium in various environments

Resistant to   Not resistant to

Acid solutions

HNO_3, all conc. up to b.p. H_2SO_4 > 10 %, HCl > 10 %, HF

Aqua regia, room temp.   Fuming nitric acid, high temp.

H_2SO_4 < 10 %, HCl < 10 %, room temp. H_3PO_4 > 30 %, $35^\circ C$

H_3PO_4 < 30 %, $35^\circ C$ H_3PO_4 > 5 %, boiling

H_3PO_4 < 5 %, boiling   Trichloracetic acid, boiling

H_2CrO_4. Acetic, oxalic,   Oxalic acid, boiling

lactic and formic acids, room temp.   Formic acid, boiling

Alkaline solutions

Diluted, room temp.   Concentrated, hot

solutions   solutions

NaClO

Salt solutions

Most salt solutions, also   Fluorides, e.g. AlF_3

chlorides and oxidizing salts $AlCl_3$, conc. boiling

up to b.p., e.g. $FeCl_3$, $CuCl_2$. $MgCl_2$,   "   "

                                         $CaCl_2$,   "   "

Gases

Moist Cl_2, ClO_2 F_2, dry Cl_2

Air, O_2 < $425^\circ C$ Air, O_2 > $500^\circ C$

N_2 < $700^\circ C$ N_2 > $800^\circ C$

H_2 < $750^\circ C$ H_2 > $750^\circ C$

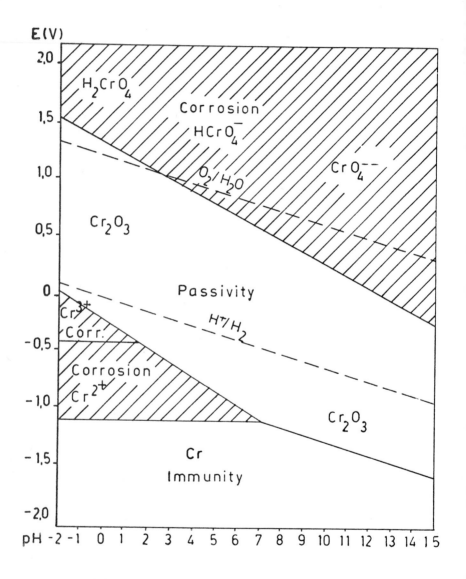

Fig. Q4. Potential-pH diagram for Chromium.

Corrosion resistance of Chromium in various environments

Resistant to   Not resistant to

Acid solutions

HNO_3 < 50 %, < 75°C   HCl, HBr, HI

H_2SO_4 + $CuSO_4$ Conc. HNO_3, high temp.

H_2SO_4 + $Fe_2(SO_4)_3$ H_2SO_4 > 5 %, > 50°C

H_2SO_4 < 5 %, aerated, room temp.   HF, H_2SiF_6, $HClO_3$

SO_2-solutions H_3PO_4 > 60 %, > 100°C

H_3PO_4, aerated, room temp. H_2CrO_4

Alkaline solutions

Deaerated, dilute   Aerated, concentrated

alkali solutions   alkali solutions at high

at room temp.   temperature

Salt solutions

Most non-halide salts   Halide salts. Oxidizing
                                                ($FeCl_3$, $CuCl_2$, $HgCl_2$, NaClO)
                                                and acid salts ($ZnCl_2$, $AlCl_3$)
                                                cause general corrosion.
                                                Other halide salts cause
                                                pitting and crevice corrosion.
                                                Thiosulphates and dithionites

Gases

O_2 < 1100°C O_2 > 1100°C

H_2O < 850°C H_2O > 850°C

SO_2 < 650°C SO_2 > 650°C

H_2S, S_2 < 500°C H_2S, S_2 > 500°C

NH_3 < 500°C NH_3 > 500°C

Cl_2, HCl < 300°C Cl_2, HCl > 300°C

F_2, HF < 250°C F_2, HF > 250°C

Note that the corrosion resistance of stainless chromium steels is
similar to that of chromium.

254

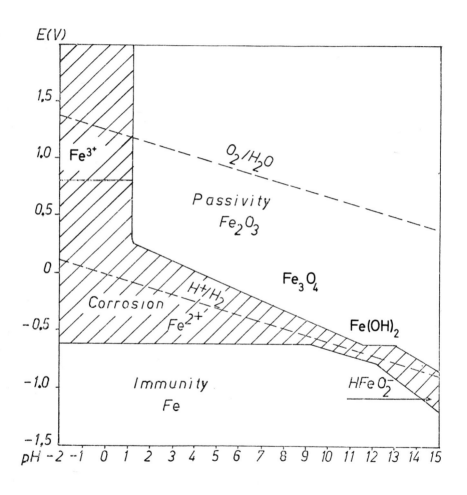

Fig. Q5. Potential-pH diagram for Iron.

Corrosion resistance of Iron in various environments

| Resistant to | Not resistant to |

Acid solutions

H_2CrO_4

HNO$_3$, conc.

H_2SO_4 > 70 %

HF > 70 %

Acids except those mentioned
to the left

Alkaline solutions

Most alkaline solutions

Hot concentrated alkalis
if in stressed condition
(caustic embrittlement)

Salt solutions

$KMnO_4$ > 1 g/l

H_2O_2 > 3 g/l

K_2CrO_4

$KMnO_4$ < 1 g/l

H_2O_2 < 3 g/l

Oxidizing salts, e.g. $FeCl_3$,
$CuCl_2$, $NaNO_3$

Hydrolyzing salts, e.g.
$AlCl_3$, $Al_2(SO_4)_3$, $ZnCl_2$, $MgCl_2$

Gases

Air < 450°C

Cl_2 < 200°C

SO_2 dry, < 300°C

NH_3 < 500°C

$H_2O_{(g)}$ < 500°C

H_2S < 300°C

Air > 450°C

Cl_2 > 200°C

F_2

SO_2, moist

NH_3 > 500°C

$H_2O_{(g)}$ > 500°C

H_2S > 300°C

256

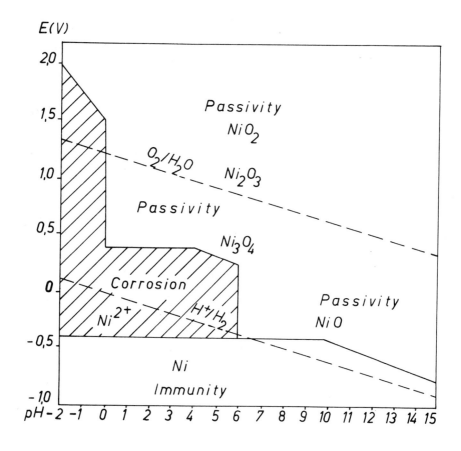

Fig. Q6. Potential-pH diagram for Nickel.

Corrosion resistance of Nickel in various environments

Resistant to   Not resistant to

Acid solutions

Dilute, non-oxidizing acids   Oxidizing acids

H_2SO_4, deaerated, < 80 %, room temp. HNO_3

HCl, deaerated,< 15 %, room temp. H_2SO_4 > 80 %

HCl, aerated, < 1 %, room temp.   HF, high temp.

HF, room temp.   Hot, conc. H_3PO_4

Deaerated dilute organic acids   Aerated organic acids

Pure H_3PO_4, deaerated, room temp.

Alkaline solutions

LiOH, NaOH, KOH, NH_4OH > 1 %

all concentrations up to b.p.

NH_4OH < 1 %

Salt solutions

Most non-oxidizing salts   Most oxidizing salts

$NaClO_4$ ($FeCl_3$, $CuCl_2$, $K_2Cr_2O_7$)

$KMnO_4$, room temp.   NaClO

Gases

Dry halogens, < 200°C   Moist halogens and hydrogen

Dry hydrogen halides,< 200°C   halides

$H_2O_{(g)}$ < 500°C $H_2O_{(g)}$ > 500°C

H_2 < 550°C Cl_2 > 450°C

SO_2 < 400°C H_2S > 65°C

S_2 < 300°C NH_3, high temp.

                                                  S_2 > 300°C

258

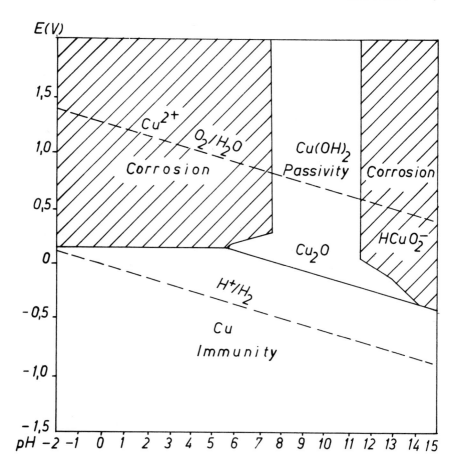

Fig. Q7. Potential-pH diagram for Copper.

Corrosion resistance of Copper in various environments

Resistant to	Not resistant to

Acid solutions

Deaerated, non-oxidizing acids:	HNO_3.
$HCl < 10$ %, $< 75^\circ C$	H_2SO_4, hot, conc.
$HF < 70$ %, $< 100^\circ C$	Aerated acids
$H_2SO_4 < 60$ %, $< 100^\circ C$	$HCl > 10$ %
H_3PO_4, room temp.	
Acetic acid, room temp.	

Alkaline solutions

Diluted solutions of NaOH, KOH, Na_2CO_3, K_2CO_3	Strong solutions of NaOH, KOH, NH_4OH, NaCN, KCN, NaClO

Salt solutions

$KMnO_4$, K_2CrO_4, $NaClO_3$. Deaerated, stagnant solutions of sulphates, nitrates, chlorides. Sea water	Most oxidizing salts, e.g. $FeCl_3$, $Fe_2(SO_4)_3$, $CuCl_2$, $Hg(NO_3)_2$, $AgNO_3$. Aerated and agitated salt solutions

Gases

Most dry gases: CO, CO_2	Moist gases, e.g. SO_2, H_2S, CS_2, CO_2
F_2, Cl_2, Br_2, SO_2.	F_2, Cl_2, Br_2.
Pure H_2	H_2, containing O_2.
$O_2 < 200^\circ C$	Dry $O_2 > 200^\circ C$
OF_2, ClF_3, ClO_3F	

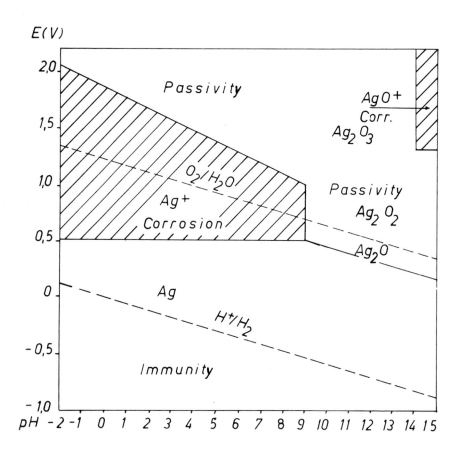

Fig. Q8. Potential-pH diagram for Silver.

Corrosion resistance of Silver in various environments

Resistant to   **Not resistant to**

Acid solutions

HCl, dilute, room temp.   HCl, conc., high temp.

HF, low temp., deaerated   HF, high temp., aerated

H_3PO_4, room temp.   Dilute HNO_3, room temp.

H_2SO_4, room temp. H_3PO_4, hot,conc.

Organic acids H_2SO_4, conc., high temp.

Alkaline solutions

LiOH, NaOH, KOH, NH_4OH, Na_2S, NaCN

all concentrations up to b.p.

Salt solutions

Most non-oxidizing salts.   Oxidizing salts (e.g. $K_2S_2O_8$,

$KMnO_4$, room temp. $FeCl_3$, $CuCl_2$, $HgCl_2$).

                                        Complexing salts(e.g. cyanides,

                                        polysulphides, thiosulphates,

                                        ammonium salts)

Gases

F_2, Cl_2 and Br_2 at room temp.   HCl and Cl_2 > $200^{\circ}C$

HCl < $200^{\circ}C$ H_2S and S_2 at room temp.

SO_2, room temp. SO_2 at elevated temp.

Air, O_2

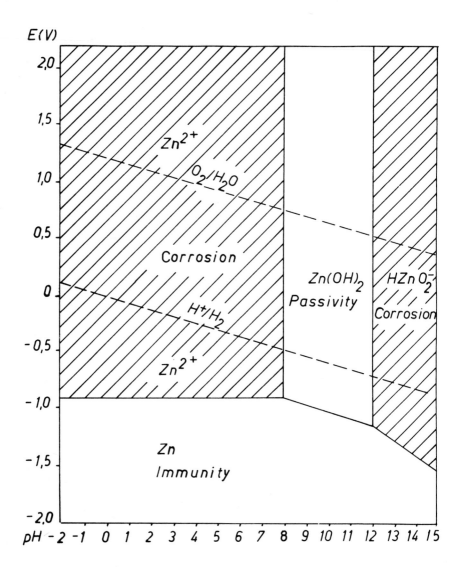

Fig. Q9. Potential-pH diagram for Zinc.

Corrosion resistance of Zinc in various environments

Resistant to	Not resistant to

Acid solutions

	Any of the common inorganic and organic acids

Alkaline solutions

pH < 12	pH > 12

Salt solutions

Na_2CrO_4, $Na_4B_2O_7$, Na_2SiO_3, $(NaPO_3)_6$ (inhibitors) 1 g/l, room temp.	Aerated salt solutions in general

Gases

N_2, CO_2, CO, N_2O, Dry Cl_2 Dry NH_3	Moist Cl_2 Moist C_2H_2

264

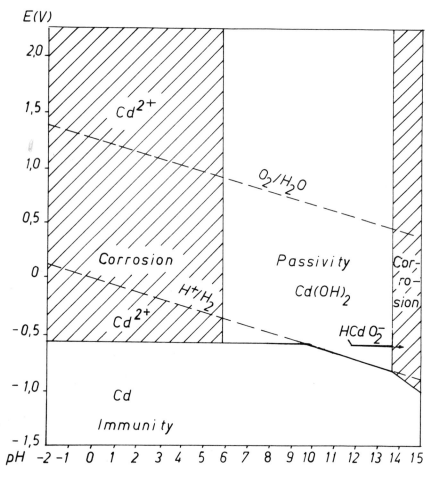

Fig. Q10. Potential-pH diagram for Cadmium.

Corrosion resistance of Cadmium in various environments

Resistant to   **Not resistant to**

Acid solutions

Any of the common inorganic
and organic acids

Alkaline solutions

Dilute LiOH, NaOH, KOH,   Conc. LiOH, NaOH, KOH
NH_4OH

Salt solutions

Na_2CrO_4, $Na_4B_2O_7$,   Aerated salt solutions in
Na_2SiO_3, $(NaPO_3)_6$ general
(inhibitors)
1 g/l, room temp.

Gases

Dry NH_3 Cl_2, Br_2
H_2, N_2 SO_2, moist
Air, O_2 < 250^oC
Dry SO_2, room temp.

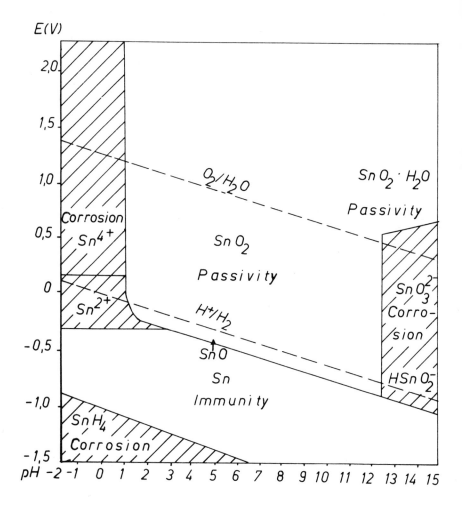

Fig. Q11. Potential-pH diagram for Tin.

Corrosion resistance of Tin in various environments

Resistant to   Not resistant to

Acid solutions

Dilute, deaerated   Oxidizing acids.
non-oxidizing   Aerated mineral and organic
inorganic and   acids
organic acids

Alkaline solutions

pH < 12   pH > 12
Higher pH values
in the presence of
silicates, phosphates
and chromates

Salt solutions

Phosphates, chromates,   Chlorides, sulphates,
borates   nitrates (black spots).
                                     Salts of metals, more noble
                                     than tin.

Gases

$F_2 < 100^{o}C$ Cl_2, Br_2, I_2 at room temp.
                                     $F_2 > 100^{o}C$
                                     $O_2 > 100^{o}C$
                                     $H_2S > 100^{o}C$

268

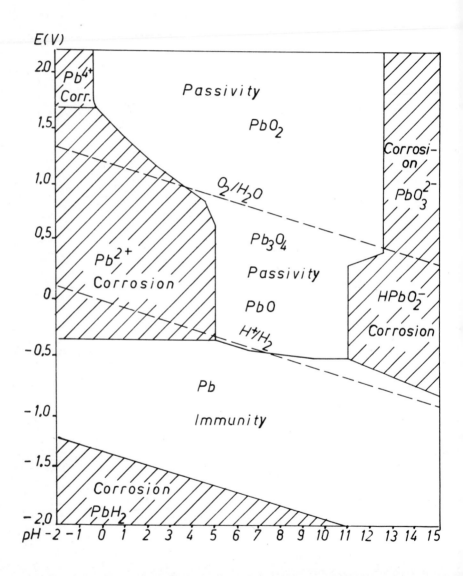

Fig. Q12. Potential-pH diagram for Lead.

Corrosion resistance of Lead in various environments

Resistant to   Not resistant to

Acid solutions

H_2SO_4 < 96 %, room temp. H_2SO_4 > 96 %, room temp.
H_2SO_4 < 80 %, $100^{\circ}C$ H_2SO_4 > 70 %, boiling
Commercial H_3PO_4 (ctng.   Pure H_3PO_4
some H_2SO_4) HNO_3 < 80 %
H_2CrO_4 HCl
HF < 60 %, room temp.   Organic acids
H_2SO_3

Alkaline solutions

pH < 11   LiOH, NaOH, KOH, pH > 12
NH_4OH < 1 % NH_4OH > 1 %
Na_2CO_3
Concrete

Salt solutions

Sulphates, carbonates, $FeCl_3$
bicarbonates $NaClO_4$ with NaCl
Pure $NaClO_4$ Nitrates
                                                  Acetates

Gases

Cl_2, moist or dry, < $100^{\circ}C$ Cl_2 > $100^{\circ}C$
Br_2, dry, room temp. Br_2, moist or at higher temp.
SO_2, SO_3, H_2S HF

GENERAL REFERENCES

Handbooks

Butler, G and Ison, H C K, Corrosion and its Prevention in Waters, Leonard Hill, London 1966.

Evans, U R, The Corrosion and Oxidation of Metals, Edward Arnold, London 1960.

Evans, U R, An Introduction to Metallic Corrosion, Edward Arnold, London 1963.

Fontana, M G and Greene, N D, Corrosion Engineering, Mc Graw-Hill, New York 1967.

Godard, H P, a.o. (Ed.), The Corrosion of Light Metals, John Wiley & Sons, New York 1967.

LaQue, F L and Copson, H R (Ed.), Corrosion Resistance of Metals and Alloys, Reinhold, New York 1963.

Rabald, E, Corrosion Guide, Elsevier, New York 1968.

Shreir, L L (Ed.), Corrosion, Vol. 1-2, George Newnes, London 1963.

Tomashov, N D, Theory of Corrosion and Protection of Metals, MacMillan, New York 1966.

Uhlig, H H, Corrosion and Corrosion Control, John Wiley & Sons, New York 1963.

Journals

British Corrosion Journal (London)

Corrosion (Houston, Texas)

Corrosion Science (Oxford)

Materials Protection (Houston, Texas)

Protection of Metals (English translation of the Russian journal Zaschita Metallov, Moscow)

Abstract Journals

Corrosion Abstracts (Houston, Texas)

Corrosion Abstracts (Stockholm)

Conversion factors from metric to English or American units

Length: 1 micrometre (μm) = 1 micron = 0.03937 mils
1 millimetre (mm) = 0.03937 inches = 39.37 mils
1 centimetre (cm) = 0.0328 feet = 0.3937 inches
1 decimetre (dm) = 0.3281 feet = 3.937 inches
1 metre (m) = 1.0936 yards = 3.281 feet
1 kilometre (km) = 0.6214 miles

Area: 1 square millimetre (mm^2) = 1550.00 sq. mils
1 square centimetre (cm^2) = 0.1550 sq. inches
1 square decimetre (dm^2) = 15.5000 sq. inches = 0.10764 sq. feet
1 square metre (m^2) = 10.7639 sq. feet = 1.1960 sq. yards

Volume: 1 millilitre (ml)=1 cubic centimetre (cm^3) = 0.06102 cu. inches
1 litre (1) = 1 cubic decimetre (dm^3) = 61.024 cu. inches =
= 0.035315 cu. feet = 0.2200 Brit. gallons =
= 0.2642 U.S. gallons (1 gallon = 4 quarts = 8 pints)
1 cubic metre (m^3) = 35.315 cu. feet = 1.3080 cu. yards

Mass: 1 gram (g) = 15.43 grains = 0.03527 ounces
1 kilogram (kg) = 2.2046 pounds = 35.274 ounces
1 ton (t) = 10^3 kg = 0.9842 (UK or) long tons = 1.1023 (U.S. or)
short tons

Concentration: 1 g/1 = 0.16036 ounces/gallon (Brit.) = 0.13353 ounces/gal-
lon (U.S.)

Pressure: 1 kp/cm^2 = 14.223 pounds/sq. inch = 32.809 feet of H_2O (39.2^oF) =
= 28.959 inches of Hg (32^oF)

Tensile stress: 1 kp/mm^2 = 1422.33 pounds/sq. inch = 0.71117 tons
(short)/sq. inch

Current density: 1 A/cm^2 = 6.4516 A/sq. inch; 1 A/dm^2 = 9.2902 A/sq. foot;
1 A/m^2 = 0.09290 A/sq. foot

Temperature: $^oF = 1.8\,^oC + 32$ $^oC = 0.5555(^oF - 32)$

SUBJECT INDEX

Leading word is indicated by a dash.